Disaster to Deliverance

*90 Days of Hope &
Healing*

Dale J. Brown, Ph.D.

Beat Dog Press
2020

Beat Dog Press

Disaster to Deliverance: 90 Days of Hope & Healing

Copyright © 2020 by Dale J Brown

Library of Congress Cataloging-in-Publication Data

Brown, Dale J., 1961—

Disaster to Deliverance: 90 Days of Hope & Healing / Dale Brown.

p. cm.

ISBN: 978-1-7323194-2-4 (ebook)

ISBN: 978-1-7323194-3-1 (Soft cover)

1. Devotional calendars. 2. Devotional literature, English. I. Title.

BV4811. A535 1993

242.'2—dc20 93-18858

Dedicated To

Survivors and thrivers and the rest of us
who are somewhere in-between.

Acknowledgements

A GREAT MANY PEOPLE build into our lives and wise is the person who recognizes these contributions. This, of course, is impossible on a comprehensive level. The threads of our social fabric are tightly woven and intricate indeed. All this to say, hundreds, if not thousands of people make us who we are. One of the joys of heaven is that I will know who these people are in my life and have opportunity to thank them.

One person comes to mind, however, to especially be thankful for this book, my wife, Kelly. She is a ray of sunshine and her simple unabashed joyful faith has kept me going when hard work and continued trust in God have wavered as I kept working on this project.

My heart expands and soul opens up when I am with her. In the midst of untold heartache and heartbreak, God gave me a living example of Jesus to love and nurture me. Thank you, Kelly—you are the love of my life.

You start with a darkness to move through,
but sometimes the darkness moves through you.

Dean Young

Contents

WHERE TO FIND TOPIC SERIES

INTRODUCTION

In the day when I cried out,
You answered me, and
made me bold
with strength
in my soul.

Psalm 138.3

MAE WEST SAID, *"YOU only live once, but if you do it right, once is enough."*

After having lived for 57 years at the time of this writing, once is definitely enough for me. I wholeheartedly reject the idea of reincarnation. Who would want to do this again? Once is enough for me but I want to give this one shot all I've got. And I want to finish well.

What does *doing it right* look like? How do we know if we have done it right? I have a feeling that Mae West and I might disagree on what 'doing it right' looks like!

Since a fair portion of life consists of suffering, whatever 'doing it right' must have something to do with surviving suffering in a redemptive manner—that is, suffering in a way that at least doesn't lead to our destruction and may even benefit us and those around us. Since suffering is in inevitable part of life, somehow our response to suffering must be significant.

Why we suffer and how we should manage it are questions as old as humanity. Societies past and present have differing views on what suffering means and how to survive it. All societies have an approach

1

to suffering that is redemptive, that is, they teach that suffering has a purpose. All societies except for ours, that is.[1]

Tim Keller notes that *Traditional cultures perceive the causes of suffering in highly spiritual, communal, and moral terms.*[2] Western secular culture has rejected the spiritual, elevated the individual and made morality completely relative and self-referenced. This radical shift in worldview has enormous implications for suffering. Most notable is that suffering is seen as an unpleasant interruption in one's relentless pursuit of happiness. Suffering is to be mitigated, litigated and hopefully eliminated at all cost.

And... suffering is not to be complained about, expressed or verbalized in any significant way. Especially if you are a man. But extreme suppression of emotions is not the way we are made. Eugene Peterson notes that:

> *The biblical way to deal with suffering is to transform what is individual into something corporate. Most cultures show a spontaneous comprehension of this. The suffering person is joined by friends who join their tears and prayers in a communal lament. They do not hush up the sound of weeping but augment it. They do not hide the sufferer away from view but bring him or her out into the public square in full view of everyone.*
>
> *If others weep with me, there must be more to the suffering than my own petty weakness or selfish sense of loss. The community votes with its tears that there is suffering that is worth weeping over.*[3]

---

[1] My primary audience for this book are people living in the midst of modern secular culture which include but are not limited to the United States, the United Kingdom, most of Europe, Australia and New Zealand. The reason for limiting the audience is that how societies view and respond to suffering is greatly varied between fully secularized cultures and those that are not. My hope, however, is that anyone anywhere reading this book will benefit from it.

[2] Timothy Keller, *Walking with God through Pain and Suffering*, (New York: Penguin, 2013) 20.

[3] Eugene H. Peterson. *Five Smooth Stones for Pastoral Work*, (Grand Rapids: Wm. B. Eerdmans Publishing, 1980) Kindle Locations 1363-1365.

The only 'grief event' that our Western culture deems worth acknowledging is the death of a family member—and that for only a few days. This lack of ability of our culture to rightly place suffering in the larger philosophical, theological and psychological contexts adds to the sufferer's pain. This is especially true of men in our world but will become more so for women as women embrace the male spiritual journey.

As a pastor for over 35 years, I have helped people through intense suffering and wrestled with what their suffering meant. Then came 2014 when I began an extraordinary period of personal loss and pain.

If I believed that I didn't have a soul, that I was alone in this vast empty universe and that nothing was ultimately right or wrong, I would have despaired in disturbing ways, possibly choosing to end my life.

Though I still wrestled with that option, my solid foundation of faith given to me by my parents and my church provided a place to land when my heart was crushed. I clung to God in my moments of deepest pain. He was the anchor to which my soul was desperately attached as my life swung wildly to and fro. He was the foundation upon which I rested when I was exhausted from the hurting in my soul and anguish in my body as I heaved great tears of lament.

Now, emerging from my own torturous journey five years later, I believe more firmly than ever that part of doing life right is to push through the disasters well. But what does this mean?

It means at least that we survive and that we do so with authenticity and honesty. It means that we don't do further damage to ourselves and to others. And it means we push past survival into thrival (a new word I just made up). Survive, then thrive. Survive—then let your scars tell their stories to heal others. Be comforted so you can be a comforter. Be healed so you can be a healer. Be a survivor so you can show others how to survive and thrive.

We all wrestle with why bad things happen to us. Someone has said that every religion is an effort to explain and deal with suffering. Substitute the word *philosophy* for *religion* in the above statement and I believe it is true.

Christianity cannot always explain suffering but our faith fervently believes that light pushes out the darkness. While we can't always explain the source or reason for the darkness, we know that light makes the darkness flee.

The Apostle Paul makes this point in his second letter to the Corinthians:

> *Praise be to the God and Father of our Lord Jesus Christ, the Father of compassion and the God of all comfort, who comforts us in all our troubles, so that we can comfort those in any trouble with the comfort we ourselves have received from God. For just as the sufferings of Christ flow over into our lives, so also through Christ our comfort overflows.*
>
> *If we are distressed, it is for your comfort and salvation; if we are comforted, it is for your comfort, which produces in you patient endurance of the same sufferings we suffer. And our hope for you is firm, because we know that just as you share in our sufferings, so also you share in our comfort.* (2 Corinthians 1:3–7)

My aim—in the spirit of the passage above—is that my suffering not be wasted. The suffering I have experienced and God's amazing comfort can be shared with you, thereby sharing and relieving some of the terrible burden you bear.

In the end, *doing it right* is really about **peace in the soul**. Unfortunately too many Christians have made faith all about conforming to rules. While it is true that our lives go better if we play within God's rules, it's also true that suffering comes to all. Playing by the rules will not spare us pain in this world.[4] In fact, when we play by the rules and still suffer, we may feel even more deeply wounded by God.

How can we have peace in suffering? How can we find rest for our souls and resist the urge to explain, overcome, mitigate and eliminate our pain? Peace comes through a deep, unbreakable friendship with God. This friendship with Abba begins with knowing you are loved, accepting his promised presence, and learning to hear his voice so that

---

[4] As a friend of mine said, *If you're going to be stupid you better be tough.* But even smart people suffer.

eventually you do less talking and more listening to him. Just as the deepest places of suffering go beyond human language to describe, so too does an authentic walk with God escape our attempts to express it, much less codify it. One aim of this book is to help you take steps toward being friends with God.[5]

Doing it right is also about **resilience**. Resilience is the ability of a material (such as metal) to bounce back after it has been stressed. Applied to the soul, resilience means that when we suffer a blow we move through it in God's timing along the path he chooses for us in such a way that we are eventually back in the game. Resilience is about celebrating God as our Deliverer.

By finding God's peace and getting back into life, we accomplish the larger goal of suffering which is to glorify God. To glorify God in the midst of pain is sometimes unspeakably difficult and I, for one, readily admit failing many times. But in the end, if God is glorified, we can count ourselves among the resilient.

The view from 30,000 feet is that *doing it right* is also about **finishing well** for the generations that follow. It's about leaving a legacy because what you leave behind matters. Research shows that how we handle difficult times and how we pass these stories down to our children builds resilience in children and is a predictor of their success.[6] Children who know about their family's successes and challenges learn that hard times come to everyone, but by sticking together and pushing through, they too can survive and thrive through life—and have some stories to tell their children.

Before we go too much further, I need you to know that I know what suffering is. To demonstrate my intimate knowledge of suffering I will express suffering on the following page:

---

[5] Charles Spurgeon wrote, *A close relationship with Christ is a certain cure for every trouble. Whether it is the bitterness of affliction, or the sickening excess of earthly delight, close fellowship with the Lord Jesus will take sharpness from the one, and dullness from the other.* Charles Spurgeon, *Morning and Evening: Updated Language Edition* (Grand Rapids: Discovery House, 2016) Kindle Location 2826.

[6] Bruce Feiler, *The Secrets of Happy Families*, (New York: William Morrow, 2013), 36-39.

You who have suffered know what I mean by that big black empty space. Simply put, I have no words to adequately describe the human soul lost in anguish. Philosophers, poets, theologians, song writers and many others try to describe the soul in pain—but all fail. Deep suffering is beyond description—at least in human language.[7]

Paul aptly describes this when he says in Romans 8.26: *We do not know what we ought to pray for, but the Spirit himself intercedes for us with groans that words cannot express.*[8]

Previous to 2014, I had heard of people being so grief-stricken that their sobbing took their breath away. Since then I have cried these kinds of tears, and it hurts.

But just because suffering really hurts—and sometimes hurts beyond words—doesn't mean you can't get through it and even beyond it to a new place of hope and healing. Though deep grief feels like you are dying, you are not. This book is designed to help you push past what feels like death into a new hope. But in my efforts to help you survive and then thrive beyond suffering, never for a moment think that I am trivializing your pain. If you believe I have done that, please send me an email! You have my permission to call me out.

In fact, one of my complaints of resources addressing grief is that too often it seems pain and suffering are belittled. It is possible to hurt beyond words. Nothing in this book is intended to minimize a pain that words cannot express. It is the nature of human communi-

---

[7]C.S. Lewis wrote: *I had been warned—I had warned myself—not to reckon on worldly happiness. We were even promised sufferings. They were part of the programme. We were even told, 'Blessed are they that mourn,' and I accepted it. I've got nothing that I hadn't bargained for. Of course it is different when the thing happens to oneself, not to others, and in reality, not in imagination.* C.S. Lewis. *A Grief Observed* (Collected Letters of C.S. Lewis) (New York: HarperCollins, 2009), 48.

[8]Tim Keller notes that *Pain and evil in this world are pervasive and deep and have spiritual roots. They cannot be completely reduced to empirical causes that can be isolated and entirely eliminated. As Hamlet said, "There are more things in heaven and earth than are dreamt of in your philosophy..."* Perhaps even more to the point is a line in J. R. R. Tolkien's novel *The Lord of the Rings*: "Always after a defeat and respite, [evil] takes another shape and grows again." Timothy Keller, *Walking with God*, 79. The Psalmist writes (Psalm 55:5-8): *Fear and trembling have beset me; horror has overwhelmed me. I said, "Oh, that I had the wings of a dove! I would fly away and be at rest. I would flee far away and stay in the desert; I would hurry to my place of shelter, far from the tempest and storm.*

7

cation that words must be used to communicate. But as miraculous and amazing as human language is, words cannot capture the depth of pain and suffering. Where my words fail to do so, it is not my intention.

My own journey of trauma and loss began on December 16, 2013 when I left a regular monthly meeting of my church's leadership. I was stunned to learn that this group of people I had served and served with for twelve years had been meeting behind my back and was actually investigating me for 'crimes' of which I was never informed. This intrigue led to my completely unexpected forced termination of the church I had pastored for over a decade. I was devastated.

But on that December night in 2013 I certainly wouldn't have predicted that less than two years later my wife of 32 years would leave me as well (October 2015). An unexpected and unwanted divorce was finalized May 20, 2016, one day before what would have been our 33rd wedding anniversary. The next day she was at a Journey concert with High School friends. I wasn't feeling so chipper.

Through those events I would eventually lose so much—my hard-earned reputation, my career, hundreds of thousands of dollars, and so much more. But I would also gain much. I gained a deeper walk with God—much deeper. I would gain the most wonderful woman in the world, my wife, Kelly, who is a burst of sunshiny encouragement, peace and hope. I would write a book, *Daily Survival Guide for Divorced Men: Surviving & Thriving Beyond Your Divorce*.

When I asked my un-divorced friends to critique my book, they inevitably said that though they were not divorced, the stuff in it helped them in their time of need.

Thus was born this new book—a daily dose of hard-earned wisdom to help us all get through the deep valleys of pain into a spacious place of hope and healing.

When my world fell apart the moorings upon which I had tied my life shredded. I felt adrift, alone, lost, uncertain, frustrated and angry. Very angry. It is in those moments that we choose to hang on for dear life or get lost in self-destructive behaviors that end up hurting us and those around us much more than we could imagine in the moment.

When I look back on those weeks and months that follow my

termination as Lead Pastor of the church I loved and then the abandonment of my wife of 32 years, I ask myself:

- What would have happened if I had chosen self-destruction rather than reconstruction?

- What was saved in my life then, now, and in my future by the compassionate and courageous help given to me by the few friends and family who dared walk this dark road with me?

- What could God bring out of such deep pain and loss that could help others in their moments of unspeakable pain?

My friend, I cannot explain the darkness. As John Eldredge says, *being on the planet is like arriving at a movie 20 minutes after it started. Sometimes the movie feels like a comedy. At others, it is a deep tragedy.*[9] I have some ideas on why this is and those ideas come from the Bible and we will explore them later. But for now I know one thing and that is that *the light pushes against the darkness.* It was in this revelation that I found my next steps in a world where every path I had ever known was shut off like a 5,000 foot cliff that suddenly dropped behind me. But there is a path in front of me—and it is a path filled with people like you who need a hand, a word, a hug.

I invite you to push against the darkness by embracing the light of Jesus. If you are not sure about that or if that even seems repulsive to you, don't worry. We have time—God has time—and he is patient and tender with his wounded sheep.

Right now you are in pain and you are looking for relief. Know this: Our God who created a world of immense variety has many tools to get back on your feet and back in the game. And he will do it! **You will get through this!**

Through this process you will be transformed in remarkable ways. You may be thinking: *I've been hammered with everyone telling me to change! I'm sick of it! I don't have the desire or energy to change!*

Maybe some things in you really do need to change—patterns of thinking and behaviors that contributed to the suffering you are

---

[9]John Eldredge, *Restoration Year: A 365-Day Devotional* (Nashville: Thomas Nelson, 2018), page 217.

enduring. The last thing you want to hear from me is that you need to change!

I get that. That's why I used the word *transform* instead of *change*. What I don't mean by the word "*transform*" is to make you feel guilty or ashamed or afraid. When people change out of guilt, shame or fear, it doesn't last. And that kind of 'transformation' is not what is really needed or wanted. What I mean by *transformed* is the changing of your inward soul through a love relationship with God that is soul-nourishing and soul-building. Transformation is about God's good and powerful grace reshaping your mind, heart, soul and emotions for his glory and for your good. That's a good thing. It's good for God, good for you, and good for the world.

One of my favorite authors, Chris Tiegreen, writes, *Our minds must fit the eternal patterns of heaven, not the momentary aberrations of earth.*[10]

In time and with your cooperation, God will re-format your mind to *fit the eternal patterns of heaven*. In fact, if you ride this kayak all the way to the ocean, you will actually be thankful for the pain you are in right now because you will recognize that what you have gained in really knowing and being known by God is far better than anything bad the world can throw at you and anything good the world can entice you with.

Weird huh? That God can take something so terrible as your unspeakable loss and bring something spectacular out of it? But that's our God! He can take the crucifixion of his Son on Friday and turn it into a glorious resurrection on Sunday.

Just to be clear as to where we are headed with all this: God doesn't want to squeeze you from the outside until you fit some kind of mold that is acceptable to the people around you who have been squeezing you ever since you can remember. God wants to move in your life in a way you may have never experienced, and through his powerful and amazing love, shift your heart and life in a direction that you will find deeply satisfying and fantastically rewarding. As God does this work inside you, all the outside stuff will naturally

---

[10]Chris Tiegreen, *The One Year Worship the King Devotional* (Carol Stream: Tyndale Momentum, 2010), 19.

change. Some people will like what they see you becoming. Others will not. Oh well! We want to please God *first*.

Now is your chance to grow into the person God intended you to be. You will discover that *the person he wants you to be* is the person *you really wanted to be all along*. You will experience a confidence and peace that seems to 'fit' you and your particular universe. You will experience a solid grip that holds firm through the storms that try to uproot you and send you out to sea.

God's work in your soul is his energy operating in the unseen depths of your innermost being. God is not a drill sergeant who wants to erase who you are inside so you conform to some external standard. God's energy in you is motivated by his persistent love which relentlessly pursues you—his beloved daughter or son—so he can lavish his love on you and so you can really know him as your dad, perhaps the dad you never had.

Are you ready to experience God's love this way? Maybe all this seems daunting to you, perhaps overwhelming right now. As I look back on those first months following December 2013, I remember that all I wanted was (1) relief from the pain and (2) hope for the future. Surviving through each day was about as much as my soul could grasp. I also remember that taking a few minutes each morning to spend time with God *saved my life from suicide, gave me comfort knowing that I was loved beyond imagination, and kept alive a tiny ember of hope that this terrible time in my life would not last forever.*

You may be down, but you are not out. You may be crushed, but my friend, you are not dead. You may be face down on the turf, but *you will get up, take a deep breath, and get back in the game.* Know this: *No life has failed if God transforms and transmits his grace, love and power to, in and through you.*

When we enter this process something amazing happens: As we experience God's gracious healing and gentle conviction, he begins to use us to clean up our messes and help repair others. I know this sounds daunting right now but it is doable by

- Taking one day at a time,

- Seeking God's grace and strength, and

11

- Holding on to hope in this moment and for the future.

Life is hard, sometimes unspeakably hard. So many times I have wanted to give up, to resign myself to what appeared to be the inevitable, to throw in the towel and just go to sleep. But deeper than those urgings is the desire to push through and actually thrive. I want to live again, to be back in the game, and use what has happened to me to help others. I want you to keep going. God has a bright future for you and me.

Nulla tenaci invia est via...
For the tenacious, no road is impassable.

How to Use This Guide

> **Choose a time**... morning, lunch, evening. Mornings are best because you can usually control when you get up and you have the advantage of starting your day with God. Everything in your mind and body will tell you that getting up 30 minutes earlier than normal is *not normal!* Trust God to make up the energy you lose from a little lost sleep, and he will do it. I promise.

> **Find a quiet place**... free from distractions.

> **Settle your mind**. Ask God to quiet your thoughts. Don't worry if your brain is still cluttered. God is just glad we show up.

> **Ask God to give you peace**. Take a deep breath and rest in his care. This is tough because we want to be in control. Surprise! You are not in control and in the end, that's a good thing. Recognize this reality by giving yourself into God's care. Imagine him giving you a huge bear hug.

> Listen to, play or sing along with some **worship songs** if this is helpful.

> **Read this Daily Guide** beginning with the first day. The readings are designed to carry you along a journey of healing. Note that some days will involve more reading than others. Hang in there and read each day completely. Nothing is more important than your recovery, so giving yourself time to it is a worthy investment.

> **Take time to pray**. Prayer is not complicated. Just tell God what you want to tell him. If you are new to this, this will be a

one-way conversation—you will talk and God will listen. With time and patience, however, you will begin to hear the voice of the Shepherd.

- ➤ If writing stuff down (**journaling**) helps, do it. For decades I've heard how wonderful journaling is. Frankly, I've been too busy to journal. But if it helps to put your thoughts down, do it. You may write out what is going on in your life or perhaps write a prayer to God.

- ➤ **Take your time!** This devotional is not your ordinary devotional. We will delve into topics with more depth than most devotionals. That said, you don't have to read a day in a day. Take two or three days to do one day if you need. God may have you pause on one of the topics we cover to do some work in your soul. This is about transformation, not performance. Let God lead.

A Few Notes on What to Expect

> ➤ Some of the quotes will not be expressions of what I believe to be true. They are meant to get you to think. Take them as they are and consider whether they express truth or not.

> ➤ Many of the readings are designed to be in a short series. In other words, we will explore one topic over a series of several days. Each day will give you something to think about and help you on this road to recovery. But some days may not be wrapped up neatly. Keep reading, keep thinking, keep praying! A table with the series titles and places they show up is found on page xv.

> ➤ This is a more thoughtful and thorough devotional than most. Some of the days will be longer than others. Remember that you don't have to do a day in a day! Take your time. Let God lead as he will.

The journey you are on is hard. Remember that you will get through this. You will survive and thrive beyond your troubles.

What you are experiencing now doesn't define you and will not last forever. Healing and hope are ahead of you. Believe it because it is true. I know. I've been there.

CRITICAL THINGS TO THINK ABOUT NOW

Crises, traumas, tragedies, catastrophes, disasters, heartbreaks—whatever you want to call them—bring us to our knees. When we feel we are in a free-fall, many thoughts come crashing into our mind. When that happens commit to the following habits. Make these rock-solid convictions from which you will not deviate.

> **Invest in time with God.** Spending time with God will give you energy, not take it away. Getting up 30 minutes earlier each day to be with God will *not* make you more tired. Your true strength comes from God. Time with him will put energy *into* you, not take it away.

> **Lower your expectations of what you can accomplish.** No one expects a patient after open-heart surgery to run a marathon the next day. Or week. Or year. Dial back what you expect to accomplish in this tough season of life. This will most likely *not* be the most productive time in your life. That's OK. As you heal, strength will return. There will be times of amazing productivity in the future. It is winter now, not spring. Be easy on yourself. For more on this **GO TO DAY 15.**

> **Exercise.** I can't emphasize enough how sweating will give you energy. Don't go for the marathon, just get moving at least a little every day. Small steps lead to big strides. You will be surprised how a little physical energy invested when you least feel like it will energize you for the rest of the day. For more on this **GO TO DAY 57.**

> **Sleep.** A common experience for those going through a terrible time is to want to curl up in bed and escape through sleep. This is normal since your mind is working hard to process all that is

happening. You definitely need sleep, but don't sleep too much. If you *just* want to sleep that could be a sign of depression. You will need more sleep but not too much. For more on this **GO TO DAY 56.**

➤ Don't waste your energy or money on anxiety, drugs, alcohol, pornography, buying stuff or escaping to the Caribbean. That's stupid and only makes things worse. Don't make things worse.

Sources for Immediate Help

If you are in immediate crisis and you think you may do harm to yourself or someone else, call one of the numbers below or go to their website now (services listed below with only a website do not have a crisis phone line):

> For direct and immediate help, **Dial 911.**

> **National Suicide Prevention Lifeline**: 800-273-8255
> *www.suicidepreventionlifeline.org*

> **Homicide Prevention Hotline & website**: 800-273-8255
> *www.savingcain.org*

> **Alcoholics Anonymous**: *www.aa.org*

> **Celebrate Recovery**: *www.celebraterecovery.com*
> A Christian-based recovery program for all addictions meeting in local churches.

> **Divorce Recovery**: 800-489-7778
> *www.divorcecare.org*

> Help with Pornography:

> — Be Broken Ministries, Jonathan Daugherty,
> *www.2.bebroken.com*

> — Faithful & True Ministries, Mark Laaser
> *www.faithfulandtrue.com*

> — Pure Desire Ministries, Ted Roberts,
> *www.puredesire.org*

> Sexual Abuse: 800-656-HOPE (4673), www.rainn.org

> Domestic Violence: 1-800-799-7233, www.thehotline.org

Day 1: You Will Get Through This Because God is For You

The Word

In the day when I cried out, you answered me,
and made me bold with strength in my soul.

— Psalm 138.3

Thought for the Day

You start with a darkness to move through,
but sometimes the darkness moves through you.

~ Dean Young

The most important question on my mind growing up was, "Am I good enough?" The answers from my dad and others were conflicted. On one hand, I was told I was special and nothing could stop me. I would be spectacular. On the other hand, if I was anything less than spectacular, it was my fault. Given the deluge of criticism I received, it seemed that though I was special, I never seemed to measure up to my specialness!

Not to kick a dead horse till its teeth fall out, but most of us grew up with this double message from our parents, our schools, our peers. To be accepted we had to jump through hoops that were just out of reach. The message we received was, *you can do it... but you probably won't.*

Implicit in this message was that people were both for me and against me, both my friend and my enemy, my companion and my challenger. People were as likely to push me down as they were to help me up.

God is not like that. Did you get that? God is not a super-sized human who acts like the people who raise us and cast us off into adulthood. God is for you. He is with you. He is on your side. He wants you to win, to succeed, to have peace. He is not capricious, he does not change his ways or his thoughts. He is not human. He is God.

So what about this God? Whose side is he on? Romans 8.31 says, *If God is for us, who can be against us?* God IS for you!

This is the truth you need to let sink deep in your soul: God IS for you, and because he is for you, you will get through this.

Paul goes on to say in verse 32, *He who did not spare his own Son, but gave him up for us all—how will he not also, along with him, graciously give us all things?*

Perhaps you are in your painful circumstances because you made a bad choice. Maybe your pain is part of living in this sin-soaked world. Maybe someone betrayed you. And then there is just living in a fallen and mortal world where things decay and die including our bodies, our dreams, our loved ones.

Whatever your situation, whoever you think are, God is for you. He wants you to know him and experience his presence and his power to sustain you through this time and transform you into the person he made you to be.

Just start with this simple reality: God is FOR you.

If you don't believe that right now, give God some time and space to work. Ask him to show himself to you. He will do it, I guarantee it!

In the day when I cried out, you answered me, and
made me bold with strength in my soul.
Psalm 138.3

THINK ABOUT IT . . .

- Who do you imagine God to be?

- If you were face-to-face with God, what would he look like? What would he say? What would he do?

- Where do you think your images of God came from?

LIFE COMMITMENT:

I choose to believe God is for me and that he is on my side. I choose to believe that despite what circumstances may say about my life, God has my best interests in mind and I can trust him with my present and with my future.

Day 2: Pain and What to Do with It

The Word

What I feared has come upon me; what I dreaded has happened to me. I have no peace, no quietness; I have no rest, but only turmoil.

— Job 3.25–26

Thought for the Day

All meaning seems to have evaporated leaving behind in its wake an empty sinking hollowness filled with darkness.[11]

~ Mark LaRocca-Pitts

Wikipedia defines pain as "a distressing feeling often caused by intense or damaging stimuli...."

But you don't know pain until you have experienced pain. Then you *know* pain.

The moment I knew I was being divorced, my soul was transported to a place it had never been before. The pain I experienced cannot be explained, only experienced. Millions of people experience this pain, but it goes unspoken and unaddressed because our culture says that we cannot feel that way. But I did.

After about six months of spiraling black thoughts, emotions tumbling all over the place and living through the sheer agony of what I was going through, I wondered what would happen if I just started posting *all* my thoughts on Facebook. What if I posted raw, unfiltered comments on what I thought, what I felt, and what I considered doing?

---

[11] Mark LaRocca-Pitts, Four FACTs Spiritual Assessment Tool, *Journal of Health Care Chaplaincy*, 21:2, 2015, 51-59.

The few times I actually did reveal my inner reality through posting on Facebook, the pushback was swift and trite—the theme of the message being, *"God will take care of you, suck it up, have faith. Get over it."*[12]

In other words, *We don't really want to hear about your problems, and we certainly don't want to listen to you whine about them.*

But the reality is that I was dying inside. My heart was crushed, my soul was disintegrating inside me.

Then I found this verse in Job.[13] I think of Job as a fairly manly guy. I mean, he was super successful and seemed to be a genuinely good and humble man, but strong as well. But when his world came crashing down, he told it like it was: *What I feared has come upon me; what I dreaded has happened to me. I have no peace, no quietness; I have no rest, but only turmoil.*

If you think you are not in pain, check again. If you think you cannot feel your pain, step back and observe what you are feeling. If you think it is a sign of weakness to name your pain and try to offload it, then consider Job. Job hurt and he said how much he hurt.

Here's the thing: *God did not cause your pain but he knows about it.* And he knows that he can do something with your pain—like ease it up over time and transform it. God doesn't waste pain. Think about that: *God does not waste pain.*

One of my favorite thinkers states, *You will be wounded. Your work is to find God and grace inside the wounds.*[14]

You're in pain—deep pain. The world may not want to hear about it or even care, but God does. Tell him about your pain. Then ask him to do something with it. If you keep your heart open, you will *find*

---

[12] For more insight, see Andrew Root, *"There's No Crying on Social Media!"* accessed March 24, 2017, http://www.christianitytoday.com/ct/2017/march/theres-no-crying-on-social-media.html?utm_source=ctweeklyhtml\&utm_medium=Newsletter\&utm_term=14285049\&utm_content=502739904\&utm_campaign=email.

[13] The story of Job (pronounced like it rhymes with 'robe') is found in the Bible, the 18th book in the Hebrew Bible (the Old Testament). Job was a righteous, prosperous man who loved God. But Job lost everything—his family, his wealth, his health—very quickly to various disasters.

[14] Richard Rohr, Joseph Durepos, and Tom McGrath, *On the Threshold of Transformation: Daily Meditations for Men* (Chicago: Loyola Press, 2010), p. 255.

God and grace inside the wounds. That's what this journey is about. Hang in here with me. But much more important is to hang in there with God.

THINK ABOUT IT . . .

> ➤ Think back to a time when someone or something caused you pain. What did you feel? Anger? Sadness? Resignation? Hopelessness? Helplessness?

> ➤ What did you do? Rage? Retreat? Learn something new?

> ➤ What do you feel right now?

LIFE REALITY CHECK:

I acknowledge my pain. It hurts and it hurts deep in my soul.

Day 3: Transformed or Transmitted?[15]

The Word

A bruised reed he will not break, and a smoldering wick he will not snuff out. In faithfulness he will bring forth justice; he will not falter or be discouraged till he establishes justice on earth.

— Isaiah 42.3–4

Thought for the Day:

*We can choose to throw stones, to stumble on them,
to climb over them, or to build with them.*

~ William Arthur Ward

PAIN COMES TO ALL living creatures, some caused by us, some visited upon us by others and some just because we are on planet Earth. Whatever the source, the question before you is, *What will I do with my pain?* This is an extraordinarily hard question to answer and however you answer it now will be challenged in the days, weeks and months ahead. You will be asking this question of yourself many times and will have to struggle with the answer each time.

When others have answered this question poorly, untold misery has been visited upon our world. That's because of a fundamental law of the universe: *Pain that is not transformed is transmitted.*[16]

---

[15] This phrase comes from Richard Rohr whose wisdom and ability to turn a phrase I greatly admire. I can't think of a better way to say this so with humility I shamelessly borrow from Fr. Rohr. He gave me permission!

[16] "Richard Rohr Quote." A-Z Quotes, accessed December 28, 2016, http://www.azquotes.com/quote/814475.

Untransformed pain turned *outward* becomes violence against others. Pain turned *inward* turns to violence against oneself. Both are destructive and potentially deadly options.

Untransformed pain lashes out at others and self. Untransformed pain only multiplies as the victims of our untransformed pain must decide what to do with the pain *we* have inflicted on *them*. And so the cycle that began in the Garden continues into the world today.[17] Untransformed pain is like spilling oil on a pond—it keeps spreading and is impossible to put back into the jar.

We lash out at others because we think that if we unload our pain we will be rid of it. But hurting others only increases our pain, it never diminishes it. If we turn our pain against ourselves, we somehow believe that we can kill our pain with pain. That's like trying to quench your thirst by not drinking. To think we can use pain against others or ourselves to lessen our own pain doesn't make sense. But this is what most of us do.

You hurt. Like Job you *have no rest, only turmoil*. What to do with your hurt? There is a better way. Today, would you commit to continuing the journey to find that better way?

THINK ABOUT IT . . .

As you begin your journey toward recovery, think about what you are doing with your pain...

> ➤ In what ways are you offloading your pain onto *others*?

    __ I lash out at others.

    __ My mind is dominated by thoughts of revenge.

    __ I am seeking ways to hurt those who have hurt me.

---

[17] The 'Garden' to which I refer is the Garden of Eden. The story of humanity's creation, fall and redemption starts in this remarkable story found in Genesis, the first book of the Bible, the first four chapters (Genesis 1-4). I recommend reading these chapters. It explains a lot of how we got here, what went wrong, and God's purpose in bringing us back. For a different (but I believe to be thorough and true) view of these chapters, see John H. Walton, *The Lost World of Genesis One: Ancient Cosmology and The Origins Debate* (Downers Grove, IL: IVP Academic, 2009) and John H. Walton, *The Lost World of Adam And Eve: Genesis 2-3 and the Human Origins Debate* (Downers Grove, IL: IVP Academic, 2015).

➤ In what ways are you turning your pain inward onto *yourself*?

    __ I have serious thoughts of suicide. (If so, call the Suicide Prevention Hotline: 800-273-8255)

    __ I am depressed.

    __ I am choosing risky behaviors, not caring what happens to me.

    __ I am medicating myself with alcohol and/or drugs.

➤ Is your strategy working?

    __ Yes, I feel better and believe that lashing out is a productive strategy for dealing with my pain.

    __ No, though it seems that transmitting my pain would get rid of it, I still feel the pain.

    __ I'm not sure... still thinking about it.

LIFE COMMITMENT:

I have a choice as to what to do with my pain. Though at this moment I don't fully understand what this means, I choose to let God transform my pain. I choose not to transmit it.

Day 4: Giving Your Pain Away

The Word

Therefore, since we are surrounded by such a great cloud of witnesses,
let us throw off everything that hinders and the sin that so easily entangles,
and let us run with perseverance the race marked out for us.
Let us fix our eyes on Jesus, the author and perfecter of our faith,
who for the joy set before him endured the cross, scorning its shame,
and sat down at the right hand of the throne of God.
Consider him who endured such opposition from sinful men,
so that you will not grow weary and lose heart.
— Hebrews 12.1–3

Thought for the Day:

Even if the whole world refuses to understand or validate the anguish one is
experiencing, yet Jesus Christ never changes. He always understands and
remains willing to help and bring healing to every throbbing emotion.[18]
~ Keturah Martin

IT WAS THE LAST run of the day. The sun was setting, the slopes
beginning to clear of skiers. I pushed off the mountain and fairly
screamed down the course. All was well until the bottom of the run.
My ski caught the top of a stump protruding through the snow. I
tumbled end-over-end, the skis whirling around me. Blood gushed
down my face when I sat up. Damage assessment revealed a deep
gash on my head.

---

[18]Keturah C. Martin, *Jesus Never Wastes Pain but Can Bring Eternal Gain*
(Bloomington: Xlibris, 2014), 392.

An hour later a doctor used needle and thread to sew my head back together. It hurt.

I got through it by focusing on something else: the amazing story I would tell back in school!

When we hurt we naturally focus on ourselves and the source of our pain. But when we hurt because of our poor choices or the betrayal of someone close to us, there is no glory in the pain, only the pain. This frustrating dynamic of pain can tempt us to transmit our pain to the ones who have caused it, including ourselves. And rare is the person (including myself) who has not transmitted their pain in some way—or a lot of ways.

There is another way, a third element that can lift us out of the cycle of feeling pain and transmitting it, only to get slammed again, and transmitting it... you get the picture. It is possible to break this cycle through the transformation of our pain. The catalyst (and source) of our transformation is Jesus himself.

Let us fix our eyes on Jesus...

When I was sitting in the doctor's office about to have my head sown up, my pain was transformed by fixing my eyes on myself and the glory the story would bring to myself.

When you are sitting alone with much worse pain, you may fix your eyes on yourself out of pity or guilt, or you may fix your eyes on those who have caused your pain out of anger. There's no glory in that.

There is a another way. Look to Christ and consider what he did with his pain. Jesus was perfectly innocent—he had never sinned. Yet he suffered the worst injustice—and the most painful consequences—death on a Roman cross. What did he do with his pain?

Jesus knew God was transforming his pain into glory for God and for our good. Through the amazing story of Jesus' sacrifice for us, God would be the hero of the greatest love story ever told, and the object of his suffering (us), would be saved from an eternity in hell and, instead, spend eternity in heaven.

Jesus didn't focus on the people who nailed him to the cross. Jesus lifted his eyes to God. God's glory came first, not personal revenge. To Jesus, our salvation was a higher priority than personal comfort.

Jesus could sit with his pain knowing that enduring his pain well would glorify God and save us from hell.

You are in pain. There is no personal glory in this pain, no great story to tell your friends when you get back to school. Your pain is embarrassing, frustrating, maddening. But your pain is not beyond transformation and redemption. Take your eyes off yourself and *consider him who endured such opposition from sinful men, so that you will not grow weary and lose heart.*

Reality check: I know this may be nearly impossible to read much less think about actually doing. In fact, you may be about to throw this book through the window! Hang in there with me. God will do a work in you. It will take time.

By looking to Jesus, you are taking your eyes off yourself and those who have caused the pain in your life. In the days ahead we will explore exactly how to focus on Jesus, but for now, commit to looking to Christ rather than focusing on yourself or others. Again, I reiterate that this is a goal difficult to achieve.

THINK ABOUT IT . . .

➤ Who is Jesus to you? Was he weak or strong? Was he a man or a wimp?

➤ What do you think Jesus thought when he was being nailed to the cross? If you were Jesus, what would you have been thinking?

➤ What would have happened if Jesus had chosen revenge while hanging on the cross, sending death angels to take out those who had unjustly nailed him on those wooden beams?

LIFE COMMITMENT:

Though I don't understand all that this means right now, I choose to let God transform my pain by fixing my eyes on Jesus. I deliberately choose to trust that Jesus can transform my pain for God's glory, my good, and the good of the world.

Day 5: What You Hear is Important

The Word

Whether you turn to the right or to the left,
your ears will hear a voice behind you, saying,
"This is the way; walk in it."

— Isaiah 30.21

Thought for the Day:

Those who trust his voice must learn to hear it above all other voices out
there. And the only way to do that is to hear the other voices and still
choose His.

~ Chris Tiegreen

ELIJAH WAS A MIGHTY prophet. He risked everything for God in the face of an overwhelming enemy. You may recall the story—he went head-to-head with evil King Ahab and the priests of Baal. He challenged them to a cosmic dual between Baal and Yahweh. The scene was the top of Mt. Carmel. The priests of Baal built an altar for their god. Elijah built one to Yahweh. The god who burned up the offering would be the winner. The losers would be slaughtered.

The priests called upon Baal to rain down fire. Nothing happened. They cried out more, Elijah taunted, still nothing. Then Elijah called on Yahweh. Fire fell down consuming every part and parcel of the sacrifice. God and Elijah won!

But there was this woman named Jezebel. She was the queen and when she heard the news from Mt. Carmel she was furious. She sent word to Elijah: *I'm coming after you.* And what did this mighty man of God do in response? He ran for his life (1 Kings 19)

Elijah hit the mother of all lows: *He came to a broom tree, sat down under it and prayed that he might die. "I have had enough, Lord," he said. "Take my life; I am no better than my ancestors." Then he lay down under the tree and fell asleep.* (vs. 4–5)

Life can turn on a dime. We can go from the mountaintop of success to the pit of despair with just a few shifts in circumstances. We can go from amazing strength and confidence to debilitating weakness. In those moments it may seem God has left us. *Exactly the opposite is true.* God is ready to fill us up when we are emptied out.

In Elijah's 'broom tree' moment God gave him food and sleep. Then God called him to the mountain:

> *And the word of the Lord came to [Elijah]: "What are you doing here, Elijah?"*
>
> *He replied, "I have been very zealous for the Lord God Almighty. The Israelites have rejected your covenant, broken down your altars, and put your prophets to death with the sword. I am the only one left, and now they are trying to kill me too."*
>
> *The Lord said, "Go out and stand on the mountain in the presence of the Lord, for the Lord is about to pass by."*
>
> *Then a great and powerful wind tore the mountains apart and shattered the rocks before the Lord, but the Lord was not in the wind.*
>
> *After the wind there was an earthquake, but the Lord was not in the earthquake.*
>
> *After the earthquake came a fire, but the Lord was not in the fire.*
>
> **And after the fire came a gentle whisper.** *When Elijah heard it, he pulled his cloak over his face and went out and stood at the mouth of the cave. (1 Kings 19.9–13, emphasis mine)*

Earth, wind and fire... we live in a cacophony of sound. Just look at a cable news channel. On a single screen at least seven inputs of information jump at you—a talking head, pictures, tickers, sidebars. Unbelievable!

God is not in this noise. His voice is above and beneath and beyond the noise.

God wants to guide you. He longs to show you the way. The key is to be still and listen for his gentle whisper. The key is to be still and listen for his *above and beneath and beyond voice.* If you are under the broom tree wishing you had never been born, *you can expect God to speak to you.*

When he does, you can be amazed but don't be surprised. His conversation with us is to be the norm, not the exception.[19]

God knows your troubles. He hears your cry. He is ready to provide for you (food and sleep) and to talk with you (*after the fire came a gentle whisper*). At the right time he will give you a new mission, a new purpose for the rest of your life. And he will let you know that you are not alone.

As you read the end of Elijah's story (below), look for these actions of God:

> *When Elijah heard [God's voice], he pulled his cloak over his face and went out and stood at the mouth of the cave.*
>
> *Then a voice said to him, "What are you doing here, Elijah?"*
>
> *He replied, "I have been very zealous for the Lord God Almighty. The Israelites have rejected your covenant, broken down your altars, and put your prophets to death with the sword. I am the only one left, and now they are trying to kill me too."*
>
> *The Lord said to him, "Go back the way you came, and go to the Desert of Damascus. When you get there, anoint Hazael king over Aram. Also, anoint Jehu son of Nimshi*

---

[19]Willard reminds us that *God wants to be wanted, to be wanted enough that we are ready, predisposed, to find him present with us. And if, by contrast, we are ready and set to find ways of explaining away his gentle overtures, he will rarely respond with fire from heaven. More likely, he will simply leave us alone; and we shall have the satisfaction of thinking ourselves not to be gullible.* Willard and Johnson, *Hearing God: Developing a Conversational Relationship with God* (Downers Grove: Intervarsity Press, 1999), 273.

*king over Israel, and anoint Elisha son of Shaphat from
Abel Meholah to succeed you as prophet.*

*Jehu will put to death any who escape the sword of Hazael,
and Elisha will put to death any who escape the sword
of Jehu. Yet I reserve seven thousand in Israel—all whose
knees have not bowed down to Baal and all whose mouths
have not kissed him."* (1 Kings 19.13–18)

THINK ABOUT IT . . .

> How has God spoken to you in the past?

> What did Jesus mean when he said in John 10.27 *"My sheep
listen to my voice; I know them, and they follow me"?*

> If you have not heard God speak to you, ask him to. Then take
some time to read the Bible (his main voice to us), be still in
his presence, and open your heart and mind to the possibility
that he really does want to speak to you, guiding you through
this storm and giving you a new purpose for your life.

LIFE COMMITMENT:

*I believe God wants to speak with me, guiding me through this storm
into a future with a mission and purpose.*

Day 6: When You Hurt Your World Shrinks

The Word

> *Then Job took a piece of broken pottery*
> *and scraped himself with it as he sat among the ashes.*
> — Job 2.8

Thought for the Day:

> *When we're in the middle of adversity, it feels all consuming.*
> *Faith flickers, hope falters, courage burns low.*
> *It sometimes seems as if the dark times will never end.*
> *And these are the hours when the enemy of our soul*
> *whispers his lies of discouragement and despair.*
>
> ~ Joni Erickson Tada

UNINVITED AND UNMITIGATED SUFFERING shrinks our world. When things are good, we feel we are in a 'spacious place.' We feel freedom to move, dream, spend, engage. Then the disaster happens and our world of hurt shrinks us to this moment, this place, this pain.

Time slows down to *this moment*. If we think about the *past* it hurts—either we deeply regret the mistakes that led to our pain or we grieve the hard work we put in to avoid such a catastrophe.

The *future* is so uncertain and painful, we can't think about it. Whatever we had planned for our future is now off the table. The pain of the past and the uncertainty of a frightening future compress time to the terrible *now*.

When we hurt, **<u>space</u>** also compresses. Forget the vacation trip to Colorado, forget the plans to remodel the kitchen, forget organizing my desk. Pain is the heat that shrinks our space around us.

This was driven home to me when I was asked by a family to visit their 32-year-old son who was dying of a rare form of cancer. I went to the hospital, introduced myself, and began to chat it up. He seemed disengaged from what I was saying. Then, without a word, he stood up, pulled up his hospital gown, and urinated into a plastic urinal as if I wasn't there.

For this 32-year-old man, time and space had shrunk to this moment and to his hospital bed. He didn't care about anything I said. He just needed to pee, so he did. Two days later he died.

When the Old Testament figure of Job had lost everything, his world shrank to an ash heap (see the scripture for today).

If this is the way you feel, then...

> Know that it is normal to feel like time and space have shrunk to this moment and this little space.

> When terrible pain is upon you, you may feel like time needs to shrink to nothing and that you need to leave the space. We call this option *suicide*, and it is a bad and terrible idea. It is OK to experience compressed time and space, just don't let the pain squeeze the life out of you. If you feel like this at this moment, read the next point...

> You will not always feel like this. The process of healing will re-expand time and enlarge your space. *I promise you that you will not always feel like this.* But if you are considering suicide as a viable option to your suffering, call the National Suicide Prevention Hotline now: 800-273-8255.

THINK ABOUT IT . . .

- When you have suffered in the past, did you experience pain shrinking your time and space?

- If you are further down the road of recovery, are you experiencing an expansion of time and enlarging of your space?

LIFE COMMITMENT:

It is normal for pain to compress time and shrink my space. I commit to living through this moment, but I pray to God that he will deliver me from this pain, and I trust he will do it. I will hold on.

Day 7: When You Hurt You Become Super Sensitive

The Word

Why is life given to a man whose way is hidden, whom God has hedged in? For sighing comes to me instead of food; my groans pour out like water. What I feared has come upon me; what I dreaded has happened to me. I have no peace, no quietness; I have no rest, but only turmoil.

— Job 3.23–26

Thought for the Day:

We rarely start with God. We start with the immediate data of our lives—a messy house, a balky car, a cranky spouse, a recalcitrant child.

~ Eugene Peterson

I HAVE WALKED WITH many men and women through the heartbreak of divorce, death, illness, financial devastation. One couple in particular comes to mind. Both were super-achievers. Each had tried to overcome tremendous adversity the world's way, and had ended up in more pain than when they started. They finally found Christ and things between them improved.

But staying together was not to be. For whatever reasons, anger rose up and lashed out and both found themselves filing restraining orders against the other as tensions exploded.

It was a long and painful season for them both. The church staff and I reached out in every way possible. We met with them, recommending counselors, nursing each through their pain. Church folks watched their kids when things were imploding at home. All this to say, we gave them our best time and energy.

So it came as a shock when a fellow staff member and I received a scathing seven page single-spaced email from the wife. My staff member walked into my office and stated that this was the longest email she had ever received! After all the time and energy we had put into this woman, my first response was anger. But then we realized the pain this woman was in had made her hurt so deeply that the smallest thing would seem super painful to her. Intense pain had made her super sensitive.

When your world comes crashing down, time and space shrink and you may become hyper-sensitive to your environment and those around you. I know I did when I went through a painful divorce. I couldn't believe that most of my friends made no effort to reach out. And most of those who did venture forth simply didn't get the intense pain I was in. It angered me and pushed me further into isolation.

Looking back now I understand a little better. I now realize how my pain drove me to seek someone, *anyone*, who would understand. Few did. But the few who did saved my life.

If the people in your life seem insensitive or not to care, don't be surprised. Some really don't care. Some may care but are uncomfortable sitting with someone who is in such intense pain. Others shy away because they don't want to be reminded of what could happen to them.

But a few will get it. A few will understand. Thank God for these few. Seek them out. Ask them questions. Let them into your heart.

And release everyone else from the burden of sharing your burden. God knows who you need to help you through. Find those folks and be grateful to them and to God for what they give you.

THINK ABOUT IT . . .

- Who among your friends and/or family has failed to reach out to you? Release them from your anger. They don't understand and you can't make them understand. Instead...

- ... Ask God to send you a few, maybe even just one, to get you through. And...

41

- ... Determine that you will not be insensitive to the hurting. Further down the path, when God puts hurting people in front of you, love them as you have been loved. (Remember 2 Corinthians 1.3-7).

PRAYER:

Not everyone will understand. Not everyone will get it. God, thank you for the few who do. As I heal, help me to be one of those 'few' to the hurting and suffering in this world.

Day 8: When You Hurt You May Lash Out

The Word

Teach me knowledge and good judgment for I believe in your commands.
— Psalm 119.66

Thought for the Day:

There are too many people today who instead of feeling hurt are acting out their hurt; instead of acknowledging pain, they're inflicting pain on others. Rather than risking feeling disappointed, they're choosing to live disappointed.

~ Brené Brown

No one likes to take their dog to the vet, least of all, the dog! We have all been shocked when our normally loving and tail-wagging dog suddenly bares his teeth and emits a low, menacing growl. What causes our adorable pet to transform into a frightening beast? The short and simple answer is, *pain*. When normally benign animals are cornered or hurt, they turn ugly. So do we. Hurt people hurt people.

When my life crashed around me my first reactions were benevolent. I tried to understand why others were coming against me. I tried to be gracious to those who had betrayed me. But then the reality of what I had lost began to sink in and I became angry.

I can illustrate this through a Facebook Messenger conversation with a longtime friend. It started with me explaining what had happened in my life the past two years. My friend acknowledged the difficulty of the situation, then wrote,

I will remind you that our God is big. Really big. He came to reconcile and leaves us with a ministry of reconciliation. He is most glorified when we are most like him.

My response?

If I did not know God was big I would have put a .40 caliber bullet through my head a few months ago. Having to go through this with you just brings it all back so maybe I should just give the lite answer when someone I know hasn't heard.

It should come as no surprise that I didn't get a response from him.

What happened in this conversation? My friend tried to understand, then he off-loaded the 'Sunday School answer' to my pain in a way that I heard as condescending and trite. This infuriated me more, and when he let the conversation drop, my anger only increased. I did *not* feel like a minister of reconciliation. I felt like I wanted to hurt him and all those who had wounded me so deeply.

When we are in severe pain we need to express it in ways that don't further alienate us from those trying to help. Ask God to give you the one or two people who can absorb your pain without further hurting you.[20]

And then release anger through other means. For me, my bike is my outlet. I let the hurt anger flow from my head down through my legs and into the pavement. My record rides have come when I have been most angry. I can't over-emphasize the value of sweating. Channel that angry energy away from others and into the pavement or weights or yoga. *When you are angry and frustrated, get moving.*

And if you are on the receiving end of someone who has been severely wounded, *leave the trite answers at home.* Instead, absorb their pain, even if it is directed at you. Hurt people lash out. Let them. Then, when the time is right, God will use you to mitigate some of their pain.

---

[20] Brené Brown writes, *Most of us were never taught how to hold discomfort, sit with it, or communicate it, only how to discharge or dump it, or to pretend that it's not happening.* Brené Brown, *Rising Strong: How the Ability to Reset Transforms the Way We Live, Love, Parent and Lead* (Random House, 2017), Kindle Location 859.

Think About It . . .

> What do you do when you are really hurt?

> What are some physical ways you can let pain out that are legal and only moderately dangerous?

> Who is the friend or counselor who is mature enough to sit with you in your pain?

> Who in your life needs you to sit with them in their pain?

Life Commitment:

I commit to releasing my hurt in as constructive a way as possible.[21]

---

[21] To read more, go to this website: http://www.charismanews.com/opinion/the-pulse/53573-15-ways-hurting-people-hurt-people.

Day 9: When You Hurt You May Be Willing to do Anything to Get Out of the Pain

The Word

Blessed is the man who does not walk in the counsel of the wicked or stand in the way of sinners or sit in the seat of mockers. But his delight is in the law of the Lord, and on his law he meditates day and night. He is like a tree planted by streams of water, which yields its fruit in season and whose leaf does not wither. Whatever he does prospers.

— Psalm 1.1–3

Thought for the Day:

Our search for significance shows up in a lot of misdirected ways.

~ Tony Dungy

As we all know, the Chinese characters for the word *crisis* mean *danger* and *critical point.*[22]

Crises push us to critical points where we have opportunity to choose well or not.

Suffering comes from a variety of reasons. Perhaps your suffering is a direct result of some bad decisions you made. Perhaps you are the victim of a wayward or misguided person in your life—a spouse, a child, a parent. Maybe you got fired or laid off or your house burned

---

[22] See https://en.wikipedia.org/wiki/Chinese_word_for_%22crisis%22 for a brief discussion about the common misinterpretation of this phrase.

down. Maybe a natural disaster devastated your home and all those around you for miles. We all suffer the death of loved ones. Perhaps your pain is from the loss of someone close to you. In any painful situation, you and I have choices to make from this point forward. The problem is that our intense pain can push us to make poor decisions with long-term consequences.

If there ever is a time when you need to slow down and seek God's wisdom and the wise direction of others, this is it. The intensity of the pain can falsely make you believe you must make decisions *now*. Don't make any huge decisions now. Stop, pray, talk with wise friends, seek out a counselor. Don't make any major decisions when you are hurting the most.

Paul Tripp says, *We all tend to surrender to and serve what we think will give us life.*[23] In your pain you may be led to believe that what gave you life before has radically failed, and it's time to try something new. If what you believed would give you life is anything less than God, then, yes, it's time to try something new, or rather, *Someone* new. God is ready for you to surrender to him and find your life and significance in him.

One thing is guaranteed: If we think we will find life in things less than God, we will be disappointed, betrayed, damaged, and eventually, destroyed. Alcohol, drugs, sex, shopping, work, hobbies... these *horizontal* things will not deliver what only our *vertical* God can deliver.[24]

And remember this: *Thinking and doing are two different things.* You have probably *thought* of doing one or more (or all) of the things listed above. But *thinking* and *doing* are two different things. You may *think* of doing a lot of things. Just *don't do* them.

Consider these things in your moment of crisis:

➤ How do you want to be remembered?

---

[23] Paul David Tripp, *New Morning Mercies*, Kindle Location 4163.

[24] Something is deeply wrong in our country. Deaths by alcohol, drugs and suicide have dramatically increased in the past 20 years. See https://www.usatoday.com/story/news/health/2019/03/05/suicide-alcohol-drug-deaths-centers-disease-control-well-being-trust/3033124002/this article for more information.

➤ How do you want your kids to think of you now?

➤ What is the cost of choosing poorly now?

We suffer because we have lost something or someone. We have lost something that gave us significance. Take the advice of Wayne Stiles who writes, *We need a different goal: faithfulness rather than significance.*[25]

In your time of crisis, choose to be faithful to God. In the end, faithfulness to him will pay off *now* and for *eternity.*

THINK ABOUT IT . . .

➤ Consider these good words from Paul David Tripp:

No person can be the source of your identity.

No one can be the basis of your happiness.

No individual can give you a reason to get up in the morning and continue.

No loved one can be the carrier of your hope.

No one is able to change you from the inside out.

No human being can alter your past.

No person is able to atone for your wrongs.

No one can give your heart peace and rest.[26]

Asking another human being to do those things is like requiring him to be the fourth member of the Trinity and then judging him when he falls short. It simply cannot and will not work.[27]

LIFE COMMITMENT:

I commit to finding my significance in God and not in another person, place or thing. From this point on my choices will be driven by being faithful to God, not on easing my pain.

---

[25] Wayne Stiles, *Waiting on God: What to do When God Does Nothing* (Grand Rapids: Baker Books, 2015), 24.

[26] Tripp, *New Morning Mercies*, Kindle Location 3962.

[27] Ibid., Kindle Location 3960.

Day 10: When You Hurt You May Question Everything

The Word

*Trust in the Lord with all your heart and lean not on your own
understanding; in all your ways acknowledge him, and he will make
your paths straight. Do not be wise in your own eyes; fear the Lord
and shun evil. This will bring health to your body and nourishment
to your bones.*

— Proverbs 3.5–8

Thought for the Day:

*We say that there ought to be no sorrow,
but there is sorrow, and we have to accept and
receive ourselves in its fires.*

~ Oswald Chambers

THEY SAY THAT THE little toe was given to us by God to show us
where the furniture is in the middle of the night. If I slam my toe
into furniture in the dark, the pain transmitted to my brain will cause
me to question several things. *Have I lost my sense of direction in the
dark? Has someone moved the furniture without me knowing? Am I
getting old and losing my mind?*

The point is, every pain we experience causes us to question
something. The deeper the pain, the more penetrating the questions.

When I was a chaplain at Children's Medical Center in Dallas I
talked with a very confused father. His daughter was dealing with
juvenile diabetes, and she was struggling. Her struggle was serious

but not life threatening. Just a few hundred feet away the kids in the liver transplant unit fought for every moment of life.

But this dad was angry and upset, disproportionally so. As he looked out the window he shook his head and said to me, *I don't get it. I started going to church. I started giving money, lots of money. And my daughter is still sick.*

Without knowing it, this father had tried to bargain with God: *God, I will give my life to you, I will give my money to you. And if I do my part, you must do your part, and your part is to take this sickness away from my daughter.*

When his daughter remained sick, he questioned God. Instead of questioning God, however, he should have questioned his bargain with God. God cannot be manipulated into doing our bidding.

But this dad was hurting for his daughter, and his pain caused him to ask some tough questions.

Don't be surprised if you find yourself doubting deeply held beliefs. I know I did. I had given my life to the church. When I was booted out of the church I had faithfully served, I had serious doubts about the church at large. I had followed the right path regarding marriage. I had followed the rules. But my marriage didn't turn out the way I had been promised it would. All I had believed about marriage was up for review in my mind's eye.

When your ground is shaken, allow yourself to ask the hard questions, *but always come back to God.* Even if you doubt him, come back to him and ask him to give you what you need to settle your heart and quiet your mind.

Take a look at Psalm 73. Here is a man who, in his pain, was questioning everything. Finally, he says, *When I tried to understand all this, it was oppressive to me till I entered the sanctuary of God; then I understood...* (Psalm 73:16–17)

God doesn't mind our questions. In the midst of our hard questions he always invites us into his sanctuary to experience his love and grace.

Think About It . . .

> ➤ What foundational beliefs have you questioned through this painful process?

> ➤ How can you know what beliefs should be ditched and which should be kept?

Life Commitment:

I commit to the truth. I commit to shedding old, false beliefs and finding the truth in God.

Day 11: When You Hurt You Don't Care

The Word

My people are fools; they do not know me. They are senseless children; they have no understanding. They are skilled in doing evil; they know not how to do good.

— Jeremiah 4.22

Thought for the Day:

Discouragement focuses more on the broken glories of creation than it does on the restoring glories of God's character, presence, and promises.

~ Paul David Tripp

As LONG AS YOU are feeling your pain, you care. As long as you are questioning what you believe in, you care. As long as you are fighting to do the next right thing, you care. As long as you are struggling with decisions, you care.

But if you stop feeling, if you stop questioning, if you stop thinking, if you stop struggling, you don't care anymore. Even a person stuck in self-pity cares—if only for him/herself.

A person who doesn't care is a dangerous person indeed.

But it's easy not to care. It's easy to throw up your hands and walk away—*the world (and God) be damned.* It's easy to fall into the pity pit and curl up in a ball and die. The easy way is not to care. The easy way is to give in to despair. The easy thing is to give up.

When you feel like that, *or if you stop feeling anything*, stop, pray, and find someone to talk with. And if you haven't gotten to this place, know that you very well might. Several times.

Don't give in to this strong pull to give in to the despair. Know that our enemy (Satan) wants to destroy you. His primary targets are families, churches, fathers, mothers, children. If you are human you are a target, and Satan's goal is destruction.

Push back. You are in a fight bigger than yourself. More is at stake than your immediate pain. What you do, how you respond, the choices you make will reverberate far wider *now* than you know and far *longer* than you can imagine.

Don't let your pain shrink your time and space to this tiny moment and this pinpoint of space. Allow God to expand your perspective of time—there is more to your life than this painful, present *now*.

Allow God to enlarge your space. If you give in to despair your space shrinks to nothing. If you push back and allow God to lead you through this, your place of positive, life-giving influence will expand far beyond what you can imagine.

THINK ABOUT IT . . .

> ➤ When have you despaired? What triggered that emotion? An email from your boss? A text from your bank warning of an overdraft? A bill from your lawyer? An ignored text to your child? A dire medical report?

> ➤ What did you do? Dwell on it? Or give it to God?

> ➤ If you feel your time shrinking, pray. Breathe deeply. Relax into God and allow him to love you back into a larger time frame. If you feel your space shrinking, take a walk. Get outside and let God use the beauty of his creation to expand your space.

PRAYER:

God, I am tempted to give in to the despair. The pain is too much, or so it feels that way right now. Give me strength to push back. Give me hope. Give me encouragement—put courage into my heart again. Help me see the bigger picture. Help me see beyond this moment. Help me see the future you have for me. Help me see the influence you can have through me to my children and to the world. Deliver me from the enemy.

DAY 12: SURVIVAL

THE WORD

This poor man called, and the Lord heard him;
he saved him out of all his troubles.
The angel of the Lord encamps around those who fear him,
and he delivers them.[28]
— Psalm 34:6-7

THOUGHT FOR THE DAY:

You see, if you quit, you lose. But so long as you stick it out,
you're still in with a chance.

~ Bear Grylls

This poor man called... When I read this verse I hear the cry of a guy who has had to deal with so much he just hangs his head and sings, *"Nobody knows the trouble I've seen, nobody knows but Jesus."* I've been that poor man!

Much of our time is spent managing circumstances to prevent disasters. In spite of our best efforts, disaster strikes. The pain is a body

---

[28]To fear God in the Bible means to have a reverential awe of him. Part of that awe is to literally fear him—he is the most powerful being in the universe and is rightly feared (Matthew 10.28). At the same time, to be in awe of God is to be amazed by him and his handiwork in creation and beyond. William Eisenhower says, *As I walk with the Lord, I discover that God poses an ominous threat to my ego, but not to me. He rescues me from my delusions, so he may reveal the truth that sets me free. He casts me down, only to lift me up again. He sits in judgment of my sin, but forgives me nevertheless. Fear of the Lord is the beginning of wisdom, but love from the Lord is its completion.* William Eisenhower, "Fearing God," *Christianity Today*, March 1986

blow that takes you to the mat. Our first priority is to survive this take down and eventually get back on our feet to fight another day.

Thankfully I have never been in armed combat, but I understand that when a soldier goes down, several things happen. First, the wounded man cries for help. Next, his buddies respond by immediately coming to his aid. Third, they protect their fallen comrade from further harm. Fourth, they stabilize the wounded man and, lastly, they get him out.

A terrible event is not the same as an RPG going off in your Humvee, but the impact of the disaster on your soul is a slashing wound which cuts through your heart. In the midst of your pain, call on God. When you call on the Lord, he sets into motion the same process that happens on the battlefield.

He **Hears**. God hears all our prayers, but when he hears the cry of a desperate person, he bends his ear in a way that gives special attention to the one crying out. God hears that cry, whether the pain is of the body or of the soul. Like a mother who instantly recognizes the wail of her baby from ten other screeching babies, your cry to God is instantly heard and given special attention.

He **Encamps**. When a soldier goes down, his buddies immediately surround him with weapons facing outward to protect the wounded warrior from further harm. In the same way, God surrounds you. He is a refuge, a place of safety. The attacks may continue but the impact of those attacks on your soul are shared by God who is beside you and all around you. He's got your back (and your front).

He **Saves**. The Hebrew word used here means *victory*. The poor man is surrounded by God's mighty protecting angels and help is immediately given to heal and restore. Just as treatment of the wounded soldier begins on the battlefield, so does God begin to stop the bleeding in your soul *right now*.

He **Delivers**. The Hebrew word basically means *he gets you out of there!* Just as powerful forces are marshaled to get a wounded soldier off the battlefield and into a field hospital, so too God gets us out of the painful place we are in. It will take a while, but to know you will not always be in pain is a ray of hope giving you resolve to hang on.

Survival begins with calling out to God. As proud people who are defined by our ability to go it alone and live a self-sufficient life, this is a hard and humble place to be. But the smart poor man or woman is going to do one simple thing: *Call on the Lord.* God is coming to your aid right now.

One other thing: If you are in survival mode, **set realistic expectations.** No one expects a wounded soldier to function at the same level he was before he was shot. In the same way, when you are in the middle of your pain, your ability to function will be diminished. Learn to be OK with that.

When things were really hard in recent disasters, I had less energy or motivation to do things. I wanted to sleep more and things looked gloomy, even good things. I lost a big chunk of that *oomph* that I relied on to get through the day. To cope, I cut the things in my daily schedule that weren't necessary. But I kept doing the things that I knew gave me life—my morning time with God, strumming my guitar, eating right and exercising, and fulfilling my commitments to work.

Think About It . . .

> ➤ Where are you in the journey? Have you just been 'hit' and are lying on the battlefield with serious wounds? If so, have you called out to God for help?

> ➤ How have you experienced God's rescue before?

Life Commitment:

I am calling on the Lord for help right now. Just as there is no shame for the wounded soldier to admit he is hit and needs immediate help, I declare that there is no shame for me to call on God to save, deliver and heal me. God, help me!

Day 13: Resilience

The Word

I am able to do all things through Him who strengthens me.
— Philippians 4:13

Thought for the Day:

The special characteristic of a great person is to triumph over the disasters and panics of human life.
~ Seneca

To put it simply, resilience is the ability to bounce back. Technically, the definition goes like this: *Resilience is the capability of a strained body to recover its size and shape after deformation caused especially by compressive stress.* The Latin base of *resilient* is *salire*, a verb meaning to *leap.*[29]

Resilience is the ability of the football player who has been 'shaken up' to shake it off and stand up to play again. It is the ability of the runner to push through the last mile of the race.

I love the White Mountains of New Hampshire. One of my favorite hikes is up Mt. Lafayette. Combined with Mt. Lincoln and Little Haystack, it's a grueling nine miles with 3,860 feet of elevation.

One particular trip I was leading a group from my church. One of the men, Mike, slipped off a wet rock and twisted his knee. He grimaced in pain as we assessed what to do. Nearly halfway through the

---

[29] *Merriam-Webster Dictionary, s.v.* "Resilience," accessed January 16, 2017, https://www.merriam-webster.com/dictionary/resilience.

hike, Mike determined to keep going. As happens with the wounded, Mike lagged.

As we began our descent I was with two of Mike's kids further along the trail. The kids and I stopped for a breather. Mike eventually caught up to us. As Mike approached, one of his kids said, *Hey look, Dad's alive!* Mike *was* alive, and still in the game, though moving slower than the rest of us. Mike was resilient![30]

Quitters are remembered for, well, quitting! And then they are quickly forgotten. But those who persevere are remembered not for what put them down but how they managed to get back up.

How will you get through this? Where does your resilience come from?

The only enduring answer is that our ability to bounce back comes from God. When we *reach the end* of our strength, smart folks *reach out* to God. If my survival is up to me, my strength is limited which means I will give up which means I will not be resilient.

Not so God. His strength is unlimited as is his unswerving commitment to you. For his **glory** he wants you to endure. For your **good** he wants you to bounce back. He is invested in your success, and your success depends on you getting back up. And getting back up depends on God.

When Paul wrote *I am able to do all things through Him who strengthens me,* he was not talking about leaping over tall buildings or building a wildly successful corporation. He was talking about resilience. *Through Christ* I can get back up and keep going. Tell God right now that you need him to pick you up. Tell him that you need his strength to get through this day. Then take a deep breath. You are in good hands.

THINK ABOUT IT . . .

- ➤ When have you been down and then gotten back up? How did it feel to get back in the game?

- ➤ When have you walked away from the challenge to get back up? Do you regret the decision to quit?

---

[30] In case you are wondering, we didn't abandon Mike on the trail! My team took turns helping him along the way.

- What does getting back up look like right now?

- What does relying on God for your strength look like?

LIFE COMMITMENT:

The easiest thing to do when down is to stay down and then slink off unnoticed. I will not do the easy thing. With God's strength, I will get back up and get back in the game.

Day 14: Wisdom

The Word

Get wisdom, get understanding; do not forget my words or swerve from them. Do not forsake wisdom, and she will protect you; love her, and she will watch over you. Wisdom is supreme; therefore get wisdom. Though it cost all you have, get understanding. Esteem her, and she will exalt you; embrace her, and she will honor you.

— Proverbs 4:5–9

Thought for the Day:

Talent is God-given. Be humble. Fame is man-given. Be grateful.
Conceit is self-given. Be careful.

~ John Wooden

A DISTINCT MEMORY I have of my first days at the University of Texas was that I was sure all the other incoming freshmen had it figured out and I was the only one who was still trying to. Much to my surprise, I learned that everyone else was still trying to figure it out too!

Thirty-five years later as a hospice chaplain I sit with the old to the extremely old. I have learned that they are still trying to figure it out too. Even the 99-year-old retired pastor had his moments of wondering. Somehow that is both comforting and disturbing.

Wisdom is of two elements: *seeing clearly* and *deciding correctly*. To make wise decisions takes clarity of vision.

During this time when your life has been turned upside down by death, divorce, illness, unemployment, you need clarity.

But just because you have clarity doesn't mean you will make winning decisions. Wisdom means more than just seeing the world clearly. Wisdom entails making decisions based on the right motivation.

A friend of mine was a mechanic at Carswell Air Force Base in Fort Worth, Texas. One day he came to church shaken. I asked what happened. He said that the day before, a French pilot was training in a fighter. The pilot came screaming over the runway upside down, then the pilot pulled 'up.' The problem was that 'up' to the pilot was, in reality, straight down onto the tarmac just outside the hanger where my friend was working on a plane. Imagine an F-16 slamming into the pavement at that kind of speed. This disaster happened because the pilot thought he was right-side-up when he was really up-side-down.[31]

Though the pilot was far more qualified and accomplished than probably almost anyone reading this, the *lack of clarity* on his part led to death and destruction. He visualized the path ahead upside down, and that is where he ended up... or rather down.

But let's say that the pilot really did understand that he was flying upside down but he flew his plane into the tarmac anyway. Why would he make such a decision? The only answer would be that he wanted to take his own life. In that case, he was clear about where he was, but his darkened heart led him to make a terrible decision.

It is critical during this time of upheaval that you make wise choices. You need to think with a clear head and decide with a pure heart.

To do this requires that you look outside yourself for wisdom. You must relocate the source of your wisdom from yourself to God. The source of all wisdom is God, and God showed himself most clearly to us in his Son, Jesus Christ. If you want to know how to live wisely in this world, listen to everything Jesus said and watch what he did.[32]

---

[31] *"List of accidents and incidents involving military aircraft (1980–89)."* Wikipedia, accessed January 05, 2017, https://en.wikipedia.org/wiki/List_of_accidents_and_incidents_involving_military_aircraft_%281980%E2%80%9389%2.

[32] Dallas Willard writes, *[Jesus] is not just nice, he is brilliant. He is the smartest man who ever lived. He is now supervising the entire course of world history (Rev. 1:5) while simultaneously preparing the rest of the universe for our future role in it (John 14:2). He always has the best information on everything and certainly also on the*

Will you relocate the source of your wisdom from yourself to God? Will you follow Jesus in finding clarity and courage to make wise decisions?

If so, you can take some steps right now to make that happen:

> **Ask God for wisdom.** Expect him to give it.[33]

> **Read the Bible.** A good place to learn about Jesus is to begin reading the book of John. Just read a few verses each day asking yourself *"What did Jesus say and what did he do?"*

> **Find a church** that is following Jesus. Go and listen. Ask questions.

> **Find some other people** who are following Jesus. Get together to bounce your ideas off them. Allow God to use other godly people to help you gain clarity of mind and purity of heart.

Wisdom is the art of being successful, of forming the correct plan to gain the desired results. Its seat is the heart, the centre of moral and intellectual decision. [34]

THINK ABOUT IT . . .

> *First we make our choices, then our choices make us.* Consider the past year. What choices did you make and what were the consequences?

> If you made poor choices, determine now to make better choices from this moment on (beginning with following the steps above for gaining wisdom!)

---

things that matter most in human life. Let us now hear his teachings on who has the good life, on who is among the truly blessed. Dallas Willard, *The Divine Conspiracy: Rediscovering Our Hidden Life in God* (San Francisco: HarperSanFrancisco, 1998), 96.

[33] *If any of you lacks wisdom, he should ask God, who gives generously to all without finding fault, and it will be given to him. But when he asks, he must believe and not doubt, because he who doubts is like a wave of the sea, blown and tossed by the wind. That man should not think he will receive anything from the Lord; he is a double-minded man, unstable in all he does.* (James 1.5–8)

[34] D. A. Hubbard, *"Wisdom,"* ed. D. R. W. Wood et al., *New Bible Dictionary* (Leicester, England; Downers Grove: InterVarsity Press, 1996), 1244.

LIFE COMMITMENT:

I can choose my source of wisdom. I choose to follow Jesus. He's a lot smarter than me! Choosing Jesus is my first good choice!

Day 15: Expectations of Yourself

The Word

*And we, who with unveiled faces all reflect the Lord's glory,
are being transformed into his likeness with ever-increasing glory,
which comes from the Lord, who is the Spirit.*
—2 Corinthians 3.18

Thought for the Day:

Do I really dare to let God be to me all that he says he will be?
~ Oswald Chambers

As you move into the future, what can you expect of yourself? Of others? Of God? We will answer these questions the next several days.

What does your future look like to you right now? If you're in the middle of your pain, the future can look distressingly bleak. The losses are piling up and those losses have a way of snuffing out what tiny rays of hope that may remain.

Don't despair. Whatever is *now* will change. Whatever you feel will *not last forever*, or even for very long. Whatever losses you have incurred can be restored with God's help and blessing.

What can or should you expect from yourself in this time? Expectations can be disappointing if we set them as standards by which we choose to measure ourselves. On the other hand, expectations can and should be aspirational—expectations can lift us up to think and do things that are good for us. Expectations can be targets to aim for. We know that without a target we lose focus and direction.

Without goals we are always successful... at nothing. Expectations help us set targets that pull us forward.

With these things in mind...

Expect yourself not to give up. Paul J. Meyer, founder of the Success Motivation Institute, says, *"Ninety percent of those who fail are not actually defeated. They simply quit."*[35] Most people don't quit. Most people keep going. Be one of those people. Though it feels like it is almost too much to bear, at some point you will realize that it was *only* almost too much to bear. You will get through this.

Expect yourself to grow. Tell yourself that you will be a different person at the end of all this, and that you *want to* and *will be* a *better* person. You owe that to yourself, to your kids, and to the world at large.

Expect yourself to know God better. Like Jacob by the Jabbok River (Genesis 32.22-32), expect to wrestle with God. Like Jacob, expect God to both wound you and bless you. Expect God to take you down a bit and lift you up a lot.

Expect to hurt. There is no way to simply forget all this and not hurt anymore. But as time goes by, the pain will be less intense and less frequent.

Expect to feel better. The sharp, penetrating sting of grief and loss will lessen in frequency, intensity and duration.

Expect yourself to be a contributor to the world. Expect God to invite you into a partnership with him that will bring him glory, bring you good and bring good through you to the world. Expect God to make this a win-win for everyone. Expect to feel good about living the second half of your life for someone other than yourself.

I like the encouragement John Maxwell brings to us:

> ➤ You certainly can't control the length of your life—but you can control its width and depth.

> ➤ You can't control the contour of your face—but you can control its expression.

---

[35] Quoted in John C. Maxwell, *The Maxwell Daily Reader: 365 Days of Insights to Develop the Leader Within You and Influence Those Around You* (Nashville: Thomas Nelson, 2007), 220.

> You can't control the weather—but you can control the atmosphere of your mind.

> Why worry about things you can't control when you can keep yourself busy controlling the things that depend on you?[36]

THINK ABOUT IT . . .

> On a scale of 0 to 10, how hopeful are you about your future, zero being completely unhopeful and 10 being completely confident of God's plan for you and your future healing?

0—1—2—3—4—5—6—7—8—9—10

> Read through the expectations listed above. Which of these expectations do you see happening in your life right now? Which are on the radar? Which seem beyond reach?

> Ask God to move you toward each one of these expectations.

LIFE COMMITMENT:

I hurt but I know it won't be forever. I am down but I know I will get back up. I have been wounded but I know someday I can forgive. I have sinned greatly, but I know I am forgiven and I can make amends. I am hopeful about what God will do in my future, and I expect both him and I to make it together. The best is yet to be.

---

[36] Ibid., 193.

Day 16: Expectations of Others

The Word

*Now while [Jesus] was in Jerusalem at the Passover Feast, many people
saw the miraculous signs he was doing and believed in his name. But Jesus
would not entrust himself to them, for he knew all men. He did not need
man's testimony about man, for he knew what was in a man.*

—John 2.23–25

Thought for the Day:

Maybe ever'body in the whole damn world is scared of each other.
~ John Steinbeck, *Of Mice and Men*

WE ARE ALL EMPTY cups desperately wanting to be filled. Our problem
is that we go to the wrong source for filling.

We mistakenly expect other people to be faucets of clean, clear,
soul-quenching water. What we fail to realize is that *they* are empty
cups as well and *they are seeking to be filled from us!* When our
expectations of other people are not met, we are hurt, angry and
disappointed. We blame the other for not meeting our expectations.

It is at this point that we might try to get our cups filled with
things, rather than relationships. We call this *addiction*. The heart of
addiction is that we build a relationship with an object (drugs, alcohol,
stuff, work, etc.) and make people objects.[37]

---

[37] Craig Nakken, *The Addictive Personality: Roots, Rituals, and Recovery.* (Center City,
MN: Hazelden, 1988). Nakken writes, *Addiction is an emotional relationship with
an object or event, through which addicts try to meet their needs for intimacy. When*

Paul David Tripp is right when he says, *Many people say they believe in God, but they shop horizontally for what can be found only vertically.*[38] Satisfaction, security, strength and fulfillment can only be found in a solid relationship with God.

God certainly uses people in our lives. In the hands of God, people can become amazing sources of help to us and we to them. But they are the gift, God is the Giver. We trust God to place people in our lives to meet certain needs, and we trust God to place us where we can be of most help to others. But we must understand that because of our sin, God's tools (people) are flawed and temporary.

With this in mind, what can you expect of people? **We can expect them to meet some needs in our lives but not *every* need.** God uses people to meet some of our needs, but God is always the source.

Because all people are sinners (Romans 3.23) **we can expect people to fail us.** We remember the wisdom of John Gardner: *Most people are neither for you nor against you; they are thinking of themselves.*[39] We really want to believe people will be strong, loyal, honest and true to us. This simply will not be a reality this side of heaven.

A Buddhist saying has helped me: *The glass is already broken.* In other words, at some point, the glass that holds my water will break. When it does, I am not surprised because I knew this moment would come. People will disappoint. If you expect this, you won't be as overwhelmed when it happens.

We can learn to walk the line between trust and cynicism.

---

looked at in this way, the logic of addiction starts to become clear. When compulsive eaters feel sad, they eat to feel better. When alcoholics start to feel out of control with anger, they have a couple of drinks to get back in control. (22) My definition of addiction... is as follows: addiction is a pathological love and trust relationship with an object or event. (24) Because addiction is an illness in which the addict's primary relationship is with objects or events and not with people, the addict's relationships with people change to reflect this. Normally, we manipulate objects for our own pleasure, to make life easier. Addicts slowly transfer this style of relating to objects to their interactions with people, treating them as one-dimensional objects to manipulate as well. Nakken, *The Addictive Personality*, 26.

[38] Tripp, *New Morning Mercies*, Kindle Location 3701.

[39] "John Gardner's Writings," accessed August 06, 2017, http://www.pbs.org/johngardner/sections/writings_speech_1.html.

God calls us to love and trust one another. But he also knows that trust is earned and can be broken. Trust *first* in God, and when people disappoint, expect it and forgive. In doing this, we can walk the fine line between blind trust of people and we can stay away from the depressing pit of cynicism.

There is hope, but it begins with God and then moves to the people he places in our lives. When people disappoint, God is there to catch us, renew us, and get us ready for our next encounters where we have the opportunity to be to people what they need, which is to say, we have the opportunity to represent our kind, benevolent awesome God to others.

THINK ABOUT IT . . .

> What are you expecting from others?

> How and when have people let you down?

> How can you learn to walk with realistic hope and expectations of others and stay out of the pit of cynicism?

LIFE COMMITMENT:

My commitment is first to God then to others. I will get my soul filled from God and then let him use me to fill others and let him use others to fill me. I will remember that he is the Giver and people, including myself, are the gifts.

Day 17: Expectations of God

The Word

In the day when I cried out, you answered me,
and made me bold with strength in my soul.
— Psalm 138.3

Thought for the Day:

The Lord will make a way for you where no foot has been before.
That which, like a sea, threatens to drown you,
shall be a highway for your escape.

~ Charles Spurgeon

On October 3, 2003 performer Roy Horn was attacked by a tiger while performing the famous Siegfried & Roy show in Las Vegas. Fortunately Roy survived. Many people blamed the tiger. But comedian Chris Rock nailed it when he said, *That tiger ain't go crazy; that tiger went tiger!* [40]

Tigers do tiger things. Guess what? *God does God things.*

And what God does is show up in the middle of our crises, traumas and disasters. The reality is that we don't usually come to God in good times. We come to God when our lives fall apart. It's just the way it is.

When it all hits the fan, we get humble and needy. At that point the smart people cry out to God and God rescues us. These are the places where we can expect God, our Rescuer, to do his rescuer thing.

---

[40] Chris Rock, *"Chris Rock Tiger Gone Crazy,"*
https://www.youtube.com/watch?v=kGEv5dC0lo4, accessed October 22, 2017.

So what can you expect of God as you continue down this pathway?

Expect God to Show Up.

Every Christmas we celebrate that God showed up. Christmas is all about God's Son, *wrapped in flesh*, leaving heaven and inserting himself into the mess of humanity, not just to visit but to stay with us: *The Word became flesh and made his dwelling among us. We have seen his glory, the glory of the One and Only, who came from the Father, full of grace and truth.* (John 1.14)

Jesus didn't do a lot of explaining about why the darkness is dark. But he knew that light pushes out darkness. You may not know why your life is the way it is right now, but Jesus is light and he will show up with you to push back the darkness.

Expect God to Comfort You.

Terrible things happen to good people and it hurts in ways words can't express. When we are hurt we are desperate for comfort. Take King David, for example. There was no more manly man than King David. He whipped a giant warrior over nine feet tall. He led men into battle many times. When it comes to manly men, David rates! Yet he wrote about God: *He heals the brokenhearted and binds up their wounds.* (Psalm 147:3) Yep, manly men hurt, and manly men need God to heal our manly, broken hearts.

If you let God comfort you, you will have an experience like no other.

Eugene Peterson observes that *We don't have to wait until we get to the end of the road before we enjoy what is at the end of the road.*[41] Heaven is a pain-free place of comfort. You can enjoy heaven on earth *now*. God loves to comfort his people.

Expect God to Make a Way.

The Israelites were up against the Red Sea on one side and a charging Egyptian army on the other. When all seemed lost, God made a way.

---

[41]Eugene H. Peterson, Dale Larsen, and Sandy Larsen, *A Long Obedience in The Same Direction: 6 Studies for Individuals or Groups, With Guidelines for Leaders & Study Notes* (Downers Grove, IL: InterVarsity Press, 1996), Kindle Location 1711.

He is doing this for you and will continue to do it for you, for his Glory, for your good and for the good of the world. (See Exodus 14-15)

Expect God to Call You to a Special Mission.

God doesn't waste pain. Only you can waste your pain by not following God's mission for your life. Our world is a damaged and hurting place. God calls his people to be *wounded healers* to our dark world. God will take what has happened to you and call you to help others who only you can help:

> *Praise be to the God and Father of our Lord Jesus Christ, the Father of compassion and the God of all comfort, who comforts us in all our troubles, so that we can comfort those in any trouble with the comfort we ourselves have received from God. For just as the sufferings of Christ flow over into our lives, so also through Christ our comfort overflows.* (2 Corinthians 1.3–5)

Expect God to Empower You.

If God calls you he will equip and empower you. He certainly did this for me. After an unexpected job termination and divorce, I was physically, emotionally and spiritually exhausted. And yet I heard his clear call to write this book. He not only gave me the energy to get up at 4:30 every morning to write it, he woke me up to get on with it!

Tony Dungy writes:

> *When we focus on the obstacles in front of us, they seem to grow larger and larger until we give up. But if we focus on what God can do through us—and on His promise that if we delight in Him, He will give us the desires of our hearts—we become confident and able to achieve whatever we were designed to achieve. Start each day by focusing on what needs to occur that day. Set your mind on what you are attempting to achieve and where you want to go. If it's a God-honoring goal and you are following His leading,*

believe that He wants you to achieve it. And you will begin to see your heart's desires fulfilled.[42]

THINK ABOUT IT . . .

> ➤ How is God showing up in your life right now?

> ➤ If you don't see him at work in your life, find a trusted friend or pastor to help you see God's hand in your life. We live in a muddy, foggy world. God is at work but sometimes we need help seeing him do his God thing.

> ➤ Have you heard God's call on your life? If not, give him time. In his timing he will call you.

PRAYER:

God, my life is in tatters. So much has been lost. So much damage has been done. But despite the hurt and pain, I believe you not only will show up in my life, I believe that you want to show up. I open my life and heart to you. I desire your comfort. I know you will call me. And I look forward to you rebuilding, renewing and restoring my life, for your Glory, for my good, and for the good of the world.

---

[42] Tony Dungy and Nathan Whitaker, *The One Year Uncommon Life Daily Challenge* (Carol Stream: Tyndale House Publishers, 2011), Kindle Location 2468.

Day 18: Walden Pond
or the North Atlantic?

The Word

> *There is a time for everything,*
> *and a season for every activity under heaven.*
> — Ecclesiastes 3.1

Thought for the Day:

> *I believe in process. I believe in four seasons. I believe that winter's tough,*
> *but spring's coming. I believe that there's a growing season. And I think*
> *that you realize that in life, you grow. You get better.*
>
> ~ Steve Southerland

I CAN'T REMEMBER WHERE I read it, but someone said that while we yearn for a peaceful life on Walden Pond, real life is more like the North Atlantic in winter! For the most part, we try to live on Walden Pond, and for most of our lives we may be able to manage life closer to Walden than the North Atlantic.

But inevitably something happens that flings you into the North Atlantic where the waves are huge and the water frigid.

Divorce did that for me. All the things I had worked for, the *stability and security* I sought, slipped right out of my hands. Maybe you had this same experience. You worked hard to provide for your family. You tried to be there for your kids, you sacrificed to secure a safe and stable home. Then the bottom dropped out. Or you diligently exercised only find you have a serious heart condition. Or you gave your life to your children only to have one turn against God and against you.

The reality is this: Walden is an illusion. But so is the North Atlantic. Life is never as peaceful as Walden and it is never as completely terrifying as the North Atlantic.

I've had a 'Walden Pond' moment or two. It was great, but fleeting and still not deeply satisfying.

For three years I was flailing around in the North Atlantic with wind, water and waves crashing all around me. But just as Walden was not as great as promised, the North Atlantic was not as terrifying as imagined. The reason Walden disappoints and the North Atlantic not so terrifying is that our security and stability are not found in earthly circumstances.

Look at Psalm 46:

*God is our refuge and strength, an ever-present help in trouble. Therefore we will not fear, **though the earth give way** and **the mountains fall into the heart of the sea**, though its waters roar and foam and the mountains quake with their surging.* (Psalm 46:1–3, emphasis mine).

Did you get that second sentence? *Therefore we will not fear, though the earth give way and the mountains fall into the heart of the sea.*

Earth and mountains are supposed to be *stable.* Their collapse represents the Psalmist's worst calamity. But, he says, *because God is our refuge,* we will not fear *even if the most stable things we can imagine actually do collapse.*

If your life is more like flailing in the North Atlantic than sitting peacefully by Walden Pond, know that God is your refuge and strength and that, ultimately, nothing can shake you.

THINK ABOUT IT . . .

> ➤ Where are you right now: Walden Pond, the North Atlantic, or somewhere in between?

> ➤ Have you experienced moments of true peace due to positive circumstances? Did the peace last?

➤ When circumstances have felt like drowning in the North Atlantic, how did you feel? What did you do?

➤ What does it mean that God is our *refuge and strength*?

Life Commitment:

I am coming to realize that life is never as peaceful as Walden nor as completely terrifying as the North Atlantic. Security and safety are only found in turning to God to be my refuge and strength.

Day 19: Between Fear and Hope

The Word

So do not fear, for I am with you; do not be dismayed, for I am your God.
I will strengthen you and help you;
I will uphold you with my righteous right hand.

— Isaiah 41.10

Thought for the Day:

Everything can be taken from a man but one thing: the last of the human
freedoms—to choose one's attitude in any given set of circumstances,
to choose one's own way.

~ Viktor E. Frankl

Think about this (I realize this is a big bite, but it's worth it!):

Hope is a disposition of the soul to persuade itself that what
it desires will come to pass, which is caused by a particular
movement of the spirits, namely, by that of mingled joy and
desire. And fear is another disposition of the soul, which
persuades it that the thing will not come to pass.

And it is to be noted that, although these two passions are
contrary, one may nonetheless have them both together,
that is, when one considers different reasons at the same
time, some of which cause one to judge that the fulfilment
of one's desires is a straightforward matter, while others
make it seem difficult.[43]

---

[43] René Descartes et al., *The Passions of The Soul: And Other Late Philosophical*
Writings (Oxford: Oxford University Press, 2015), 264.

78

Every person lives between hope and fear. When things are going well, hope dominates your 'brain space.' When things get tough, fears can (and do) set in. Your brain is saturated by worrying thoughts provoked by fear.

Your soul is always in a tug-of-war between hope and fear. Usually these two emotions are in balance. But when something really bad or really good happens, hope and fear get out of balance. This creates a sense of disequilibrium that is unsettling to our soul.

There are two things to say about this:

First: Know deep in your soul that **God is the God of hope**, and *he will not be moved.* Consider these words from the Psalmist:

> *Many are saying of me, "God will not deliver him." But you are a shield around me, O Lord; you bestow glory on me and lift up my head. To the Lord I cry aloud, and he answers me from his holy hill. I lie down and sleep; I wake again, because the Lord sustains me. I will not fear the tens of thousands drawn up against me on every side.* (Psalm 3.2–6)

God is your anchor, your rock, your foundation. He will not be moved. Though you waver between hope and fear, God will not waver. He is solid when we are not.

Second, know that your goal is to keep moving.

There are two ways hope and fear can paralyze your life. First, if hope runs rampant, complacency and laziness can slow or halt our growth. As Descartes says, *When hope is so strong that it altogether drives out fear, its nature changes and it becomes complacency or confidence.*[44]

On the other hand, if fear completely takes over, paralysis can lead to self-destruction. Descartes writes: *When fear is so extreme that it leaves no room at all for hope, it is transformed into despair; and this despair, representing the thing as impossible, extinguishes desire altogether, **for desire bears only on possible things.***[45]

---

[44] Ibid.
[45] Ibid. Emphasis mine.

God is the critical ingredient Descartes leaves out. God is the bearer and bringer of impossible things, therefore **all things are possible for you that fit within God's will**. Since God is unequivocally for you and on your side, you can be sure that his will is good and right and true.[46]

When fear comes crashing in, take a deep breath, pray to God for comfort, peace and wisdom, and allow him to reassure you that you will make it and you will be OK. God will do this. He *longs* to do this for you.

THINK ABOUT IT . . .

> ➢ Are you more hopeful or more fearful right now?

> ➢ What fears are roiling around your head right now?

> ➢ What hope is God giving you?

LIFE COMMITMENT:

I will always live between hope and fear. I choose to give my fears to God and allow him to replace them with hope in his good will toward me and his desire to fulfill his purpose for me.

---

[46] *Therefore, I urge you, brothers and sisters, in view of God's mercy, to offer your bodies as a living sacrifice, holy and pleasing to God—this is your true and proper worship. Do not conform to the pattern of this world, but be transformed by the renewing of your mind. Then you will be able to test and approve what God's will is—his good, pleasing and perfect will.* (Romans 12.1-2)

Day 20: God is Your Anchor

The Word

We have this hope as an anchor for the soul, firm and secure.
It enters the inner sanctuary behind the curtain,
where Jesus, who went before us, has entered on our behalf.
— Hebrews 6.19–20

Thought for the Day:

Ultimately, spiritual maturity is not about memorizing the Bible and
mastering the spiritual disciplines. These are healthy things to do, but they
are still only means to a greater end, which in itself is learning to love with
God's love and learning to serve with God's power.

~ Gary Thomas

For a few years I had the privilege and joy of restoring a 28-foot sailboat and learning to sail it. There is nothing like the feeling of a massive boat moving silently through the water under the power of the wind alone.

After the boat was habitable, my two older children and I would spend nights on Lake Travis. Lake Travis was formed upon the completion of Mansfield Dam in 1941. The dam backed up water between limestone hills. Most of the shoreline of Lake Travis is rocky cliffs. Spending the night on the lake made me suddenly aware of the extreme importance of correctly setting the anchor of my boat so we didn't end up smashed into those rocky cliffs!

I had never given much thought to how to anchor a boat. I just thought you tossed the anchor overboard and it would hold. But when you are on a sailboat surrounded by rocks, correctly setting the anchor takes on new meaning. The last thing you want is to wake up with the boat smashing against the rocks with your two kids inside.

On one trip a cold front was predicted to come in that Friday afternoon. Sure enough, the winds went from a southerly breeze of 10 mph to a northerly howler of at least 25 mph. We were determined to spend the night on the boat anyway, so we motored to our favorite spot. But I knew that with a strong northerly wind predicted through the night, setting the anchor was critical. I took my time choosing the spot and then worked to make sure the anchor would hold.

Through the night the wind buffeted our boat but the anchor held. The next morning we were where we planned to be—safe in the cove, ready for a breakfast of pancakes and sausage. All through the night the winds had buffeted our sailboat. And through the night our boat swung back and forth, *but not too far back and forth because the anchor held.*

If you have set your anchor on one of the Four P's—Possessions, Perks, Prestige, and Power—you have wrongly set your anchor. The only anchor for your soul that will hold is God himself: *We have this hope as an anchor for the soul, firm and secure.*

The Greek word translated *firm* is formed from the negative of *fail.* In other words, the writer says that Jesus is our anchor that will not fail. The Greek word we translate as *secure* means *stable* and relates to walking on stepping stones that are sure and secure. In other words, both from the negative and the positive side, the writer of Hebrews is confirming for us as clearly as possible that God is our only hope, an anchor that will hold us secure in the storm.

Like my sailboat, you and I may swing about when the winds blow, but if we remain anchored in God we will not be set adrift to crash into the rocks.

THINK ABOUT IT . . .

➤ Into what is your anchor set? Is your anchor holding?

➤ What steps can you take to set your anchor in God? (Reading this book is a good start!)

➤ Go back and re-read Day 19. How can anchoring yourself in God help you live between fear and hope?

LIFE COMMITMENT:

God is my anchor, my rock, my sure foundation. He will not be moved. Though I may waver between hope and fear, God will not waver. He holds me secure.

Day 21: How Thinking Works (1)

The Word

Then God said, "Let us make man in our image, in our likeness, and let them rule over the fish of the sea and the birds of the air, over the livestock, over all the earth, and over all the creatures that move along the ground." So God created man in his own image, in the image of God he created him; male and female he created them.

— Genesis 1:26–27

Thought for the Day:

The difference between losers and winners is often determined between the ears.

~ Tony Dungy

ONE OF THE MOST amazing events to watch is the launch of the Space Shuttle. I have even interrupted staff meetings so we could all marvel at this magnificent sight on the TV screen. Not everyone on my staff had the same appreciation as me.

At launch the Space Shuttle and launch vehicle weigh 4.4 million pounds. The fuel, which weighs 20 times more than the shuttle itself, propels the shuttle from zero to 17,500 mph in just over eight minutes. That, my friend, is simply stunning! The engines generate 37 million horsepower. Just the fuel pumps alone deliver 71,000 horsepower!

Why do I rattle on about the space shuttle and its amazing launch? Simply because *this magnificent event started in someone's brain.* Someone thought of the idea of the space shuttle. The reality we witness on television began as a thought in someone's head. That's amazing!

In fact, your brain is the second most incredible thing in all the universe. Did you get that? That three-pound mass of cells in your head is the *second most astounding thing in the entire universe!* The first is, of course, God himself.

Only the human brain can remember the past and make meaning from those memories. Only the human brain can project into the future with an imagination powerful enough to shape that future. Only the human brain can conceptualize spiritual reality and tap the resources of the soul to access that reality. Only the human brain can think abstractly and from that abstraction and careful observation, describe reality with mathematical equations and scientific laws.

All this is because we are created in God's image. Dogs are wonderful and they think, but they don't think like us. Dolphins are cool and smart. But dolphins don't build dolphin hospitals or dolphin universities. Our ability to reason is above and beyond any other created thing.

We are more than our thoughts but in our lived experience, we are *mostly* our thoughts. That's because if you are awake, you are, by definition, thinking. This is a blessing and a curse.

We try to maintain our thoughts by controlling our external environment so inputs are comprehendible and manageable. We regulate our thinking by slowing our thoughts enough to process them. We try to control our emotions with our thoughts so emotions don't send our thoughts cascading into a downward spiral of chaos.

But when circumstances run out of control, thoughts come fast and furious and conflicting emotions build one upon another until everything in us—mind, emotions and soul—are overwhelmed. In those moments our thoughts can go in multiple directions which adds to the cascading effect. This out-of-control spiral can lead to drastic and destructive behaviors.

On January 28, 1986, the Space Shuttle *Challenger* lifted off the Florida launchpad only to disintegrate in a massive fireball 73 seconds into its flight, ending the lives of seven extraordinary people. A small separation at an O-ring allowed flaming gas from the solid rocket booster to burn through to the external fuel tank, causing cascading structural failures.

The Space Shuttle transformed much of what we know of space and brought everyday discoveries to useful applications in our everyday lives. But on that January day in 1986 things got out of control and disaster was the consequence.

Over the next few days we want to explore how we think and how we can keep our thoughts on track so we don't let our thoughts take us out in a ball of fire.

Today, however, think about this: Your brain is the second most amazing and incredible thing in all the universe! That's amazing!

THINK ABOUT IT . . .

> What do you think is amazing? How much more amazing is your brain than the most amazing thing you can think of?

> How does knowing you have the second most amazing thing in all the universe change how you think of yourself?

LIFE COMMITMENT:

Even though I may feel emotionally out of control at times, in reality I know that I possess the second most amazing thing in all the universe! That, in itself, is enough to get some positive thoughts going!

Day 22: How Thinking Works (2)

The Word

We demolish arguments and every pretension that sets itself up against the knowledge of God, and we take captive every thought to make it obedient to Christ.
— 2 Corinthians 10:5

Thought for the Day:

Feelings, and feelings, and feelings. Let me try thinking instead.
~ C. S. Lewis

Someone said, *There is nothing so easy as thinking, and there is nothing so hard as thinking well.* We all wake up thinking, but how many of us learn to think well?

The **first step** in thinking well is to **become your own observer.** By that I mean that you step back from yourself and analyze your thoughts, emotions and actions. You step outside yourself and evaluate yourself as if you were studying someone else.

Then you think about what you are thinking. Are my thoughts productive? Is my thinking leading me down a path that is helpful or harmful? If I doggedly pursue this line of thinking, what will be the result?

The **second step** in thinking well is to realize that **you make your thoughts**.

Because our thoughts are so close to us, we forget that we are making them. You make your thoughts like you make a toy car in the workshop or a cake in the kitchen. The inner 'you' is making thoughts.

The proof of this is that you can think a thought. You can choose this moment to think about what you are reading or where you will watch the football game coming up this weekend or a cooking show this evening.

The **third step** is to recognize the unproductive thoughts you are making and then **throw them out**! Like a birdhouse that looks like a rat trap, **you can throw your thoughts away!** Like a cake that is a disaster, you throw it out!

This is what the writer of Psalm 42 does:

Why are you downcast, O my soul? Why so disturbed within me?
Put your hope in God, for I will yet praise him, my Savior and my God.
(Psalm 42:5–6)

The writer tells himself to throw out those bad thoughts!

I love woodworking but I'm not great at it. A few times I have started a project that, despite my best efforts, was not coming together. When I decided that my work was beyond hope, everything I made so far went into the scrapheap.

If a line of thinking is just not doing it for you, throw it out.

The process for this to happen is that you take a step back and evaluate what you were thinking. You think about where this line of thinking is taking you. If you're not satisfied with the direction of your thinking, choose to push those thoughts out and begin a new thought.

Inside your head is the second most amazing thing in all the universe! Why waste it by letting negative thoughts pile up?[47]

THINK ABOUT IT . . .

> ➤ Pause every few hours and just observe yourself as you would someone else. What are you doing? What are you feeling? What are you thinking?

---

[47] *Resilient people are self-aware enough to notice when their thinking is counterproductive. They don't fall into thinking traps such as jumping to conclusions or making assumptions. Instead, they gather the facts they need to move around obstacles and face the challenge head on.* "Things Resilient People Do" Beliefnet, accessed January 15, 2017,
http://www.beliefnet.com/inspiration/galleries/5-things-resilient-people-do.aspx.

LIFE COMMITMENT:

I choose to think about what I am thinking and throw out thoughts I make that are not helpful.

Day 23: How Thinking Works (3)

The Word

"For my thoughts are not your thoughts, neither are your ways my ways,"
declares the Lord. "As the heavens are higher than the earth, so are my
ways higher than your ways and my thoughts than your thoughts."

— Isaiah 55:8–9

Thought for the Day:

> *Deep in the human unconscious is a pervasive need*
> *for a logical universe that makes sense.*
> *But the real universe is always one step beyond logic.*
>
> ~ Frank Herbert, *Dune*

WHAT IS THE SHORTEST distance between two points? A straight line, right? That's what I learned in geometry. But in God's geometry, the shortest distance between two points may not be the *best* way to get between two points.

Take the Israelites under the oppression of the Egyptians for example. God rescued them, promising them a homeland in what is today modern Israel. From modern Cairo (Egypt) to Jerusalem is only 264 miles. But in God's plan, the trip took 40 years and covered hundreds of miles.

To us this is insane! We want to get the job done as quickly and efficiently as possible. We don't stop for potty breaks on the family vacation because we have a destination to reach! We don't plant flowers in our garden. You can't eat flowers. What's the use of flowers?

Humans are built to think, to analyze, to figure things out. We are driven to understand our world and what is happening to us. In the three years of my greatest travail, my mind worked overtime trying to figure out the *hows* and the *whys*. I didn't get it. I simply didn't understand.

Albert Einstein said, *Any fool can know. The point is to understand.* But I didn't understand. I didn't even know all the facts but I worked hard at trying to discover them.

Søren Kierkegaard wrote, *Life can only be understood backwards; but it must be lived forwards.* OK, but I can't wrap my mind around what happened. I don't understand why people would do what they did.

Here's the deal: *You and I won't understand.* No matter how much we dissect and analyze and try to figure it out, we can't. Much of the information we would need to figure it out is inaccessible to us. We can't get into the heads and hearts of those who have caused us pain. Even if we had all the info, our own thinking processes are distorted. We even struggle to understand our own ways of thinking and the true content of our hearts.

Tens of thousands of doctors, scientists and researchers spend countless hours trying to understand why our bodies get diseased. We have made great progress but the bottom line is that we don't know why biology goes bad and we suffer disease, illness and death.

If your happiness and ability to move forward depend on you understanding what happened, you will be unhappy and stuck where you are. Instead, *start letting go of your burning need to figure it out* and let God take what is *now* and build a better future for you.

God's thoughts are not our thoughts and his ways are not our ways. The key is to trust that his thoughts are better than our thoughts and his ways better than our ways.

Paul David Tripp writes, *There will be moments when you simply don't understand what is going on. In fact, you will face moments when what the God who has declared himself to be good brings into your life won't seem good. It may even seem bad, very bad.*[48]

---

[48] Paul David Tripp, *New Morning Mercies*, Kindle Location 615.

It's here that you must push against everything that is driving you to figure it out and rest in him who knows it is best to stretch a 264-mile journey to many hundreds of miles. Trust in the God who can take a terrible Friday (the Crucifixion) and transform it into a victorious Sunday (the Resurrection). If you're in Friday, Sunday is coming. On Friday you won't get it. But come Sunday morning when Jesus is standing in front of you, you *will* get it!

Tripp tells us: *You need to remind yourself again and again of his wise and loving control, not because that will immediately make your life make sense, but because it will give you rest and peace in those moments that all of us face at one time or another—when life doesn't seem to make any sense.*[49]

God promises through Isaiah: *You will keep in perfect peace him whose mind is steadfast, because he trusts in you. Trust in the Lord forever, for the Lord, the Lord, is the Rock eternal.* (Isaiah 26.3-4)

Confession: Even as I am writing this I am still frustrated that I can't figure it out! I was born and bred on the scientific method. I spent decades reading and learning and thinking and writing. I'm not stupid. I should be able to figure this thing out. Dang it.

Think About It . . .

> How much of your time and energy is going to figuring it out?

> What would change even if you could figure it all out?

Life Commitment:

I confess that though I am hard-wired to figure it out, this time I won't be able to despite my best effort. I commit to resting in God's better thoughts and ways. He has it figured out. He's got me covered.

---

[49] Ibid., Kindle Location 629.

DAY 24: UNDERSTANDING YOUR EMOTIONS (1)

THE WORD

*A happy heart makes the face cheerful,
but heartache crushes the spirit.*

— Proverbs 15:13

THOUGHT FOR THE DAY:

*We should allow feelings and emotions to run their course, teaching us and
forming us. No feeling lasts forever. Feelings are not right or wrong; they
have no moral meaning. They are merely indicators of what's happening
in our lives on other levels.*

~ Richard Rohr

I AM AMAZED AT how sensitive we are to temperature. A few degrees
up, we are hot. A few degrees down, we are shivering.

When I feel warm, I don't get up and start yelling at the thermometer. Instead, I go to the thermostat and turn it down so the air
conditioner kicks on.

A thermometer only tells you how fast air molecules are bouncing
around—the faster they go, the higher the temp. The slower they go,
the lower the temp. A thermometer cannot *change* anything, it only
reveals something—the speed of moving air molecules.

The same is true for your emotions. Emotions are real. They
exist because something in the 'atmosphere' of your life is happening.
The part of you that God gave to you to react to that 'something'
going on inside you is reacting. You cannot not have emotions just

as you cannot not have moving air molecules (I realize this is terrible grammar but it makes the point, hopefully!)

Modern humanity relishes the science of moving air molecules. We study this phenomenon, measuring it, making up equations to describe it, using it to produce something. But when it comes to our emotions, we pretend we don't have them. We push them down and we tell others they should not have them either—think of when we tell our kids they should not be angry or upset. That's like telling air molecules moving at the speed that makes the thermometer read 100° that they shouldn't be moving that fast. We instantly recognize the absurdity of commanding molecules not to move at a particular speed. But we fail to recognize the same absurdity in commanding ourselves not to feel what we are feeling.

The reality of our emotions is independent of whether or not you acknowledge their existence. But because emotions are *only* like a thermometer—telling us something about ourselves—they are not to be feared or denied, just acknowledged and appropriately expressed.

Emotions in and of themselves are morally neutral. It's not wrong to feel angry, irritated, sad or happy. Those emotions are only reflecting what is happening inside us as we engage our world. What we *do* in response to our emotions, however, has huge moral and practical implications. But the actual emotion itself is only telling us something about ourselves.

This may be completely new information to you:

- Emotions are real.

- Emotions are like a thermometer, only indicating to us what is happening inside us.

- Emotions are morally neutral.

In the Bible we read of men and women who experienced anger, fear, jealousy, lust, terror, hatred, greed, depression, guilt, resentment, bitterness, pride, sorrow, peace, happiness, joy, contentment and the list goes on and on.

If you are still not convinced you have emotions, go to this website for a comprehensive list: https://bit.ly/2Vsrgv3.

Think About It . . .

> - What emotion or emotions are you experiencing right now?

> - What emotions have you experienced through the events and processes that are causing you so much pain?

> - If someone were to be asked what one emotion they see in you, what would they say?

> - What have you done in response to your emotions?

> - What emotions do you want to experience?

Life Commitment:

I will acknowledge I have emotions and recognize that my emotions (and the emotions of others) are only like a thermometer, telling me something about myself, not defining who I am or who I am destined to be.

DAY 25: UNDERSTANDING YOUR EMOTIONS (2)

THE WORD

Do not be anxious about anything, but in everything, by prayer and petition, with thanksgiving, present your requests to God. And the peace of God, which transcends all understanding, will guard your hearts and your minds in Christ Jesus.
— Philippians 4.6–7

THOUGHT FOR THE DAY:

... for there is nothing either good or bad but thinking makes it so.
~ William Shakespeare, *Hamlet*, Act 2, Scene 2

THE PROPHET ISAIAH LIVED through incredibly tumultuous times. After a period of prosperity, Israel was overrun by the Assyrians. Isaiah served through several governmental administrations, most of them dysfunctional and destructive.

Though Isaiah's world was chaotic and unpredictable, his message was always the same: *God is with you and for you. Trust in him.*

Isaiah makes an important point when he writes, *You [God] will keep in perfect **peace** him whose **mind** is steadfast, because he trusts in you.* (Isaiah 26:3)

The critical connection here is between *mind* and *emotions.* If you set your mind (thoughts) on God, you will experience peace (an emotion).

Here's the underlying dynamic at work: *Almost every emotion begins with a thought.* You can't feel something without the initial thought. Thinking comes before feeling. In fact, most of our thoughts will be reflected *back to us* and *out to those around us* as emotions. We think something and that thought generates an emotion. That emotion is experienced by us and, if we outwardly express it, by those around us.

A few days ago we said that the first step in training yourself to think well is to **become your own observer**. Step outside yourself and ask yourself what you are thinking.

Today take this one step further. When you feel an emotion, put a label on your emotion (anger, sadness, exuberance) and then *trace that emotion back to the thought that preceded it.*

Remember that you think first, and whatever you are thinking produces an emotion. You cannot have an emotion without a thought. Your emotions are linked to your thoughts.

THINK ABOUT IT . . .

> ➤ Is it possible to have an emotion without first having a thought?

> ➤ What emotion do you experience most? What thoughts usually precede that emotion?

LIFE COMMITMENT:

Today I will step back and analyze what I am feeling. I will then trace what I am feeling back to the thought that produced that feeling.

DAY 26: UNDERSTANDING YOUR EMOTIONS (3)

THE WORD

Like a city whose walls are broken down is a man who lacks self-control.

— Proverbs 5.28

THOUGHT FOR THE DAY:

Your reactions determine your reach.

~ Lysa TerKeurst

I HAVE LOTS OF friends in Africa, fellow pastors mostly. One of my African friends made his first trip to a developed country when he came to America as part of a seminary training program. He—along with dozens of other pastors from around the world—convened at a seminary in the southeastern US for their six weeks of classes. They were housed in student dorms on the seminary campus while the regular students were on summer break.

They had a problem: they nearly froze to death even though it was summertime! The dorm was equipped with air conditioning, and it really worked. In fact, it kept their rooms at 60° F or below. Night after night the students bundled up as best they could to survive the uncomfortably cold temps.

When one of their teachers heard a student complaining about the cold, the teacher went to the dorm and showed the majority world visitors how to use the thermostat. Yep, it was that simple!

Most of us reading this will be amazed that these students didn't know how to use a thermostat. But we who may laugh at these students fail to understand a simple truth about ourselves: *our emotions operate like a thermometer and thermostat.* Our emotions are like a thermometer—they simply tell us what is going on inside us. Like the uncomfortably cold air in the dorm rooms of the students, our emotions can't be ignored for long.

But like that cold air in the dorm, our emotions can be controlled, but you have to know how.

We are like the students who were clueless as to how first world air conditioning works. We experience our emotions and then rage about what we are feeling! Don't rage at the thermometer, instead, let's figure out how to use the thermostat. The thermometer *describes* reality; the thermostat *sets* reality.

What is the thermostat for your emotions? Hint: go back and look at yesterday's reading! *Every emotion begins with a thought.* Our emotions are a product of our thoughts just like the temperature in a room is the product (in part) of where the thermostat is set.

So go back to yesterday. The challenge yesterday was to step back and analyze your emotions (that is, 'read the thermometer'). Then you were to trace what you were feeling back to the thought that produced that feeling ('see what the thermostat is set on').

The next obvious move is to reset the thermostat. How do you do that?

Go back to Day 22. If you re-read Day 22 you will recall that one of the key points is that **you make your thoughts**. You have the power to set the thermostat of your emotions through the power of your thoughts. *So, to reset the thermostat of your emotions, reset your thoughts.*

If you have negative thoughts that are producing negative and damaging emotions, *reset the thermostat of your emotions by throwing those thoughts out!*

That's what the writer of Psalm 42 does: *Why are you downcast, O my soul? Why so disturbed within me? Put your hope in God, for I will yet praise him, my Savior and my God.* (Psalm 42.5–6)

This guy has found the thermostat: he tells himself to throw out those disturbing thoughts and instead, think about the awesomeness of God (a lot more on that later!).

THINK ABOUT IT . . .

> ➤ Today add to the process you have already begun: Step outside yourself and analyze what you are feeling. Trace that feeling back to its root thought. Now throw that thought out (if it is negative) and replace it with a good thought.

> ➤ Be easy on yourself! This is a lifelong exercise.

LIFE COMMITMENT:

Today I will think about what I am feeling and then reset the thermostat of my emotions by thinking different and better thoughts.

Day 27: Understanding Your Emotions (4)

The Word

Let us hold unswervingly to the hope we profess, for he who promised is faithful.

— Hebrews 10.23

Thought for the Day:

The greatest discovery of my generation is that a human being can alter his life by altering his attitude.

~ William James

I WAS A YOUNG seminary student moving into the first home we would own, 900 square feet of vintage 1950 small town Fort Worth. First on the list of repairs was a new deadbolt lock on the front door.

Eager to impress my young wife with my handyman skills, I set out installing the new lock. First thing: drill that really big hole the dead bolt fits into. What did I do? Drill the hole TOO BIG! Dang it. It's really hard to make a smaller hole out of a bigger hole. And remember, the hole that I drilled too big was in our *front door*!

I sat there and ruminated about this situation. My thoughts were not leading to solutions and the lack of solutions let me to think angry thoughts, and my angry thoughts led to angry emotions. I then expressed my anger by throwing my screwdriver hard on the floor.

The screwdriver bounced off the floor, then up and off the couch. From there it sailed even higher and, with a thud, smashed into the door jam next to where my young wife was standing. She was definitely impressed with me, just not the kind of impression I had been aiming for. Dang.

For the record, *I never did anything as drastic or violent again.* The image of something as lethal as a screwdriver screaming uncontrolled through the air stopped me in my tracks.

Emotions are real and they are morally neutral. You cannot not have emotions. But you *can* learn to recognize your emotions and express them appropriately. Right now you may be experiencing emotions with an intensity that is new to you. As I wrote in the introduction, my own life experience in a period of three years led to a ferocity of emotions that was new to me. I felt pushed to my limits.

We *can* control how we express our emotions, no matter the intensity. Whatever you do, *don't cause damage to yourself or others in this time of intense emotions.* I guarantee you will regret it.

Here are some ways to diffuse the intensity of your emotions:

- **Talk** about what is going on to a trusted friend, counselor, and/or pastor. Like heating up a sealed pressure cooker inevitably leads to an explosion, so too does keeping all that stuff inside you lead to an emotional explosion. Talking releases the pressure inside you. *You cannot do this alone.*

- **Get moving.** Exercise is proven to release stress. Intense exercise will not make you forget but it will release pent up energy. Some of my fastest times on my bicycle have been when I have been raging inside. I have *never* ended a ride angrier than when I began!

- **Keep reading!** The truths you read here and from other sources influence your mind which controls your emotions. But you have to keep at it. Our brains can only hold so much—and our brains leak. To hold truth in our heads we have to keep it coming in.

- **Pray.** Prayer was never intended to be a fourth-down punting situation in which we ask God to bail us out of our hasty decisions. It was intended to be a first-down huddle.[50] Prayer is just talking with God. The best way to pray is to pray, that is, just start talking with God. No instructions needed, just stop and do it.

Think About It . . .

> Think back to a time when you expressed an emotion in a destructive way. How did you feel after you cut loose?

> When you feel rage or depression or some other strong emotion now, what actions have you considered to relieve that feeling? Suicide? Homicide? Alcohol? Exercise? A weekend trip? Reading?

Life Commitment:

I choose to work through my emotions instead of letting them work through me. Today, right now, I will stop and pray. Today I will physically move in such a way that my heart rate significantly increases. Today I will call someone to talk about what is going on with me.

---

[50]Neil T. Anderson and Joanne, *Daily in Christ: A Devotional* (Eugene: Harvest House Publishers, 1993), 93.

Day 28: Understanding Your Soul (1)

The Word

He has set eternity in the hearts of men; yet they cannot fathom
what God has done from beginning to end.
— Ecclesiastes 3.11

Thought for the Day:

The spiritual life cannot be made suburban. It is always frontier, and we
who live in it must accept and even rejoice that it remains untamed.

~ Howard Macey

We were on a staff retreat in a beautiful home on the shores of Lake Winnipesaukee in New Hampshire. The first question I had for my staff was simple: "What is the soul?" This would be like a professor at a medical school asking first year students, "What is the body?" I got mostly blank stares in response to my question! We don't have a solid, succinct, clear answer to this simple question, *What is the soul?*

The dictionary says that the soul is *A part of humans regarded as immaterial, immortal, separable from the body at death, capable of moral judgment, and susceptible to happiness or misery in a future state.*[51]

Despite a concerted effort to deny the reality of the human soul, we know we have one. And we know that it is invisible and yet at the core of everything we are. John Ortberg wrote a book titled, *You*

---

[51] *The American Heritage Dictionary, s.v.* "soul," accessed January 27, 2017,
  https://ahdictionary.com/word/search.html?q=soul&submit.x=24&submit.y=29.

Have a Soul: It Weighs Nothing but Means Everything.[52] That says it all.

The Hebrew word translated as *soul* or *heart* means "the center of things." Your soul is your inner self. It is the 'you' that you are talking to when you have conversations with yourself, which you have most of the time.

The Bible says God breathed his spirit into us and in so doing, brought ordinary dirt to spectacular life (Genesis 2.7). Our clearly distinctive human soul not only animates our lives in a unique way while living on earth, but it is also that which is the 'eternity' that God has set into our hearts (Ecclesiastes 3.11). Your soul is the thing that God gave us to access the spiritual world just as your body is given by God to access the material world.

Maybe you haven't thought about your soul much. You should because it is just as real and vital as your body. You need to know that the soul can be wounded, and often is, and that those wounds come from illness, betrayal, conflict, financial loss, job loss, or a seemingly unending list of bad things that visit us all.

If you crashed your car on the way to work this morning and your leg was broken and bleeding, no one would deny that you should drop everything and get your leg tended to. But our culture fails to recognize the same urgency and need for the care of the wounded soul.

Your soul needs care and careful tending... *Only take care, and keep your soul diligently.* (Deuteronomy 4.9 ESV)

When you feel deep pain right now, the *part of you* that is feeling that pain is your soul. Just as a needle through the toe will create pain in your toe, so a blow to your soul will make your soul hurt.

But there is hope! The God who made you—body and soul—can heal and restore your soul.

Dallas Willard writes:

> *The human soul is a vast spiritual (nonphysical) landscape, with resources and relationships that exceed human comprehension; and it also exists within an infinite environ-*

---

[52] John Ortberg, *You Have a Soul: It Weighs Nothing But Means Everything* (Grand Rapids: Zondervan, 2014).

ment of which, at our best, we have little knowledge. We only know that God is over it all and that the soul, if it can only acknowledge its wounded condition, manifests amazing capacities for recovery when it finds its home in God and receives his grace.[53]

Did you get that last sentence? *If [I] can acknowledge [my soul's] wounded condition, [my soul] manifests amazing capacities for recovery when it finds its home in God and receives his grace.*

THINK ABOUT IT . . .

> ➤ How would you have answered the question I posed to my staff, "What is the soul?"

> ➤ If someone were to ask you what it is that is hurting inside you because of your illness, divorce, lost job, what would you tell them?

> ➤ How is your soul?

LIFE COMMITMENT:

I know I have a soul and I know it is hurting. I commit to tending to my soul and caring for it and its recovery.

---

[53] Dallas Willard, *Renovation of The Heart: Putting on The Character of Christ* (Colorado Springs: NavPress, 2002), Kindle Location 2820.

Day 29: Understanding Your Soul (2)

The Word

Come to me, all you who are weary and burdened, and I will give you rest.
Take my yoke upon you and learn from me, for I am gentle and humble in
heart, and you will find rest for your souls.
For my yoke is easy and my burden is light.
— Jesus as recorded in Matthew 11.28–30

Thought for the Day:

A self-made man is a poorly made man.
~ Paul David Tripp

Natura abhorret vacuum. This is a Latin phrase that describes a
foundational truth of reality: *Nature abhors a vacuum.* The proof of
this is when you cook garlic, the smell pervades every room of your
house. The molecules from the garlic seek to reach equilibrium (equal
density) throughout the room.

What is true of molecules in a room is true of our souls. Your
soul is real but it is empty. It is empty because back in the beginning,
Adam and Eve decided to turn against the one Being in the universe
for whom their souls were made. When Adam and Eve believed
Satan's lie that God was not the true soul-filler, they turned away
from God.

The teaching of Christianity is that man chose to be inde-
pendent of God and confirmed his choice by deliberately

disobeying a divine command. This act violated the relationship that normally existed between God and His creature; it rejected God as the ground of existence and threw man back upon himself.[54]

We have a God-shaped hole in our souls because our first parents kicked God out of their lives. As Rick Warren says, *Your heart is designed to contain God.*[55] Anything less than God doesn't fit and won't work.

It's amazing how dense we are about this. Some of you are mechanics. You know that engines are built to amazing tolerances. A particular bolt fits in a particular hole *and anything less than a near perfect match will not work and has potential to do real damage to the engine.*

Some of you are software engineers. You know that code has to be precise or it will send commands to the CPU that will throw everything off.

Some of you are homebuilders. In your case my analogy breaks down because we all know that caulk can cover a multitude of sins!

Your soul has the same tolerance requirements as a Lamborghini. Would you put honey instead of oil in your brand new Huracán? Would you fill your tank with water instead of 90 octane (or higher) gasoline? Would you staple a tarp over your seats to protect them?

Some of you are literally shaking with horror while reading this! But when it comes to our souls we give little thought to what goes into our souls and if what we are putting in our souls is fitting or not. I can drive my car and detect the slightest noise or 'feel' and know something is wrong. But our souls can be falling apart and we are clueless.

Blaise Pascal (d. 1662) was a brilliant French Christian philosopher as well as an inventor, mathematician, and scientist. The Pascal programming language is named in his honor for his work as a mathematician and inventor of a mechanical adding machine. Pascal,

---

[54] A. W. Tozer, *The Knowledge of The Holy: The Attributes of God, Their Meaning in The Christian Life* (New York: Harper & Row, 1961), 54.

[55] Rick Warren, *"Your Heart is Designed for God to Fill,"* accessed January 27, 2017, http://pastorrick.com/devotional/english/your-heart-is-designed-for-god-to-fill.

among other things, proved that nature actually has a vacuum. What he proved of nature as a scientist he applied to the soul as a Christian. The soul, without God, is a vacuum. Only God can fill the vacuum:

> *What else does this craving, and this helplessness, proclaim but that there was once in man a true happiness, of which all that now remains is the empty print and trace? This he tries in vain to fill with everything around him, seeking in things that are not there the help he cannot find in those that are, though none can help, since this abyss can be filled only with an infinite and immutable object; in other words by God himself.*

> *God alone is man's true good, and since man abandoned him it is a strange fact that nothing in nature has been found to take his place: stars, sky, earth, elements, plants, cabbages, leeks, animals, insects, calves, serpents, fever, plague, war, famine, vice, adultery, incest. Since losing his true good, man is capable of seeing it in anything, even his own destruction, although it is so contrary at once to God, to reason and to nature.*[56]

THINK ABOUT IT . . .

> ➤ What kind of fuel are you putting into your car?

> ➤ What kind of fuel are you putting into your soul?

> ➤ Which is more important, your car or your soul?

LIFE COMMITMENT:

I will pay attention to my soul and what I fill it with.

[56]Blaise Pascal, *Pensées* (Harmondsworth: Penguin Books, 1966), 125.

Day 30: Understanding Your Soul (3)

The Word

My soul finds rest in God alone; my salvation comes from him.
— Psalm 62.1

Thought for the Day:

It is dangerous to explain too clearly to man how like he is to the animals
without pointing out his greatness. It is also dangerous to make too much
of his greatness without his vileness.
It is still more dangerous to leave him in ignorance of both.

~ Blaise Pascal

I've had my car for ten years now. It has had more stuff in it, on it and behind it as it has carried me and many friends to adventures far and wide. At the time of this writing I have driven it the equivalent of ten times around the earth. I know my car. I know precisely how it 'feels' under my hand and foot. I know every sound it makes. When it doesn't 'feel' right or I hear a new sound, however subtle, I pay attention to it and begin to diagnose possible causes.

If you are a mom you know your kids like no other human being on the planet. Your ears are tuned in to their every move, sound, gesture. You can hear your kid cry on a playground full of a hundred screaming little banshees!

Amazing how we know much more about our cars/trucks than we do about our souls. We understand our sacrificial love and giving attention to our kids more than our own souls.

Our souls are invisible. They are like the wind—we see the effects of the wind but we can't see the air molecules that make the trees move.

How do you determine the condition of your soul? This is critically important. While we spend some time with our kids, 100% of our time is spent with our own souls. According to AAA, the average American spends 293 hours per year in his/her car. In comparison, you spend 8,760 hours in your soul per year! That's 3.3% of your life in your car vs. 100% of your life in your soul.

Dallas Willard says that, *In the person with the "well-kept heart," the soul will be itself properly ordered under God and in harmony with reality.*[57]

What happens when your soul is not in harmony with God and reality? Well, just like your car has an idiot light so too does your soul.

Willard was a brilliant philosopher and theologian. But when asked how he tested the condition of his soul, Willard asked himself two questions:

Am I growing more or less irritable these days?

Am I more or less discouraged these days?

Irritability with others and discouragement within yourself are your soul's idiot lights—and worth paying attention to.

THINK ABOUT IT . . .

> ➤ What is the condition of your soul?

> ➤ Are you more or less irritable with people?

> ➤ Are you more or less discouraged?

LIFE COMMITMENT:

I commit to paying as much attention to the condition of my soul as I do to the condition of my car (and my kids)!

---

[57] Willard, *Renovation of the Heart*, Kindle Location 2790.

Day 31: The Place of Wisdom

The Word

At this, Job got up and tore his robe and shaved his head. Then he fell to the ground in worship and said: "Naked I came from my mother's womb, and naked I will depart. The Lord gave and the Lord has taken away; may the name of the Lord be praised."

— Job 1.20–21

Thought for the Day:

In the mouth of society are many diseased teeth, decayed to the bones of the jaws. But society makes no effort to have them extracted and be rid of the affliction; it contents itself with gold fillings.

~ Kahlil Gibran

In his June 3, 2017 commencement speech at his son's graduation from Cardigan Mountain School, an elite school for boys in New Hampshire, Supreme Court Chief Justice John Roberts gave some unusual advice:

> *From time to time in the years to come, I hope you will be treated unfairly, so that you will come to know the value of justice. I hope that you will suffer betrayal because that will teach you the importance of loyalty. Sorry to say, but I hope you will be lonely from time to time so that you don't take friends for granted. I wish you bad luck, again, from time to time so that you will be conscious of the role of chance in life and understand that your success is not*

completely deserved and that the failure of others is not completely deserved either.

And when you lose, as you will from time to time, I hope every now and then, your opponent will gloat over your failure. It is a way for you to understand the importance of sportsmanship. I hope you'll be ignored so you know the importance of listening to others, and I hope you will have just enough pain to learn compassion.

Whether I wish these things or not, they're going to happen. And whether you benefit from them or not will depend upon your ability to see the message in your misfortunes.[58]

This was not the usual commencement address which celebrates everyone's 'specialness' and that anyone can achieve the impossible if they only dream big enough.

Roberts spoke to these young men through the lens of an elder. His is the voice of a man well into the second half of his life. The heart of his advice is that the tough places are where wisdom is born and matured.

Oswald Chambers says it like this:

We say that there ought to be no sorrow, but there is sorrow, and we have to accept and receive ourselves in its fires.... You cannot find or receive yourself through success, because you lose your head over pride. And you cannot receive yourself through the monotony of your daily life, because you give in to complaining. The only way to find yourself is in the fires of sorrow. Why it should be this way is immaterial. The fact is that it is true in the Scriptures and in human experience.[59]

---

[58] Katie Reilly, "'I Wish You Bad Luck.' Read Supreme Court Justice John Roberts' *Unconventional Speech to His Son's Graduating Class*," last updated July 5, 2017, accessed July 17, 2017, http://time.com/4845150/chief-justice-john-roberts-commencement-speech-transcript/.

[59] Oswald Chambers, *My Utmost for His Highest: Selections for the Year* (Uhrichsville: Barbour and Co, 1992), 177.

He goes on to say, *Sorrow removes a great deal of a person's shallowness, but it does not always make that person better. Suffering either gives me to myself or it destroys me.*[60]

These are hard things to hear because our culture tells us that we deserve not to suffer, that suffering can be avoided with hard work and the right insurance, and that pain can be eliminated with the right medication.

These are all myths. Suffering and sorrow are part of our journey. Embrace your sorrows as the place where wisdom is truly born and matured. Chambers is brutal: *Why it should be this way is immaterial.* It IS this way, so embrace it and learn from it. Don't waste your pain.

Think About It . . .

> ➤ Whether or not you waste your pain is up to you. If you have chosen to allow God to use your pain and suffering to grow you, what lessons have you learned so far?

Life Commitment:

I realize that suffering and sorrows are part of the human deal. I choose to embrace this reality and allow God to use my suffering to make me a source of wisdom and strength to others.

---

[60] Ibid.

Day 32: Regaining Your Footing

The Word

Therefore, my dear brothers, stand firm. Let nothing move you.
Always give yourselves fully to the work of the Lord,
because you know that your labor in the Lord is not in vain.
— 1 Corinthians 15.58

Thought for the Day:

If you have an unsatisfied heart now, outward accomplishments won't
change a thing. Know who you are on the inside and what God has done to
make you who you are. That's where your identity comes from. Who you
are is not a vocational question. Your identity is defined by the God who
made you, and it doesn't change with circumstances.
~ Tony Dungy

It was 1992, the Barcelona Olympics. British runner Derek Redmond started off strong in the 400-meter semi-finals, but at the 150-meter mark his hamstring ripped. Pain drove him to the ground. As the medical crew approached to carry him from the track, Redmond waved them off, deciding that even if he limped across the finish line dead last, he *would* finish. In that moment he says that he thought to himself, *I remembered where I was—the Olympics—and I knew I had to finish.*

Redmond stood up and started hobbling down the track. It was then that his dad, Jim Redmond, ran onto the track, pushing past a security guard to get to his son. Father and son finished the race, Derek leaning on his father's shoulder for support. The crowd, 65,000 strong, jumped to their feet, cheering on father and son.

You may feel you are down on the track with your dreams shattered, your soul ripped to shreds, and no hope of finishing. In this moment *remember **where** you are and **who** you are and **who God your Father is***.

You are God's son, you are God's daughter, a trophy of his grace, a man or woman of God who has a mission to accomplish, a purpose to fulfill.

He is there, next to you, hand outstretched, to lift you back to your feet and get you to the finish line.

Derek Redmond says that as his dad helped him toward the finish line, his father said to him, *Don't worry, you've got nothing to prove, you are a champion to us, we'll be back to do this together.*

I can't think of any words I would want to hear more from my dad if I were limping along the track in front of 65,000 people.

God says the same to you: *Don't worry, you've got nothing to prove, you are a champion to us, we'll be back to do this together.*[61]

Ask God to give you strength to get back on your feet. Ask God to give you a steady hand to right yourself as you stand. Ask God to point you in the right direction. And ask God to give you a shoulder to lean on as you head toward the finish line.

There was no prouder man in Barcelona than Jim Redmond on the day he helped his son across the finish line. God feels the same about you.

Think About It . . .

> ➤ In your mind picture the entire race Derek Redmond ran that day. Where are you on that race? At the starting line? Hurtling down the first 150 meters? Or down on the track in agony trying to decide what to do? Limping along alone toward the finish line? Leaning on dad's shoulder as you move down the track?

> ➤ Where does God fit into your race?

> ➤ What do you believe God is saying to you right now?

---

[61]Watch this video to hear Redmond explain that day:
https://www.youtube.com/watch?v=kjkBPthoYVg

Life Commitment:

I commit to crossing the finish line. I may be slow and a bit gimpy, but I will cross the finish line with God at my side.

Day 33: Regaining Your Hope

The Word

*May the God of hope fill you with all joy and peace as you trust in him,
so that you may overflow with hope by the power of the Holy Spirit.*
— Romans 15.13

Thought for the Day:

*Hope in the Christian's life is not wishful thinking.
It is confident expectation.*

~ Henry Blackaby

HOPE IS A HARD and strange and marvelous thing. On one hand, we must live in what we call the 'real' world, that is, the world where pain really hurts, decisions have consequences, and the future seems up for grabs.

On the other hand, the Christian lives in the *real* real world. He/she knows that this is not a WYSIWYG world (a What You See Is What You Get world)—what seems permanently devastating can be used by God in amazing ways to turn our lives and circumstance around.

Our only hope is that God is not surprised by our circumstances, he loves us, is for us, and died and rose again to be with us is. But this radical hope in a materially invisible God is sometimes challenging to maintain through hard times.

The writer of Psalm 43 demonstrates the emotional roller-coaster of living through tough times while still grounding his hope in God:

Vindicate me, O God, and plead my cause against an ungodly nation; rescue me from deceitful and wicked men.

You are God my stronghold.

Why have you rejected me? Why must I go about mourning, oppressed by the enemy?

Send forth your light and your truth, let them guide me; let them bring me to your holy mountain, to the place where you dwell.

Then will I go to the altar of God, to God, my joy and my delight. I will praise you with the harp, O God, my God.

Why are you downcast, O my soul? Why so disturbed within me?

Put your hope in God, for I will yet praise him, my Savior and my God.

(Psalm 43:1–5)

Let's walk through this Psalm. The Psalmist is hurting. He has been falsely accused and the cost has been high. Real life is incredibly painful for him in the moment. For you and me, we have suffered real pain and huge losses. But then, is not God still God? The writer thinks so: *You are God my stronghold.*

But the question remains: *Why all this pain?*

The writer does what we do—he swings between anger and hope, frustration with God and radical reliance upon him:

Why have you rejected me? Why must I go about mourning, oppressed by the enemy? Send forth your light and your truth, let them guide me; let them bring me to your holy mountain, to the place where you dwell.

The writer then imagines himself further down the road. The pain is less and God is victorious:

Then will I go to the altar of God, to God, my joy and my delight. I will praise you with the harp, O God, my God.

The writer then reflects back on his previous thoughts and admonishes himself with these words:

Why are you downcast, O my soul? Why so disturbed within me? Put your hope in God, for I will yet praise him, my Savior and my God.

If your emotions are swinging wildly between amazing hope and black despair, you are not alone. Everyone swings between hope and fear (See **Day 19**). The difference between those with God and those without is that ***those whose hope is in God come back from the brink of despair to rest in God***. We settle our souls upon God and find him a place of amazing refuge, comfort, strength and enduring hope.

Eugene Peterson writes,

> *Without hope a person has basically two ways to respond to the future, with wishing or with anxiety. Wishing looks to the future as a fulfillment, usually miraculous, of desire. It expends its energy in daydreaming and fantasy. Anxiety looks to the future as a demonstration of inadequacy—present weakness is projected to the point of disaster.*
>
> *Hope is a response to the future that has its foundation in the promises of God. It looks at the future as time for the completion of God's promise. It refuses to extrapolate either desire or anxiety into the future, but instead believes that God's promise gives the proper content to it.*[62]

Your future belongs to God. **Wishful thinking** will not deliver you out of your troubles and, instead, set you up for unrealistic expectations. **Anxiety** will take energy away from what you need to do now. Instead of dreaming about a blissful future or losing yourself in anxiety, ***lean back into God. Settle your hope upon him*** and expect him to do amazing things.

Why are you downcast, O my soul? Why so disturbed within me? **Put your hope in God**, *for I will yet praise him, my Savior and my God.*

---

[62] Eugen Peterson, *God's Message for Each Day: Wisdom from the Word of God* (Nashville: Thomas Nelson, 2006), 233.

Think About It . . .

➤ Are you living in a fantasy world or, at the other extreme, overcome by anxiety?

➤ What does resting in God look like to you? How has God helped you so far?

Prayer:

Lord God, only you can deliver me out of my troubles. My hope is in you, and my promise is that you get all the glory when I am healed and restored.

Day 34: Regaining Your Strength

The Word

Do you not know? Have you not heard?
The Lord is the everlasting God, the Creator of the ends of the earth.
He will not grow tired or weary, and his understanding no one can fathom.
He gives strength to the weary and increases the power of the weak.
Even youths grow tired and weary, and young men stumble and fall; but
those who hope in the Lord will renew their strength.
They will soar on wings like eagles;
they will run and not grow weary, they will walk and not be faint.
— Isaiah 40:28–31

Thought for the Day:

It is not the critic who counts; not the man who points out how the strong
man stumbles, or where the doer of deeds could have done them better. The
credit belongs to the man who is actually in the arena, whose face is
marred by dust and sweat and blood; who strives valiantly... who at the
best knows in the end the triumph of high achievement, and who at the
worst, if he fails, at least fails while daring greatly.
~ Teddy Roosevelt

LIFE IS HARD ENOUGH as it is. Just the day-to-day regimen of work, family life and attention to personal needs takes an enormous investment of energy. At the time my troubles began I was using 110% of my energy. Then life fell apart. The next weeks and months would see my available energy drop to half or less of what it had been. Job loss and divorce sucks the life right out of your life. A diagnosis of cancer, the death of spouse, friend, or, worst of all, a child, drain your spirit to zero.

From just a logistical viewpoint, energy must be diverted to figuring out the practical matters of getting through a crisis: caregiving, medical appointments, court hearings, financial issues—the medical, legal and financial aspects of this new reality.

Emotionally, whether you wanted it or not, anxiety, worry and despair take the wind out of your sails. Just when you need *more* energy to meet enormous challenges, your energy level drops dramatically. Charles Spurgeon said, *Anxiety does not empty tomorrow of its sorrows, but only empties today of its strength.*[63] No truer words could be said.

When great loss intrudes upon your life, here are some tips on wisely investing the energy you have and working to get your strength back:

- **Invest in time with God.** Spending time with God will give you energy, not take it away. Getting up an hour earlier to be with God will *not* make you more tired. Your true strength comes from God. Time with him will put energy *into* you, not take it away. Ask God to give you the energy to wake up and spend time with him. He wants this more than anything so you can be sure he will give you good sleep to make up for what you lose.

- **Lower your expectations of what you can accomplish.** No one expects a patient who just had open-heart surgery to run a marathon the next day. Or week. Or year. Dial back what you expect to get accomplished during this time of suffering. This will most likely *not* be the most productive time in your life. That's OK. As you heal, strength will return. There will be times of amazing productivity in the future. It's winter, now, however, not spring.

- **Invest in your children.** Often when crises strike we become so consumed with our own pain that we fail to pay attention

---

[63] Quoted in Wayne Cordeiro, *Leading on Empty: Refilling Your Tank and Renewing Your Passion* (Minneapolis, MN: Bethany House, 2009), Kindle Location 835.

to our children. Given that children often become quiet as they watch the adults fall apart, we sometimes assume that their silence means they are coping with the crisis well. But this is a false assumption. Children don't know how to process and express their emotions so they often go silent. It is scary to them to see mom and dad cry and express their pain.

If you are in pain you can be sure your children are hurting too. This is the time to sit with them, holding them, giving them space to feel and permission to express themselves in whatever ways they can find. Accept what they say or do and then determine to help them. Take children to counseling to help them work through their thoughts and emotions. Love them, listen to them, hug them.

- **If you must keep working at your job**, think about what you must do at work to get you by. When you are working, *work*. Concentrate, focus, get the job done. Don't waste time at work worrying about your personal life. It is best to leave our troubles in the car when you go into the office. Ask God for strength to do your best and you will be amazed at his response!

- If there are legal, medical and/or financial issues that need attention, bear down and focus. Push through.

- **Sleep.** A common experience for anyone going through intense suffering is to want to curl up in bed and escape through sleep. This is normal since your mind is working hard to process all that is happening. Sleep, but don't sleep too much. Just wanting to sleep could be a sign of depression. You will need more sleep but not too much. **(See Day 56)**

- **Exercise.** I can't emphasize enough how sweating will give you energy. Don't go for the marathon, just move some every day. A little goes a long way. **(See Day 57)**

- When pain comes raging upon us we will work hard to find relief. If you have a history of addiction, you can be sure the urge to indulge will return. Don't give in. Buying in to the lie that your addiction will ease your pain is from the enemy. Don't waste your energy or money on anxiety, drugs, alcohol, pornography, buying stuff or escaping to the Caribbean. This will only makes things worse. *Don't make things worse.*

Pastor Wayne Cordeiro writes:

> *Each of us has a finite amount of energy to invest each day, and how we invest that will make all the difference.... I measure my energy in bursts or pockets of energy. I have found that I have about seven bursts of energy each day that I can invest. I must choose wisely where and when to invest these pockets of life vitality, because (as the used-car dealer says on the TV ads) when they're gone, they're gone.[64]*

You *will* get your strength back. It will take some time but you will be strong again. Invest the energy you have now wisely.

THINK ABOUT IT . . .

➤ How is your energy level?

➤ What things deserve your pockets of energy right now?

➤ What can you quit doing or leave off your schedule?

PRAYER:

God, I am beat. Restore to me my strength. Let me draw upon you and invest what you give me in what matters most.

---

[64] Ibid., Kindle Location 1653.

Day 35: Regaining Your Courage

The Word

Have I not commanded you? Be strong and courageous.
Do not be terrified; do not be discouraged,
for the Lord your God will be with you wherever you go.
— Joshua 1.9

Thought for the Day:

Courage is not the absence of fear, but rather the judgment that
something else is more important than fear.
~ Ambrose Redmoon

The American Heritage Dictionary says that *courage is the state or quality of mind or spirit that enables one to face danger, fear, or vicissitudes with self-possession, confidence, and resolution; bravery.*[65]

The root of our word courage comes from the Latin *cor* which means *heart*. Your heart is your inner being, your thoughts, your desires and your will. We can have a strong heart, which means a heart that is sure, confident and leaning in the right direction. Or your heart can be weak—fearful, timid, flighty, and leaning in the wrong direction.

Painful and frightening life experiences weaken our heart. Just like a blow to the leg weakens it and makes walking difficult, so do hard experiences take courage out of our hearts and make living difficult.

---

[65] *The American Heritage Dictionary*, s.v. "courage," accessed July 25, 2017,
https://ahdictionary.com/word/search.html?q=courage&submit.x=0&submit.y=0.

Discouragement takes courage *out* of our heart. *Encouragement* puts courage back *into* your heart. God wants your weakened heart to have courage. Courage comes into your heart when you believe the right things about God and about yourself.

Are you strong enough to get through this? Your answer will reveal what you believe about your strength.

Does God have your best interests in mind, making all things work for his glory, your good and the good of the world? A resounding *Yes!* to that question will put courage into your heart. A wavering or faltering *"Maybe"* will take courage away. Let God put courage back into your heart.

To have courage, believe in a mission bigger than yourself. *Courage is not the absence of fear, but rather the judgment that something else is more important than fear.* What is more important than your fear? Suffering will strip the unimportant from your life. Suffering will force you to ask what is really worth living for. What is so important in your life that will motivate you to move past your fears?

Consider your kids. They are far more important than anything you can fear. Think of God's mission for your life. Think of the amazing good God can do in your life if you give yourself to him and the task he has for you in his Kingdom. If one life is significantly changed because of your story, isn't that one life worth pushing past this fear?

Audrey Lorde writes, *When I dare to be powerful, to use my strength in the service of my vision, then it becomes less and less important whether I am afraid.*[66]

What are you really living for? Suffering will clarify your answer to this question. When you have a mission and purpose bigger than yourself, courage comes flowing in! Believe in a God big enough to accomplish his mission through you.

Consider these passages from the Bible:

> *But God made the earth by his power; he founded the world by his wisdom and stretched out the heavens by his understanding.* (Jeremiah 10.12)

---

[66] "Audre Lorde Quotes." BrainyQuote, accessed July 25, 2017.
https://www.brainyquote.com/quotes/quotes/a/audrelorde357287.html.

Finally, be strong in the Lord and in his mighty power. (Ephesians 6.10)

For God did not give us a spirit of timidity, but a spirit of power, of love and of self-discipline. (2 Timothy 1.7)

Believe in a God who will, in the end, make things right.

If you have been treated unfairly you may be tempted to put your energy into revenge. The goal of revenge is making someone pay. It's working hard to make things just. In the end this is wasted energy.

Bear Grylls writes, *Real courage is about how we react in the face of overwhelming odds. And it is impossible to be courageous if you aren't also afraid. Courage involves facing our fears, and walking through them. It is not about having no fear, but it is about doing what is necessary despite the fear.*[67]

Let God put courage into your heart today.

THINK ABOUT IT . . .

➤ What is most frightening to you?

➤ How can one or more of the truths above speak against your fear?

➤ What action(s) do you need to take to demonstrate power over your fear?

LIFE COMMITMENT:

I am not a coward and I will not be ruled by fear. My God will move me boldly into the future he has for me, and I want to be there with him, side-by-side.

---

[67]Bear Grylls, *A Survival Guide for Life: How to Achieve Your Goals, Thrive in Adversity, and Grow in Character* (New York: William Morrow, 2014), 183.

Day 36: Accepted by God (1)

The Word

Accept one another, then, just as Christ accepted you,
in order to bring praise to God.
— Romans 15:7

Thought for the Day:

People are suffering from an identity crisis.
It seems everywhere we turn we see people
striving to become someone or something
that they perceive will bring them some sort of
contentment when in reality the opposite is true.[68]

~ Perry Noble

From the beginning of my Christian experience I was told the amazing truth that I was accepted by God. Everyone seemed so excited to tell me this wonderful news. But try as I might, I could not wrap my head around what being accepted by God really meant. The reason is that my understanding of acceptance was based on my experiences of human 'acceptance.'

We are told that to accept others is a noble thing, part of our unique American experience of one another. Despite the mantra that we need to accept one another, my actual experience is that we don't accept each other for who we are. Instead, the relationships I have lived in have been unpleasantly based on a cost-benefit analysis. If I

---

[68] Perry Noble quoted in Mark Driscoll, *Who Do You Think You Are? Finding Your True Identity in* Christ (Nashville: Thomas Nelson, 2013), 7.

can do something for you, you like me. If I am of no use to you, you push me aside and move on to the next person to use. And at the bottom of it, I usually treat others the same way.

For this reason, all this talk of acceptance was muddied in my brain until I ran across the biblical way of understanding God's acceptance of us from the smart folks at an organization called Victorious Christian Living.[69]

Here's how this works: when someone says to me that God accepts me I automatically filter that statement through what I know of acceptance, which is to say, I define the word 'acceptance' by my experience of acceptance. The only experience I know of acceptance is from my life in the world.

How do I gain the world's acceptance? To get the world's ultimate approval/acceptance I follow a specific path:

First, someone in the world (an **AUTHORITY** in my life) gives me their expectations. This authority can be parents, a teacher, an employer or anyone or anything in the world that has a measure of control over my life.

Next, I have to work to meet those expectations. I strive to *do* the things that I have been told I should do. I jump through all the right hoops to reach the goal, *which is acceptance by that authority in my life.*

When I was a boy the only question on my mind was, "Am I good enough?" The answers from my dad and others were conflicted. On one hand, I was told I was special and nothing could stop me. I would be spectacular. On the other hand, if I was anything less than spectacular, it was my fault. Given the deluge of criticism I received, it seemed that though I was special, I pretty much never measured up to my specialness!

Most of us grew up with this double message from our parents, our schools, our peers. To be accepted we had to jump through hoops that were just out of reach. The message we received was, *you can do it but... you probably won't.*

---

[69]The teachings for the next several days come primary from *"Seven Areas of Life Training."* Victorious Christian Living International, accessed February 03, 2017. http://www.vcli.org/salt/.

Implicit in this message was that people were both for me and against me, both my friend and my enemy, my companion and my challenger. People were as likely to push me down as they were to help me up.

Is this your experience of 'acceptance'? If this is the way God 'accepts' me, I think I will pass!

To be continued...

THINK ABOUT IT . . .

> ➤ When you hear the word 'acceptance' what first comes to your mind?

> ➤ What have you been told you must do to be accepted by the authorities in your life? Parents? Teachers? Employers?

> ➤ When have you measured up? What were the consequences?

> ➤ When have you failed to measure up? What were the consequences?

LIFE COMMITMENT:

It could be true that what I think about God's love and acceptance for me has been informed more by my experience of how the world defines love and acceptance than by what God says about me.

Day 37: Accepted by God (2)

The Word

> *We have the free gift of being accepted by God,*
> *even though we are guilty of many sins.*
> — Romans 5.16 (NLT)

Thought for the Day:

> *I renounce the lie that I am too worthless to ever be accepted by God or*
> *people. I acknowledge that my value before God is so great He sent Jesus to*
> *die for me, and it is the value in His eyes which truly counts.*
> ~ Keturah Martin

I WAS OFTEN TOLD I was loved and accepted without condition, but it seemed to me that love and acceptance came with a lot of conditions. When I came home with A's on my report card, I got showered with praise and affection. When I came home with a C in algebra, all hell broke loose. All those A's didn't seem to make up for a single C. The question I was always asking (and still ask in my weaker moments) is, *"Am I good enough?"* And often the answer was, *"Almost."*

When I worked hard to be good enough for the **AUTHORITIES** in my life, I got **AFFIRMATION**.

Affirmation is the second step in being accepted by the world. First, authorities lay out their **expectations**. If you meet these expectations, you get **affirmed**.

This is the way the world works whether you working on a Ph.D. or trying to get into a gang. The group says, "Do this, and we will accept you." You jump through the hoops, and if you succeed, they affirm you. If you keep it up, affirmation turns into **ACCEPTANCE**. You're in!

The downside of this is that if you fail to keep jumping through the hoops, you can be pushed back out. You can go from being *acceptable* to *unacceptable*.

This is the way of the world. Authorities give us expectations. We work hard to meet those expectations. If we do, we are affirmed, and if consistently affirmed, we are accepted.

Here's the thing: The motivation behind this dynamic at work in our world is *control*. Parents, teachers, employers—they all have to control us. The way they control us is to give or take away their acceptance of us. The emotion that accompanies and drives this process is *fear*. We *fear* not being accepted, and that fear motivates us to follow the rules.

Now think about it: Do you think God accepts or rejects you based on your obedience to his authority?

If you do, please explain these words from the Bible:

> *[We] know and rely on the love God has for us. God is love.... There is no fear in love. But perfect love drives out fear, because fear has to do with punishment.* (1 John 4.16–18)

Hopefully you are beginning to realize that being accepted by God means something significantly different from how the world accepts us.

THINK ABOUT IT . . .

➤ What is the most ridiculous thing you ever did in order to be accepted by a group?

➤ What are some ridiculous things people do to earn God's acceptance?

➤ Was there a time you felt like God accepted you?

➤ Was there a time when you believed God rejected you?

LIFE COMMITMENT:

I believe God's way of accepting me must be different from the world's way of acceptance.

Day 38: Accepted by God (3)

The Word

Do you want to get well?
— Jesus, asked of a lame man as recorded in John 5.6

Thought for the Day:

If you obey for a thousand years, you're no more accepted than when you first believed; your acceptance is based on Christ's righteousness and not yours.

~ Paul David Tripp

For the past two days I have explained the way the authorities in our world accepts us. The **authorities** in our lives give us expectations. We try to meet them. If we do, we are **affirmed**. If we are affirmed enough, we are **accepted.** If we screw up, we can be unaccepted.

The purpose of this dynamic is *control*, and the emotion used to control us is *fear*.

Now, two simple questions: Is this the way God works? Is God's main goal to control you?

That leads to a next question: Do you think God can control you?

The small town of Bertram is located northwest of Austin, Texas. This little town has the irritating habit of positioning one of their police cruisers somewhere along the highway that goes through their town. The cruiser is empty. But it is menacing. Every time I go through Bertram *I know the empty cruiser will be there. And every time I see that cruiser my heart skips a beat and I slow down out of fear of getting a speeding ticket!*

If an empty police cruiser can control my behavior and strike fear in my heart, what can an all-powerful God do?

The prophet Jeremiah said,

> *God made the earth by his power; he founded the world by his wisdom and stretched out the heavens by his understanding. When he thunders, the waters in the heavens roar; he makes clouds rise from the ends of the earth. He sends lightning with the rain and brings out the wind from his storehouses.* (Jeremiah 10.12–13)

That's a powerful God! God could make you bend over double with excruciating pain right now. He could pop your head off or send you careening through space. *God can do to you whatever he wants!* So the question is, *What does God want?*

Here's what God wants: God wants you to experience his love so that you can respond to him in love.

God does not want to control you out of fear but to woo you with his love!

That's why God's acceptance of us begins with his love, not his expectations.

First John 4.16 plainly states, *God is love. Whoever lives in love lives in God, and God in him.*

In the world's way of acceptance, you must earn the approval of the authorities. In God's Kingdom, **God already approves you on the basis of what Jesus, his Son did for you on the cross.**

The authors of SALT write, *God's way starts with acceptance. He accepts you right now before you do anything. He doesn't accept you based on your ability to obey His commands. You are accepted because Christ's death on the cross made you acceptable.*[70]

When God looks at you he doesn't see your shortcomings, he sees his Son's righteousness. When God looks at you he doesn't see where you have fallen short he sees where his Son has lifted you up.

---

[70] *Seven Areas of Life Training*, Book 1, Lesson 4. VCLi, Version 2.0, 51.

That means that you have nothing to prove to God. Jesus has already earned God's approval of you. You cannot earn God's approval; his approval of you has already been purchased by his Son.

Neil and Joann Anderson say it like this:

> *We are not on a performance basis with God. He doesn't say, "Here are My standards, now you measure up." He knows you can't solve the problem of an old sinful self by simply improving your behavior. He must change your nature, give you an entirely new self—the life of Christ in you.*[71]

The world says, **Perform**! God says, **Receive**!

There is nothing you can do to add to or take away his love from you. When you do something good, God doesn't love you more. When you mess up, God doesn't love you less. His love is based on who he is *not on what you do or don't do.*

God's acceptance of us begins with his love for us, not his expectations of us.

THINK ABOUT IT . . .

➤ In what ways have you tried to earn God's approval?

➤ If you tried to earn God's approval, how did you know you got it (or not)?

➤ God's acceptance of us begins with his love for us, not his expectations of us. What could change in your life if you really believed this?

LIFE COMMITMENT:

I give up! I give up trying to earn God's approval and love. Instead, I choose to simply receive his steadfast, never-changing love for me.

---

[71] Anderson and Anderson, *Daily in Christ: A Devotional,* 105.

Day 39: Accepted by God (4)

The Word

For you did not receive a spirit that makes you a slave again to fear, but
you received the Spirit of sonship. And by him we cry, "Abba, Father."
The Spirit himself testifies with our spirit that we are God's children.
— Romans 8.16-17

Thought for the Day:

Every day you preach to yourself some kind of gospel—
a false "I can't do this" gospel or the true
"I have all I need in Christ" gospel.
~ Paul David Tripp

When my wife met me upon my return from Africa and told me she was leaving me, the weight of her rejection drove me into the ground. I had worked hard all my life to earn the approval, affirmation and acceptance of the people in my life. No person's approval meant more to me than her's.

Just a few weeks before this happened, she had been on a business trip. On the way home she posted on Facebook that she could not wait to get home and go to church to hear her favorite preacher. She meant me! I beamed inside! A month later she told me she was leaving me. Coming to grips with these double messages is a challenge yet before me.

Every single rejection stings because rejection goes against all that we have tried so hard to attain—the love, approval and acceptance of others. As now famously disgraced Lance Armstrong once said, "A boo is a lot louder than a cheer."

The only thing that kept me going through that time was knowing that God did not reject me. Even though I am a divorced pastor, God has not divorced me. Though to many people in the world I am a failure because my wife rejected me, I know that in God's eyes, I am accepted and loved *no matter what.*

God begins by accepting us out of his love for us and based on Christ's death on our behalf. When we understand this amazing truth we understand and experience God's **AFFIRMATION**. God's affirmation of us is experienced as an emotion. We *feel* God's love for us. Just like we feel the fear of the rejection of the world, we can feel God's amazing love and acceptance of us!

The Apostle Paul wrote, *The Spirit himself testifies with our spirit that we are God's children.* (Romans 8.16). This is really good news! When we experience God's Spirit testifying with our spirit that we are his kids— accepted *because we are his kids*—we experience joy, peace, gladness... and the list of positive emotions goes on.

To the depth that I felt crushed by all that I was going through, God met me equally and even beyond with his Spirit gently holding my soul and reassuring me that I would be OK. I kept hearing him say, *I love you, you are OK. Just hold on and we will get through this. I will never leave you or forsake you.* I could receive no greater affirmation than that.

God first **ACCEPTS** us based on his love for us, not our performance for him. He then **AFFIRMS** us by reassuring us that we are his kids and he will never leave us or forsake us.

Think About It . . .

> - Have you experienced God's **peace** equal to or greater than your **anxiety**?

> - Have you experienced God's **joy** equal to or greater than your **anguish**?

> - Have you experienced God's **love** equal to or greater than your **anger**?

> If not, ask his Spirit to testify with your spirit that you are his daughter, that you are his son, and that you are accepted, affirmed and loved *no matter what* anyone else may say or do. Ask him to allow you to experience this truth deep in your soul as a good and strong emotion.

LIFE COMMITMENT:

I choose to believe that God has accepted me first, and that he actually wants me to experience the reality of his acceptance of me resulting in emotions of peace, joy and love.

Day 40: Accepted by God (5)

The Word

Before I formed you in the womb I knew you,
before you were born I set you apart.
— Jeremiah 1.5

Thought for the Day:

Because the Spirit of the Lord is in you, you are free to choose to live a
responsible and moral life. You are no longer compelled to walk according
to the flesh as you were before conversion. And now you are not even
compelled to walk according to the Spirit. You are free to choose to walk
according to the Spirit or to walk according to the flesh.
~ Neil Anderson

EVERYONE DEMANDS IT FOR others but few want it for themselves. We decry others when they avoid it, but we crumple into a heap when others require it of us. We rail at others when it catches them in the act, but curl up into a ball of excuses when it exposes our shortcomings. What am I talking about? Accountability.

Everywhere we turn we hear the incessant call for more accountability. And yet when we are held accountable, we squeal and squirm. We scream at the referee who fails to call pass interference on the opposing team, but run like a hen when the finger is pointed at us.

From the world's perspective, accountability is all about fear. The boss lays down expectations. Then he holds us accountable. The thought of failing creates fear in us, and fear motivates us to meet expectations. If we meet expectations we get affirmed, and if affirmed enough, we feel accepted. Accountability is a big piece of the way the systems in the world work.

How does accountability work in God's Kingdom? If God starts with accepting us, and then he affirms us, where does accountability fit in?

Look at the first few lines of the 23rd Psalm:

The Lord is my shepherd, I shall not be in want.

He makes me lie down in green pastures, he leads me beside quiet waters, he restores my soul.

He guides me in paths of righteousness for his name's sake. (Psalm 23.1–3)

This Psalm affirms what we have said about the way God accepts us. It starts off with the assurance that God is our good shepherd, and we know that shepherds accept their sheep the way they are.

The next few lines are all about affirmation: God leads me to green, abundant pastures and quenches my thirst at no cost. Green pastures and still waters are given to all sheep regardless of how 'good' or 'bad' they have been. He restores my soul *at no cost.* In other words, God accepts us and provides for us because he loves us, not because we have done anything to earn it.

But then comes accountability. Notice how David describes accountability in God's Kingdom: *He [God] guides me in paths of righteousness for his name's sake.*

God *does* hold us accountable. He doesn't let us live without limits. But the limits he sets are *for our good* and *for his glory.* God sets boundaries for us, but the purpose of those boundaries is that we may flourish into who we were meant to be. When we grow into his Kingdom people, the world takes notice and God gets the glory!

He *guides* us—he doesn't *drive* us—into the paths of righteousness so that we may flourish and in our flourishing, he may get the glory. God wants the best for us.

I confess that a few times I disciplined my children more to release my own anger than to guide them in life. Not God. His discipline is never to vent his own anger but *always* to nudge us back onto the path toward green pastures, smooth waters and soul restoration.

What if we stray *way* off the path? The Shepherd will pursue us (not hunt us down) to bring us back to the abundant pasture and thirst-quenching stream (see Luke 15.4-7).

God holds us accountable for our good and for his glory. He is motivated by his love for us, trusting that by loving us we will respond in love back to him. There is no fear in this equation. The world operates on the basis of fear. God operates on the basis of love. The difference between the two is utterly profound.

THINK ABOUT IT . . .

> - If you go to church, why do you go?

> - If you give money to your church or another charity, why do you give?

> - If you pray, why do you pray?

LIFE COMMITMENT:

I choose to believe that God is for me and has my best interests in mind, and that he holds me accountable not out of a motivation of control but out of pure love for me.

Day 41: Accepted by God (6)

The Word

Brothers and sisters, I do not consider myself yet to have taken hold of it.
But one thing I do: Forgetting what is behind and straining toward what is
ahead, I press on toward the goal to win the prize for which God has called
me heavenward in Christ Jesus.
— Philippians 3:13-14

Thought for the Day:

Jesus paid it all! There are no bills due for your sin!
You are now free to simply trust and obey.
~ Paul David Tripp

ONE DAY I WAS driving along and I had a profoundly terrible thought.
It was terrible because it was so incredibly untrue. The thought I had
was this: *I bet I will get into heaven. I mean, I am a pastor! Don't all
pastors go to heaven because we are so good?*

The moment I thought it I realized how idiotic this was. The first
bad thing about this thought was that whatever *good* I did could *never*
add to God's love for me. I could *never* increase God's love for me by
any good thing I did. He loves me now as much as he did when he
decided in eternity past to create me. He loves me now as much as he
did when his Son hung on a cross taking the hell I rightfully deserved
for every sin I would commit in my lifetime. There is nothing good I
could ever do to increase God's love for me. He loves me, period.

The second bad thing about this thought was that I am *not nearly
as good as I had led myself to believe!* I am a self-centered sinful

creature like everyone else. Which led me to this awesome reality: *There is nothing bad that I could ever do that would take away God's love for me.* He loves me, period. His love for me never changes.

God is not like the Greek gods who were just out-sized humans who pretty much screwed up the world with their super-sized but misdirected powers. God does not act like we do—he doesn't keep track of our good deeds and misdeeds—and love us depending on the score.

The world begins with rules to follow which may or may not lead to its acceptance of us. God is just the opposite—he begins by accepting us! No hoops to jump through, no demands to meet, no fear of falling short. God *begins* with accepting you because he profoundly, deeply and relentlessly loves you.

If he wanted to control you out of fear, he could. Oh... he could! Instead of controlling you through fear he wants to woo you with his love. The basis of God's acceptance of you is love, not fear.

THINK ABOUT IT . . .

> ➤ Do you fear God or love him?

> ➤ What could you do to make God love you more?

> ➤ What does God think when you mess up?

LIFE COMMITMENT:

I will live my life based on God's unchangeable love for me, not based on the fear of not meeting his or people's expectations of me.

Day 42: Go With the Flow

The Word

See, I am doing a new thing! Now it springs up; do you not perceive it?
I am making a way in the desert and streams in the wasteland.
— Isaiah 43.19

Thought for the Day:

Often in the growth process we do not know what to do, or we do not want
to do what we know we should do. This is where the "control" of the Spirit
comes into play, and we must yield. We must submit to what the Spirit is
telling us to do and allow him to have the reins of control moment by
moment.
~ Henry Cloud

I MAPPED OUT MY life carefully. I would get educated, get married, get a steady job, have some kids, retire comfortably and die peacefully. I would spend my last days in a house by a lake, reading good books by the water in summer and by the fire in winter. My life would be predictable. My life would be peaceful. Most of all, my life would be stable.

In some ways that happened. I got educated. I pastored stable churches (or so I thought). We had the big house and the kids. I loved walking with my kids in the New England woods behind our home, working in the yard in the summer and working with wood in the basement in the winter. I really craved this stability and worked hard to get it and protect it. I wanted what scientists and engineers call *homeostasis*.

The problem with stability is that life is intrinsically unstable. Life is not a quiet pool of water. It's a flowing river. Life is in motion and motion means change.

God knows this. The Bible is about a God who is in motion and it tells the stories of this God-in-motion sending his people in motion.

God called Abram to get moving from the city of Ur to the yet-undisclosed Promised Land. He sent Jacob north to get a wife and Joseph south to Egypt by the most unlikely of means. God pulled his chosen people out of Egyptian slavery and then has them live a life of constant motion in the desert until they finally get a few hard-fought lessons under their belts.

God sent a very pregnant Mary in motion from Nazareth to Bethlehem, then he sent the young family fleeing to Egypt as refugees. Jesus sent his disciples on all kinds of missions. He is always on the move, teaching and healing wherever he is.

God scattered the early church when they became too comfortable in their Jerusalem digs. He knocked Saul off a donkey and Saul becomes Paul, the most in-motion man who ever lived, traveling well over 11,000 miles in his four recorded journeys—by foot, donkey and boat.

A persecution in Rome sent Priscilla and Aquila fleeing to Corinth and then to Ephesus. Along the way they faithfully teach about the Jesus who had saved them... and who seemed to want them to keep moving!

If your life has been turned upside down by circumstances, welcome to life. Life is about movement and change. Since nothing surprises God and God himself seems to relish movement, determine to quit fighting for stability in your circumstances and simply *go with the flow.*

God has you covered. He is *with* you and he is even *in front of you*, preparing your future for you. Stability is an illusion. Real life is in the river!

THINK ABOUT IT . . .

> How important is stability to you?

> When your life has been turned upside-down in the past, how did you handle the disruption? Did you go with the flow or fight it every step of the way?

> What possibilities do you see for God to work in your future?

LIFE COMMITMENT:

God is a God in motion. I will move with him.

DAY 43: FLOW WITH THE GO

THE WORD

But as surely as God is faithful, our message to you is not "Yes" and "No."
For the Son of God, Jesus Christ, who was preached among you by me and
Silas and Timothy, was not "Yes" and "No," but in him it has always been
"Yes." For no matter how many promises God has made,
they are "Yes" in Christ.
— 2 Corinthians 1.18–21

THOUGHT FOR THE DAY:

Security is mostly a superstition.
It does not exist in nature,
nor do the children of men as a whole experience it.
Avoiding danger is no safer in the long run than outright exposure.
Life is a daring adventure or nothing at all.
~ Helen Keller

WHEN HAMMERED BY LIFE, recovery begins with a surrender to the flow... *Go with the flow.* The only way you can go with the flow with any sense of peace is to know that God controls the flow. God is *with you*, and he is *in front of you.* He has your future—he is *in* your future preparing a way for you.

But when life is caving all around us our natural reaction is to withdraw, hunker down and ride out the storm. We tend to pull back rather than risk reaching out.

This can be deadly. We can easily get lost in booze, pornography, video games, television... anything we think can fill the hole left by the rejection of people in our lives, the guilt of our own poor choices, or the trauma of a terminal medical diagnosis. We just want to be left alone and try to forget our pain.

Another factor is fatigue. When struggling through problems our energy level drops. Getting through each day is like trudging through a snow-covered field with the wind howling around us rather than strolling through a green meadow with sunshine beaming down on us.

This is definitely not the time to make major decisions. But it is also a mistake to turtle up and get lost in booze, drugs, TV or shopping.

God knows this and so he will send you opportunities to crawl out of the hole. Say yes to these opportunities.

Bear Grylls is a man who has said *yes* to the opportunities that have come his way. Once he spent 18 months recovering from a skydiving accident. But when the opportunity came to say yes to jumping out of a plane again, he took it! His advice? *Say yes and try something, rather than saying no because you fear where a yes will take you.*[72]

He goes on to write, *More often than not, saying no means that nothing will change in your life. A yes, however, has the power to create change. And change is where we create room for success.*[73]

SAY YES! Say yes to God and the invitations he sends your way to get out of the hole. Say yes to people when they reach out to you. Say yes to opportunities to get out. Say yes to your own ideas... go take a hike, go on a trip, go to a movie. Go to church, a men's or women's conference, a small group. Take a chance! What do you have to lose?

THINK ABOUT IT . . .

- ➤ What invitations have come your way that you have said no to? Was it helpful to stay hunkered down?

- ➤ What happened when you said yes?

- ➤ What can you say yes to today?

---

[72] Grylls, *A Survival Guide for Life*, 36.
[73] Ibid.

Life Commitment:

I choose to believe that saying yes to the opportunities God puts in my path is better in the long run than playing it safe.

Day 44: The Stages of Suffering, Grief and Loss

The Word

The Lord himself goes before you and will be with you;
he will never leave you nor forsake you.
Do not be afraid; do not be discouraged.
— Deuteronomy 31.8

Thought for the Day:

If you're going through hell, keep going.
~ Winston Churchill

THE GOOD NEWS IS THAT THERE are stages of suffering, grief and loss. That is, there are certain thoughts, emotions and events you are experiencing right now that most people also experienced when they traveled this painful journey. These stages usually loosely follow a sequence or progression. It helps to know others have walked this painful road before you and have emerged on the other side intact. Many emerged even better than they were before. That's your goal—to not just survive but to thrive beyond your pain.

It also helps to know that what you are experiencing is normal. It's common to feel raw pain, anger, depression and many other emotions. When you begin to feel better you will know that it is OK to be getting better and that, for most people, the trajectory is toward recovery, not years of pain, isolation, loneliness and depression. You really will get through this. The hard part is that this is a journey and journeys are made only one step at a time.

I'm a hiker and my favorite places to hike are the mountains. I have planned many hikes for many groups of people. The scene is always the same as we gather at the bottom of the mountain—everyone is excited but also nervous. We are eager to get to the top but we also know that the way to the top is up a steep path just beyond the trailhead sign.

The first mile is difficult—your legs protest this sudden change from sitting comfortably in a car to pushing your body (plus a pack) up the mountain.

Then the body kicks in and things rock until about midway up the trail. At that point your mind knows there is no turning back but you also know you're only halfway up the mountain. A rest stop with a nice view helps renew strength and the view gives encouragement when you see how far you've come.

The last hard part is just before the summit. Your legs are exhausted, the summit seems further than possible, but you also know you're almost there. Sometimes the mind has to tell the legs to move, and they do. By pushing on, you break through the last trees to reach a granite peak with stunning views all around. The group is all smiles and mutual congratulations—you made it!

Grief is a tough mountain to climb. Like a hike, you start at the bottom and put one foot in front the other. With enough steps over enough time, you get to the top.

As you move through these stages of grief it's good to know you really are making progress. There's not much you can do to speed up the process but you *can* slow it down. Determine now to being open to experiencing each of these stages as they come and seeking the right help and doing the right things to keep moving.

Grief is a hard journey. You will think and feel things you have never thought or felt before. Allow yourself permission and space to get through this. And remember, *Don't make things worse.* You will get through this.

THINK ABOUT IT . . .

> ➤ Think back to a time when you suffered a loss. What did you think and feel when you first understood the scope of the loss?

➤ What was the process you went through to get to a point of accepting the loss and being able to move on? The way you processed that loss is probably the way you will process this loss.

➤ To see a chart outlining these stages go to https://bit.ly/2ywz1XY.

Life Commitment:

My thoughts and emotions are all over the place right now. Despite this, I am committed to pressing on through this journey. Though I'm at the bottom of the mountain with a heavy pack, I know if I put one foot in front of the other, I will summit.

Day 45: The Stages of Suffering, Grief and Loss — (1) Shock

The Word

After this, Job opened his mouth and cursed the day of his birth.
— Job 3.1

Thought for the Day:

A groan is a matter about which there is no hypocrisy.
~ Charles Spurgeon

In a space of five years both of my parents died, I lost two jobs, my career and my wife left me. This was not a good run. I distinctly remember the empty house after my wife left me. I was in total shock. I couldn't believe what I had just heard when I arrived home from a teaching trip to East Africa. My mind raced in a million directions. Raw unmitigated pain poked it's black and fiery head into my brain and fire singed my heart. But just for a moment. My brain's shock-absorbers kept most of the pain away, giving me time to think and feel through the entire terrible state of things.

When bad news is received the brain quickly scans the information. When it realizes the catastrophic nature of the event, the brain slows serious thinking. The region of the brain known as the Inferior Frontal Gyrus (IFG) has been shown to interfere with the ability of the brain to process bad news in its totality, thus protecting the soul from extreme trauma.[74] God designed us to be able to receive only small

---

[74] https://www.ncbi.nlm.nih.gov/pmc/articles/PMC2845804/, accessed June 6, 2018.

doses of catastrophic news. This is so we are not overwhelmed to the point of radical but ill-considered actions like suicide or homicide.

Though the brain filters the bad news, some bad news gets through. What follows is a flood of horrifically negative emotions.

Sean Witwer describes his own emotions when he was served with divorce papers:

> *I'm not sure how many negative emotions can flood a body at once, but this is one of those rare instances in life that can never be described sufficiently by mere words. Unless you have ever experienced it, you can't understand the mix of disbelief, rejection, grief, sadness, brokenness, and shock that hits. My heart was in a blender and my wife turned it to 'high.' My body was hit by a numbing, sick, empty feeling and I trembled inside.[75]*

The prophet Jeremiah cried out, *Oh, my anguish, my anguish! I writhe in pain. Oh, the agony of my heart! My heart pounds within me, I cannot keep silent.* (Jeremiah 4:19)

What you might feel and experience at this stage:

- Numbness, a sense of disbelief. *I can't believe this is happening.* A sense that time has slowed down.

- Anxiety and perhaps panic when you project into the future what this moment might mean in the long-term.

- A strange sense of being detached from reality. You may experience a sense of loss of reality, of being in a hazy, unreal world. You observe the environment as though watching a movie, remote and detached from the events happening around you. You are unable to wake up from this dream into the real world.[76]

- Emptiness, a feeling that usually comes when you've gone through the above emotions.

---

[75] Sean Witwer, *Divorce Recovery 101: A Step by Step Guide to Reinvent Yourself in 30 Days* (Amazon Digital Services, 2016), Kindle Locations 393-402.

[76] Bruce Fisher and Robert Alberti, *Rebuilding: When Your Relationship Ends*, 4th Ed., (Oakland: New Harbinger Publications, 2016), Kindle Locations 2064-2066.

- Possibly guilt at what happened that led to this moment. Thoughts of what you could have done differently to avoid the accident, detect the cancer sooner, placated your spouse, etc.

- Possibly rage which may be expressed in shouting, crying, throwing or damaging objects and/or the desire to hurt someone, including oneself. This emotion will come out more in men than women and is dependent on the nature of the loss.

- Thoughts of wanting to end your life. Suicidal thoughts are common after any extreme loss. If you are experiencing thoughts of taking your life, go to Appendix A to assess your risk and get help. The National Suicide Hotline is **800-273-8255.**

- Emotional fluctuation, that is, switching between thoughts of the positives of the loss and the extreme negatives. The brain is wired to try to find the good in every negative circumstance, so it is natural that we would think of something positive in the midst of the bad news. Extreme mood swings are common at this stage.

- Many people lose their appetite and struggle to sleep. Some experience a tightness in their throat. Sighing is also common.

- Relief—some may feel a sense of relief and feel guilty about it. If you were the caregiver for a parent who has been sick for a long time, it is normal to feel relief for yourself and for the one who has passed. A professor once told me that every death brings some positives, and the ones left behind should not feel guilty about embracing those positive things.

Your goal at this point is to simply survive without making decisions that will cause lasting harm.

Survival Strategies for when disaster strikes:

- Reach out for help to God and two or three wise friends, a counselor and a pastor. *Talk it out or you will take it out.* As you talk it out, don't be surprised if you repeat the story of what happened many times. Repeating the story is how our brain wrestles with accepting this new reality.

- Don't believe everything you're telling yourself about yourself or the situation. Don't project into the future what could happen. Just live in and through this moment.

Duration: Numbness and shock last a few hours to a few days. If you are stuck in shock for several weeks, seek help immediately. Being stuck is measured by intensity of emotions and functionality. If you can't go to work or do normal daily tasks, intervention is called for. Reach out to a pastor and/or counselor for help.

Success: You know you are moving through shock when you are able to acknowledge the reality of the situation enough to begin to deal with it.

Identity issue: The question you will be asking yourself at this stage is, *"What happened?"*

T.D. Jakes writes, *When the unthinkable happens, suddenly the darkest fears get unleashed from the chains of reason and kennels of faith.*[77] What fears are unleashed from the chains of reason in your mind and heart? God will rein them in. This process has an end and it is good.

THINK ABOUT IT . . .

➤ If you feel you are stuck in shock, get help from a trusted friend, counselor and pastor.

LIFE COMMITMENT:

Though the earth gives way and falls into the heart of the sea, God will get me through this (Psalm 46). I commit my present and my future to his care. And I call upon him for comfort, knowing he wants to comfort me in my pain and eventually heal me.

---

[77] T. D. Jakes, *Crushing: God Turns Pressure into Power* (Dallas: TDJ Enterprises, 2019), 6.

Day 46: The Stages of Suffering, Grief and Loss — (2) Raw Pain

The Word

> *How long must I wrestle with my thoughts and*
> *every day have sorrow in my heart?*
> *How long will my enemy triumph over me?*
> — Psalm 13.2

Thought for the Day:

The biblical way to deal with suffering is to transform what is individual into something corporate. Most cultures show a spontaneous comprehension of this. The suffering person is joined by friends who join their tears and prayers in a communal lament. They do not hush up the sound of weeping but augment it. If others weep with me, there must be more to the suffering than my own petty weakness or selfish sense of loss. The community votes with its tears that there is suffering that is worth weeping over.

~ Eugene Peterson

MOST OF US HAVE EXPERIENCED EXCRUCIATING physical pain. One time my stomach was cramping so badly I went to the ER. I was willing to do whatever it took to get out of the pain. When I arrived at the ER a team quickly mobilized to attend to me with the shared goals of diagnosis, pain relief and healing.

Everyone has experienced emotional pain as well. Though our society treats emotional pain and physical pain differently, emotional pain is just as real and damaging as physical pain. It's important for you to realize this and give yourself permission to feel your heartbreak and to expect help and relief.

We experience pain when we feel a loss of any kind. Losses introduce layers of hurt and pain that touch multiple areas of life. This stage is described well here:

> *As the shock wears off, the pain begins. This is a time of emotional upheaval.... You will experience overwhelming and excruciating pain—pain so palpable as to even feel it physically. Physical symptoms may include loss of appetite and weight loss or gain, chest pain, insomnia and extreme fatigue. Emotional symptoms of sadness, anger, guilt, anxiety, restlessness, and agitation will most likely occur. The hallmarks of this phase are rapid mood swings, intense emotions and the feeling of lost control over your life. You may even feel like you are losing your sanity.*[78]

What you might feel and experience at this stage:

- Hurt, pain, anguish, sorrow. I'm not sure any language has the words to capture what the deeply wounded soul feels at this point.

- Sadness—a heaviness, a shadow, a darkness. *Outside are sun and billowing clouds, people going about their normal lives. But how could that be? How could things be so blissfully routine and ordinary out there when you're feeling so much darkness and despair in here?*[79] Our English word 'sad' has its roots in the Germanic languages that meant 'full.' Sadness is a heaviness, a weightiness that overshadows and underlies everything in a person's life and thoughts. It 'fills' your soul with gray.

- Fear of how you will do life now, what you will tell others and what they will think of you, how you will make it financially.

---

[78] Author unknown, *The New Grief Stages: Finding Your Way Through the Tasks of Mourning*, accessed March 23, 2018,
https://www.recover-from-grief.com/new-grief-stages.html.
[79] H. Norman Wright, *Experiencing Divorce*, (Nashville: B&H Books, 2017), Kindle Locations 399-401.

- Rage which may be may be expressed in shouting, crying, throwing or damaging objects and/or the desire to hurt someone, including oneself. Like a hurt animal, hurt humans may lash out at self or others. (See Day 34)

- Regret at things said or done or not said or not done.

- Trouble catching your breath and frequent sighing.

Your experience of pain at this stage will depend on the nature of your loss. We all experience so many losses that come from so many directions. The value you assigned to the thing (or person) lost will directly determine the depth of the pain you feel when you lose that thing (or person).

For example, my daughter almost died while we were serving in Africa as professors. She was seven. It was excruciatingly painful to watch her go through suffering and I would have given anything to take her place. But I fully understood that had she died, my grief would have been on a completely different order—a place I prayed hard not to have to go to.

My parents were both 90-years-old when they died. This loss hurt but was completely expected and celebrated in a way. But if a child's mother dies when that child is five-years-old, the impact will be huge.

If you are suffering a divorce, how you process this loss will be completely dependent on your relationship with your ex-spouse. If you were in love with your spouse and enjoyed his company, you will experience the pain of separation. You will miss being with him. Like death, then, the separation caused by divorce will create separation pain in your life.

If you were unhappy with your husband and didn't like being around him, you won't experience the pain of separation as much. But you *will* experience the lost dream of being a family and all the things attendant to that.

All this to say that our society considers only one grief event to be worthy of its attention: the death of an immediate family member—and then only briefly. All other losses are secondary and considered much less painful and traumatizing. But losses come in all sorts of packages and are experienced in a huge variety of ways and degrees of intensity. How you are feeling right now has many factors involved in it. Allow yourself to experience your raw pain without guilt or remorse. It hurts! It is OK to hurt.

The major **survival strategy** in this stage is to ride it out. Don't do anything violent or permanent. Don't believe what you are telling yourself about you. Believe what God says about you. Connect with a good friend who can hear your anguish without trying to smooth over your pain with easy fixes. Find a counselor and/or pastor to sit with you in the agony.

Duration: Raw pain comes and goes for days, weeks or even months.

Success: Success looks like surviving intact without damaging yourself or others. Success is experiencing God's comforting presence. Successfully navigating through this stage doesn't mean that you will never feel the raw pain again. Success is experienced when the intensity and the frequency of the pain diminish over time.

Identity issue: The question you will be asking yourself at this stage is, *"Why me?"*

THINK ABOUT IT . . .

> Think back on a time when you experienced raw pain as a kid, teenager or adult. What did you do then? Do you regret any actions you took back then? What can you do differently now?

LIFE COMMITMENT:

I commit to riding this pain out, trusting that it won't last forever and that God will get me through it.

Day 47: The Stages of Suffering, Grief and Loss — (3) Anger & Bargaining

The Word

For man's anger does not bring about the righteous life that God desires.
— James 1.20

Thought for the Day:

Broken hearts are very vulnerable; they must be guarded carefully. When your heart has been broken, it can either become more soft and pliable to the work of God, or it can become hardened toward God and the things of God. And it is a strong temptation to harden our hearts toward God when he has disappointed us and when it feels like he has deserted us. If your heart is broken, are you willing to allow this hurt to serve as a softening agent that makes you more aware of God, more alive to his purposes, more sensitive to his Spirit at work on you and in you? Or will you let your heart become hardened so that you no longer hear his word, accept his rebuke, experience his mercy?
~ Nancy Guthrie

WHEN LIFE FALLS APART WE HURT DEEPLY. Ripped things hurt and ripped people sometimes rage. Anger is a dominant emotion among those who suffer greatly, especially among men. Some of us are caught off guard by the intensity of our anger—we may be surprised that our once placid and relatively calm personality is suddenly over-run with the heat of anger, resentment and envy.

We live in a culture without a 'theology of pain.' More to the point, we believe that we should be free from it. When pain inevitably comes to us, many of us feel violated. We may be angry because we thought we could avoid this suffering. Some of us may believe it is our innate right *not* to have to undergo suffering. As Rabindranath Tagore wrote, *We read the world wrong and say that it deceives us.*[80]

For some of us anger is so deeply embedded in our souls that nearly every negative emotion is processed and expressed as anger. Sadness may come out as anger. Grief may explode as anger. Self-pity may express itself as anger.

For better or worse, anger serves several purposes: it releases negative energy, it may get people to change or take action, it makes us feel powerful. Anger is one thing we can *do* when suffering robs us of options and rips control out of our desperately clutching hands.

It is our anger that drives us to bargaining. We may try to bargain with the people who have caused us grief or we might try bargaining with God: *I will go to church if you will* _____. *I will give my tax refund to help orphans if you will* _____.

Our kids bargain with us all the time! They will make a demand, then, when hearing a firm 'NO' they may soften their approach—that's called bargaining![81] Bargaining may be an attempt to get back what you have lost or, if the situation is inevitable (such as terminal cancer), bargaining may be an attempt to postpone what is coming.

When it becomes clear that our bargaining has failed, anger may explode in newly destructive ways. It's important to *think through every proposed action stemming from anger for its potential to harm others or yourself.*

What you might feel and experience at this stage:

- Pure anger, fury, hatred. The thoughts in your head may produce strong enough emotions that they want to be expressed outwardly in destructive ways such as physical harm to yourself or to others or to property.

---

[80] Quoted in Elisabeth Kübler-Ross, *On Death and Dying* (New York: Scribner, 2011), Kindle Location 847.

[81] Ibid., Kindle Location 1379.

- The weight of the loss (or impending loss) may drive you to attempt to bargain with people or with God to get restored what you lost or to postpone or avoid the inevitable.

- Emotional fluctuations, swinging between anger and affection, fear and boldness, sadness and hope.

- Cognitive dissonance: your mind is filled with reasons to be angry but also thoughts on how to get back what you lost or hope for what you think you can still retain.

- If you're suffering because of your poor choices, you may feel guilt, remorse, shame, embarrassment.

Duration: If you engage in bargaining it usually doesn't last too long. The impacts of great losses intrude in our lives in such a way that they cannot be ignored. The cancer will make us sick, the bank will foreclose on our home, the absence of the child will loom larger. Reality pushes us out of bargaining and into the next stage.

Success: Success at this stages means you accept that things are not going to get better. You accept the loss. Success looks like moving forward, not letting anger bind you to the past or paralyze your present. Success is finding hope in the future.

Identity issue: The question you will be asking yourself at this stage may be a return to the question you asked yourself at Stage 2, which is, *"Why me?"*

THINK ABOUT IT . . .

➤ How has anger been useful in your life in the past?

➤ How have you usually expressed anger? Violence? Shouting? Passive aggressiveness?

➤ Can you remember a time when you tried to bargain your way out of a jam? What was the result? In what ways are you bargaining right now?

165

LIFE COMMITMENT:

What has happened has left me devastated, hurt and angry. I commit to expressing my anger constructively. I can be angry without being an angry man or woman.

Day 48: The Stages of Suffering, Grief and Loss — (4) Isolation / Loneliness / Depression

The Word

I will not leave you as orphans; I will come to you. Before long, the world will not see me anymore, but you will see me.
Because I live, you also will live.
— John 14.18-19

Thought for the Day:

During my years caring for patients, the most common pathology I saw was not heart disease or diabetes; it was loneliness.
~ Dr. Vivek H. Murthy, Surgeon General of the United States

Stage 3—Anger and Bargaining—is a reaction to the events that have led to your loss. Anger and bargaining feel like you're doing something about this incredible pain in your life. You hope rage will somehow change the situation. You bargain, hoping to get your life back where it was before disaster befell you.

Stage 4 begins when you recognize that anger and bargaining haven't worked. Anger and bargaining feel like action that will produce results, namely getting out of the intense pain and solving the problem that led to your grief. When this doesn't work, your soul goes on the defense, which is to huddle, turtle, withdraw, and slink away to nurse your wounds. We are fixers—we like to fix things. Living in a world where extreme optimism in human ingenuity is coupled with boundless human energy, we fervently believe we can solve any problem life throws at us. When our efforts to fix our problem don't work, some of us slither away in defeat.

What you might feel and experience at this stage:

- Exhaustion, loss of energy and enthusiasm. Anger is exhausting. Bargaining takes huge investments of emotional energy. You are spent and simply don't care anymore.

- Worthlessness. Self-pity. Your best efforts have failed. *Why did this happen to me?*

- Sadness, grief, misery. Negative thoughts dominate.

- Everything is gray.

- You may experience feelings of intense isolation, loneliness, emptiness.

- Activities you enjoyed seem pointless.

- Food may lose its taste.

- Isolating yourself and engaging in passive activities such as watching TV or sleeping are appealing. For many people, video gaming is a welcome escape from this world into a virtual one where lives are magically reconstituted and no one really gets hurt.

- The thought of starting anything new will be met with a sigh and desire to take a nap.

- Other signs of depression are fatigue, irritability, messiness, physical pain, numbness, trouble concentrating and suicidal thoughts.

If the nature of your suffering is long-term (such as cancer, divorce, business failure, etc.) at this point in the process your friends may be tired of walking this journey with you and may abandon you or at least pull back. This adds to our isolation and gives us one more reason to turtle up. In our hurry-up, instant gratification world, friends who walk the long, hard road of grief with us are hard to find.

The major **survival strategy** at this stage is to balance your need to invest less energy in life with your need for remaining connected to people and activities that will give life again. Say *yes* to activities and invitations even though everything in you wants to say *no*.

It is here that you may experience God's unique presence. Lettie Burd Cowman was an American Christian writer and missionary in the early twentieth century. I have found her devotional *Streams in the Desert* amazingly timely and helpful. She writes regarding the Bible verse *"What I tell you in the dark, speak in the daylight; what is whispered in your ear, proclaim from the roofs"* (Matthew 10: 27):

> *Our Lord is constantly taking us into the dark in order to tell us something. It may be the darkness of a home where bereavement has drawn the blinds; the darkness of a lonely and desolate life, in which some illness has cut us off from the light and the activity of life; or the darkness of some crushing sorrow and disappointment.*
>
> *It is there He tells us His secrets—great and wonderful, eternal and infinite. He causes our eyes, blinded by the glare of things on earth, to behold the heavenly constellations. And our ears suddenly detect even the whisper of His voice, which has been so often drowned out by the turmoil of earth's loud cries.*[82]

Expect God to find you in your dark place and give you comfort, encouragement and, eventually, a new calling for the next stage of your life.

In addition to staying connected to God, you must stay connected to your counselor, pastor and loyal friends. You must *not* believe everything you are telling yourself. For years I have told depressed people, *Don't believe everything you are telling yourself right now. Your thinking is distorted. Instead, listen to what wise and trusted friends are saying to you.*[83]

---

[82]L. B. Cowman, *Streams in the Desert: 366 Daily Devotional Readings* (Grand Rapids: Zondervan, 2008), 150.

[83]For more information about depression, go to https://www.webmd.com/depression/guide/detecting-depression\#1.

Cling to hope: how you are *thinking* now will change. You will have more positive thoughts as time goes by. How you are *feeling* now will change. You will feel better in time.

If you're stuck in a pattern of negative, cynical thinking, you may be depressed. If you know you have some reasons to be positive but your mind can't go there despite your best efforts, see a counselor/therapist and your medical doctor. Living with depression is nasty, and counseling, along with medication (if needed) can literally save your life. There is no shame in getting the help you need.

Duration: Clinical depression is defined as having experiencing the above signs and symptoms for most of the day, nearly every day, for at least two weeks. If this is you, you need help. Help will include conversations with a counselor, therapist, psychiatrist and/or pastor. Treatment recommendations may include medication. This stage may last for weeks or months. The more you push back by remaining engaged with the world, the shorter this stage will be.

Success: You will know you are getting through depression when you wake up one day realizing that you have had more good days than bad and when you begin to want to engage life again.

Identity issue: The question you will be asking yourself at this stage is, *"Who am I?"*

THINK ABOUT IT . . .

> ➤ When you experienced pain in the past, what did you do?

> ➤ How strong is the pull in you to withdraw from the world?

> ➤ What is one thing you can do today to push against the urge to turtle?

LIFE COMMITMENT:

Though I feel a strong pull toward isolation, I will not give in. I will say 'yes' to any invitations that come my way to engage in life again, and I will take steps to be a part of the world again.

Day 49: The Stages of Suffering, Grief and Loss — (5) Turning the Corner

The Word

There is surely a future hope for you, and your hope will not be cut off.
— Proverbs 23.18

Thought for the Day:

Discouragement focuses more on the broken glories of creation than it does on the restoring glories of God's character, presence, and promises.
~ Paul David Trip

AT SOME POINT YOU WILL REALIZE that you are having more good moments than bad, and when the bad moments come they are less intense. Gradually life doesn't seem so hard and traumatic. Your energy slowly returns. Your sleep improves and you begin to think more clearly.

A terrible thing happened, and you won't forget this terrible thing. But in a healthy recovery process, the terrible thing doesn't dominate your brain space like it did when the event first occurred. Healthy recovery is evidenced when the pain of loss and remembrances of the events surrounding it diminish in size. They are there, but not dominating all your thinking.

As life begins to return, determine to thrive beyond your loss by working on your own issues that need to change. Don't use these glimmers of new energy to go back to old habits that may have put you in this situation in the first place. Take this opportunity to envision a new future for you and the people in your life.

A caution: Some people may experience a return to depression at this stage. Just when you are beginning to feel better, triggers can send you back to the Raw Pain stage. Don't let setbacks keep you down. Remember how far you have come and the bright possibilities for the future.

What you might feel and experience at this stage:

- Less pain, more hope.

- More energy.

- Better sleep.

- More desire to live life.

- Triggers that may set you back momentarily or for hours or even a few days.

Survival strategies include staying connected to God, family, friends, your counselor and pastor. Determine to begin the road to building a new life with healthy habits. Take on habits that will support your mission to fulfill God's calling on the rest of your life (more on this later). Turning the corner after a great tragedy is an opportunity to remake your identity. Resolve to reject old destructive ways of living and, instead, take on habits that will make a new and better you.

Duration: Turning the corner feels like a slow pivot. This is rarely a 'light bulb' moment. Light begins to dawn gradually as you begin to see hope for your future.

Success: As you begin to have glimmers of hope that you will survive this, you launch an identity separate from your identity before your loss. If your husband died, you begin to see yourself as a single woman/widow. If your business failed, you envision life without the rewards of a successful business. A new identity might emerge that actually propels you to success in life's next stage.

Identity: The question you will be asking yourself at this stage is, *"What could be in my future?"*

Think About It . . .

- ➤ Have you experienced glimmers of hope?

- ➤ Do you have more energy?

- ➤ Are you sleeping better?

- ➤ If not, don't despair. Hang on—things will get better!

Life Commitment:

When I begin to feel better and see a future for myself, I determine I will use this blank slate to let God build a better me.

Day 50: The Stages of Suffering, Grief and Loss — (6) Reconstruction

The Word

*No eye has seen, no ear has heard, no mind has conceived
what God has prepared for those who love him.*
— 1 Corinthians 2.9

Thought for the Day:

*The land of God's promises is open before us, and it is his will for us to
possess it. We must measure off the territory with the feet of obedient faith
and faithful obedience, thereby claiming and appropriating it as our own.*
~ L. B. Cowman

My hunch is that if you have reached this stage you would not be
reading this book. If you still have the reconstruction stage ahead of
you, know that *you will get through these stages of grief, suffering and
loss.* There is hope for your future. Nothing in your heart or head may
be believing this right now, but be confident: **you will survive.** My
job is to help you move beyond mere surviving into truly thriving.

As you consider your future, you have much to look forward to
in this stage. At Stage 6 you make critical choices as to what kind of
future you will have. Ask God who he wants you to be and what he
wants you to do. Bounce ideas off trusted friends. Make sure the new
things you try are healthy, not self-destructive. Build habits that are
life-giving to you and to others.

At this stage it's common to try on new 'identities.' In my own case, my losses included my career as a pastor and my wife. The core of my identity—husband and pastor—were stripped away. These were unbelievably painful losses. For about one minute I had thoughts that went like this: *Hey, I am not a pastor! I am not a husband! I can do what I want! Let's go party, drinking, drugging, sexing... let's live it up!*

In my heart of hearts I knew this wasn't me, and, frankly, I didn't want to be remembered for how I handled these losses as a guy who gave up on God and gave in to the world.

So in my reconstruction phase I stuck with God, asking him what he wanted me to do. He clearly gave me a call to write! And I went back to earlier activities that had given me life but had been suppressed because of a lack of time (from the church) or support (from my wife). I hiked, backpacked, skydived and cycled like a wild man!

I also started really learning the guitar and later, the ukulele and bass guitar. Playing music is a great outlet for my soul.

But all is not easy at this stage. Reconstruction can be tumultuous as you regain energy to move forward. You may have many ideas of what your future could be. At the same time, rebuilding is a daunting task.

What you might feel and experience at this stage:

- Fluctuating emotions as you engage the task of rebuilding your identity.

- Excitement that a new life is waiting for you.

- Conflicting desires about who you want to be.

- Desire to build your identity by trying on various experiences. If you never skydived or learned how to dance, you just might find yourself jumping out of an airplane at 14,000 fee or learning swing!

- Swinging between confidence and fear, initiative and withdrawal.

All trauma causes a foundational dis-integration of identity and the challenge of re-integrating yourself to accommodate the changes that come from loss. Getting the energy to rebuild your life from a diminished position is a challenge.

Survival strategies include remaining connected to a counselor/therapist who can help guide you to make wise choices through the reconstruction of your identity. It is here that walking closely with God is critical, as he desires to call you into the second half of your life with a clear and strong purpose (see Days 87 and 88). Being part of a local church and life group (small group) will help you discover how others have navigated the challenges of life to emerge stronger and better. Sharing your story will reinforce your faith as you recount how God saved you through these hard times.

Duration: Reconstruction can take months as your mind and soul slowly work through the process of identity formation and reformation.

Success: As you picture what successfully navigating this stage looks like, ask yourself what you want people saying about you at your funeral. Success starts with deliberately choosing habits that will build a lifestyle of God's design, passionately pursuing his mission for your life.

Identity: The question you will be asking yourself at this stage is, *"Who is God and what does he desire from me and for me?"*

THINK ABOUT IT . . .

- ➤ What stage do you think you are in right now?

- ➤ What aspects of your identity have been diminished or destroyed because of the divorce?

- ➤ What habits in your old life need to go?

- ➤ What new habits will you choose to build a better you?

- ➤ Have you heard God's call on your life as to what he wants you to do and be for the rest of your life, or at least the next few years?

Life Commitment:

God can and does use suffering to strip me down and rebuild me into the person he wants me to be. I submit to his loving hand of guidance and strong call upon my life so that I will finish well.

Day 51: The Stages of Suffering, Grief and Loss — (7) Acceptance & Hope

The Word

> *This poor man called, and the Lord heard him;*
> *he saved him out of all his troubles.*
> — Psalm 34:6-7

Thought for the Day:

> *Optimism and hope are radically different attitudes. Optimism is the*
> *expectation that things—the weather, human relationships, the economy,*
> *the political situation, and so on—will get better. Hope is the trust that God*
> *will fulfill God's promises to us in a way that leads us to true freedom. The*
> *optimist speaks about concrete changes in the future. The person of hope*
> *lives in the moment with the knowledge*
> *and trust that all of life is in good hands.*
> ~ Henri J. M. Nouwen

British Entrepreneur and motivational speaker Rasheed Ogunlaru says, *Sometimes in life there's no problem and sometimes there is no solution. In this space—between these apparent poles—life flows.*[84]

---

[84]Rasheed Ogunlaru, *azquotes*, accessed June 7, 2018,
http://www.azquotes.com/quote/673473. Our Western mindset makes acceptance
of hard events more difficult. John Reich and colleagues note that Western and
Eastern philosophies... *offer contrasting views on the nature of conscious experience
most likely to sustain well-being. Western views focus on choice and mastery over*

In the last stage of grief recovery you come to accept that this enormous loss occurred and it can't be undone. The best way forward is forward. You accept what happened and choose to move on.

The key marker of success at this stage is that your loss and the events surrounding your loss don't dominate your head space. Perfect acceptance would be that you think less often of your loss and when you do, you don't have strong feelings of anger/resentment nor do you have strong feelings of lingering desire/attachment. When remembering your loss, your emotions are more moderated.

That's the perfect scenario. The reality is that you and I will always have emotions—sometimes strong emotions—when we think of what happened to us and the impacts of our loss(es). How influential are those thoughts over our lives? Is lingering pain still being transmitted to others around us or has God transformed our pain into energy to forge into the future he has for us? Recovery will be characterized by the latter.

Another critical and difficult issue is forgiveness. If our pain is the result of our own bad choices, we must forgive ourselves. If someone else causes our hurt, we move toward forgiving them. If our loss can't be clearly assigned to us or to another human being, we may struggle with forgiving God. These are huge issues that are too much to cover here.[85]

When in the acceptance stage, you will agree that

> *Resilience transforms. It transforms hardship into challenge, failure into success, helplessness into power. Resilience turns victims into survivors and allows survivors*

---

the environment, whereas Eastern philosophies emphasize full awareness and acceptance of experience, however painful, to gain an enlightened and "joyous" view of the world. John Reich, et al, *Handbook of Adult Resilience* (New York: Guilford Publications, 2012), 8. Timothy Keller writes that *Sociologists and anthropologists have analyzed and compared the various ways that cultures train its members for grief, pain, and loss. And when this comparison is done, it is often noted that our own contemporary secular, Western culture is one of the weakest and worst in history at doing so.* Timothy Keller, *Walking with God through Pain and Suffering* (New York: Penguin, 2013), 20.

[85] The best book on forgiveness I have read is by Everett Worthington, *Forgiving and Reconciling: Bridges to Wholeness and Hope*. Downers Grove: InterVarsity Press, 2003.

to thrive. Resilient people are loath to allow even major setbacks to push them from their life course.[86]

The major **challenge** at this stage is to stay connected to God, your dream, other people. When you feel you are slipping back, talk it out. Don't let the past rob you of your future!

Duration: This stage usually begins many months after a loss but can take a long time to complete. You are on a journey and journeys have different paces at different stages. Be patient with yourself.

Success: You know you're in this stage when thoughts of your loss don't elicit strong positive or negative emotions, you're engaged in living your new identity with energy and enthusiasm, and you have growing relationships with yourself, other folks and with God.

Identity: The question you will be asking yourself at this stage is, *"How far will God take me?"*

THINK ABOUT IT . . .

➤ When you think of your loss, what emotions do you experience?

➤ Has God given you a mission and purpose for your future? If not, ask him to, and then be patient while waiting for the response.

LIFE COMMITMENT:

Though a terrible thing happened to me I know God has a plan and a future for me. I am eager to know his plan for me but also willing to be patient for him to work in my life, preparing me for his future.

---

[86] Karen Reivich, *The Resilience Factor: Seven Essential Skills For Overcoming Life's Inevitable Obstacles* (New York: Random House, 2003), Kindle Locations 114-116.

Day 52: Moving Through These Stages

The Word

Brothers and sisters, I do not consider myself yet to have taken hold of it. But one thing I do: Forgetting what is behind and straining toward what is ahead, I press on toward the goal to win the prize for which God has called me heavenward in Christ Jesus.
— Philippians 3:13-14

Thought for the Day:

Good management of bad experiences leads to great growth.
~ John Maxwell

The Greek word in the scripture quoted above that is translated with the English phrase *straining toward* is **epekteinomai**. The root of this word means *to stretch*. Interestingly this word has two prefixes attached to it, *epi* and *ek*. Without getting too technical, these two prefixes greatly intensify the meaning of the root word. In other words, Paul is saying that though he has much in his past that could haunt him, he is *really stretching toward the future*, pressing in on God's purpose for his life.

How long does it take to get through these stages of loss and grief, and do you just go right through them or is it more circular or more back and forth? It depends and maybe and yes.

We are unique humans with many factors involved in our losses. Each of us will go through these stages at different rates. And 'going through them' doesn't usually mean a straight linear progression (sorry about that you engineers!). For example, you may be in the

181

middle of Stage 5—'Turning the Corner'— and see or hear or smell something at the grocery store, sending you back to Stage 1 for a moment.

The key here is to see yourself making progress despite brief setbacks.

Another key is to measure your progress in terms of how you are functioning and how you are feeling. If your loss happened four years ago and you are barely able to crawl out of bed, you need professional help. If you are expressing your pain in destructive habits such as drinking, drugging, shopping or anything else that is less than God's best, you will be slow in progressing toward Stage 7 and you will continue doing damage to yourself and others.

How are you doing? The best way to answer that question is to have honest conversations with your pastor, counselor/therapist and a couple of good friends who love you enough to accept you as you are but not leave you where you are.

Think About It . . .

> ➤ Where do you think you are in this process?

> ➤ Now ask your friends and counselor where *they* think you are.

Life Commitment:

Paul said it 2,000 years ago. Now YOU believe it and embrace it! "I do not consider myself yet to have taken hold of it. But one thing I do: Forgetting what is behind and straining toward what is ahead, I press on toward the goal to win the prize for which God has called me heavenward in Christ Jesus."

Day 53: Suicide: Stay

The Word

The thief comes only to steal and kill and destroy;
I have come that they may have life, and have it to the full.
— John 10.10

Thought for the Day:

It is crucial to see that deciding against the principle of suicide creates its
own practical strengths: it commits one to the human project and to one's
own life in a way that gives rise to solidarity and resilience. And when one
speaks of such commitment to living, others may be encouraged to live and
to find the resources to survive pain.
~ Jennifer Michael Hecht

NATIONAL SUICIDE PREVENTION LIFELINE: 800-273-8255. The information found in the next few days can also be found in Appendix A.

If you have thoughts of taking your life you are not alone nor are you abnormal. I believe that the vast majority of people think of taking their own life at some point in their lives. But it also seems to me that some people never think of taking their lives, no matter how hard life gets. If you are one of those people who seldom thinks of suicide, please don't skip the next few days. Information you gain here could help save a friend's life and give you insight into why some of us entertain suicidal thoughts.

Early on we said that pain that is not transformed is transmitted. Suicide is simply intense pain transmitted toward oneself, sometimes with the intention to eliminate the pain or what a person perceives to be the source of the pain to oneself and/or to others.

I am one of those people who think about suicide. For about four days a few months after my divorce was final, suicide became one of several options. I was shocked at how casually I thought of this option. As I considered what to do, suicide seemed a viable choice. Death by my hand was laid out there along with the other options on how to move forward out of the pain.

A newly divorced man named Philip writes:

> *As a divorced man, I can honestly say I contemplated suicide for the first time in my life during the first year or two of my separation. It's incredibly difficult to have your entire family life—children, home and even wife—pulled away from you. Prior to the divorce, I was very happy, making a good salary and living in a nice neighborhood. Soon after the divorce, I was saddled with very high child support payments, debt from legal fees and barely enough left over to pay the rent of my small one bedroom apartment.*[87]

H. Norman Wright says that there are four main reasons for suicide:

- **Depression [Rage]**—*The person is sitting on a high level of unacceptable rage that has developed because of a series of events in life over which he or she has no control. Eventually this repressed rage is turned against himself or herself in suicide.*

- **Relief of Pain**—*Those with high levels of pain usually [believe they] have [only] three choices: a psychotic distortion that reduces the pain, drugs or alcohol, or suicide. They often say, "I don't want to die, but I don't know any other way out—I just can't stand it."*

- **Revenge**—*Some [people] feel overwhelmed by hurt or rejection from another person. Their desire to hurt back is stronger than the desire to live.*

---

[87] Jack Cafferty *Why does divorce make men more suicidal than women?*, last updated March 11, 2010, accessed July 13, 2017, http://caffertyfile.blogs.cnn.com/2010/03/11/why-does-divorce-make-men-more-suicidal-than-women/.

- **Hopelessness**—*Twenty-five percent of those who commit suicide do so after giving it quiet consideration and weighing the pros and cons of living and dying.*[88]

Teacher, author, and historian Jennifer Michael Hecht lost two friends to suicide. In her own grief she decided to research and write about it. She wrote her thoughts in a blog called "The Best American Poetry." In the blog she made an appeal to those contemplating suicide:

> *I want to say this,... Don't kill yourself. Life has always been almost too hard to bear, for a lot of the people, a lot of the time. It's awful. But it isn't too hard to bear, it's only almost too hard to bear...*
>
> *I'm issuing a rule. You are not allowed to kill yourself. When a person kills himself, he does wrenching damage to the community. One of the best predictors of suicide is knowing a suicide. That means that suicide is also delayed homicide. You have to stay.*
>
> *Don't kill yourself. Suffer here with us instead. We need you with us, we have not forgotten you, you are our hero. Stay.*[89]

When I was struggling those four days, here is (among other things) what I kept in my head that helped me choose to stay:

- *I did not want to add to the pain of others.* If trauma has caused me tremendous pain, it is fair to assume that my suicide would traumatize the people I love the most. This is not right nor fair to them. My goal should be to reduce pain in the world, not add to it.

- *I will get through this.* Life has always been almost too hard to bear for a lot of the people a lot of the time. It's awful. But it isn't too hard to bear—it's only <u>almost</u> too hard to bear. What I feel today will not be what I feel tomorrow.

---

[88] H. Norman Wright, *The New Guide to Crisis and Trauma Counseling* (Ventura, CA: Regal Books, 2003), Kindle Locations 3120-3126.

[89] Jennifer Michael Hecht, *Stay: A History of Suicide and the Philosophies Against It* (New Haven: Yale University Press, 2015), 7-8 (emphasis mine).

- *If I take my life, this is what I will be remembered for.* No matter all my accomplishments, the first thing people will think of when my name is mentioned will be that I took my life. I did not want that.

- *By taking my own life, I may contribute to someone else's suicide.* Survivors of those who take their lives are more likely to take their own life. I didn't want to potentially contribute to the death by suicide of anyone among my family or friends.

- *I will deprive the world of what God has planned to do through me.* I have much to offer this world. God showed me that I had many years to serve him and that many people would be helped if I chose to stay.

When I thought of these realities, suicide remained an option, but one among many options. If I had not considered these realities, suicide as an option could have become my *only* option, at least in my mind.

If you are thinking of suicide as one of several options, pay attention to your thinking. If you have come to the conclusion that suicide is your *only* option, your thinking has become distorted and you need immediate help. *Call the suicide prevention hotline immediately* — **800-273-8255**. Don't hesitate. Put this book down and call *now*. Don't turn temporary moments of personal anguish into a permanent state of calamity for those around you.

THINK ABOUT IT . . .

- ➤ Is suicide one of several options you are considering? God has bigger plans for you than you can imagine. Don't cheat the world of what you have to offer.

- ➤ In your mind, is suicide becoming the *only* option? You need help. Call the suicide hotline: **800-273-8255**

LIFE COMMITMENT:

"Life has always been almost too hard to bear, for a lot of the people, a lot of the time. It's awful. But it isn't too hard to bear, it's only almost too hard to bear." I commit to bearing through this terrible time of life,

knowing that what is now will not always be. God is my hope. He will see me through to new life and new hope. I choose to stay.

Day 54: Suicide—Assessing Your Risk

The Word

> *The Lord is close to the brokenhearted and*
> *saves those who are crushed in spirit.*
> *A righteous man may have many troubles,*
> *but the Lord delivers him from them all.*
>
> — Psalm 34.18–19

Thought for the Day:

It can be a tremendous comfort to learn that great minds have concluded that no individual need wonder whether his or her life is worth living. It is worth living.

~ Jennifer Michael Hecht

National Suicide Prevention Lifeline: 800-273-8255

On September 25, 2000, Kevin Hines jumped off the Golden Gate Bridge. He hit the water 220 feet below and lived to tell about it. He is only one of 33 among an estimated 2,000 people who have jumped to survive the fall. As I read his story his words leapt out at me:

> *In the midst of my free fall, I said to myself these words,*
> *words I thought no one would ever hear me repeat: "What*
> *have I done? I don't want to die. God, please save me!" As*

*I fell, I somehow possessed the mind-set that all I wanted
to do was live—by any means necessary.*[90]

I wonder how many of the more than 45,000 people who take their
lives every year in the United States have had the same thought the
moment after they jumped or pulled the trigger or hit the tree or
swallowed the pills or cut their wrists.

Are you thinking of taking your life? Take your thoughts seriously. If you are thinking any of the following thoughts or taking
any of the following actions, you are at a higher risk for attempting
to take your life by your own hand.

Carefully consider these questions:

- How much of your 'brain space' is taken up by thinking of
  suicide? Are you thinking of **how** to do it? Are you considering
  what people would say? Are you thinking about suicide a large
  portion of your day?

- Are your thoughts turning into **plans**? Have you thought of
  a **time** and a **place**? Have you thought of **how** you would do
  it? Have you thought of how you would obtain the means to
  do it?

- *Are you preparing others for your leaving?* Have you told
  anyone you will miss them? Have you written out your will?
  Have you given away personal belongings? Have you obtained
  the means to do it such as purchasing a gun or obtaining pills?
  Have you rehearsed how you will do it?

- Have you decided if you want your attempted suicide to be your
  final act on earth, or do you plan for it to be only self-injurious,
  not lethal?

If you answered **yes** to any of these questions, I urge you, I plead
with you, get help immediately. Call this number: **800-273-8255**.

---

[90] *He jumped off the Golden Gate Bridge . . . and lived!*, New York Post, last updated
June 20, 2013, accessed July 13, 2017,
http://nypost.com/2013/06/30/he-jumped-off-the-golden-gate-bridge-and-lived/.
See also his book, Kevin Hines, *Cracked, Not Broken: Surviving and Thriving After
a Suicide Attempt*, (Lanham, MD: Rowman & Littlefield Publishers, 2013).

I want you to stay. I got up at 4:30 every morning for months so that I could write this book *so that you would choose to stay.* One reason I chose to stay is to help others in the same situation choose to stay. You are wanted and needed. Please stay.

What the Psalmist wrote 3,000 years ago is as true today as it was then: *The Lord is close to the brokenhearted and saves those who are crushed in spirit. A righteous man may have many troubles, but the Lord delivers him from them all.* (Psalm 34.18–19)

In 1997 my 50-year-old sister, Jackie, took her life. Don't do what my sister did. Please stay. I did, and I am glad I did.

THINK ABOUT IT . . .

> ➤ Go back over the questions listed above. If you are considering suicide as an option I urge you get help. Call the hotline. Call a pastor, a trusted and wise friend, a counselor.

LIFE COMMITMENT:

I commit to staying. The world needs me.

Day 55: Suicide—Getting Help

The Word

*So do not fear, for I am with you; do not be dismayed, for I am your God.
I will strengthen you and help you; I will uphold you with my righteous
right hand.*

— Isaiah 41.10

Thought for the Day:

God's agenda is never elimination but transformation.

~ Richard Rohr

National Suicide Prevention Lifeline: 800-273-8255

Jesus said as recorded by the apostle John: *The thief comes only to
steal and kill and destroy; I have come that they may have life, and
have it to the full.* (John 10.10)

You and I are in a war and Satan is our enemy. Satan hates God,
but since Satan can't destroy God, his driving passion is to deface God
by defacing and/or destroying God's highest creation. That would be
you. Suicide is the ultimate destruction of God's amazing creation.

King David wrote: *When I consider your heavens, the work of your
fingers, the moon and the stars, which you have set in place, what is
mankind that you are mindful of them, human beings that you care for
them? You made them a little lower than the angels, and crowned them
with glory and honor.* (Psalm 8:3–5)

Wow! You and I are God's amazing creation! No wonder Satan
wants to take you out! **Don't let him!**

In my office I have a plastic anatomical human skull that can be taken apart. Inside is a model of the brain. Sometimes when people come into my office who are troubled and depressed, I take out my plastic skull and pull out the brain.

I say to them:

I know you are suffering and that you are in pain because of your loss. But did you know that you still have this amazing thing between your ears—your brain! Your brain is the second most incredible thing in all the universe. Did you get that? That three-pound mass of cells in your head is the second most astounding thing in the entire universe! The first is, of course, God himself. Whatever you have lost, you still have this amazing thing! And, you have God! What can be better than that?

To take your life by suicide is to destroy this second most amazing thing in all the universe! Don't do it. Don't give Satan the victory. Don't let the thief come in and destroy. Instead, cry out to God. He WILL rescue you!

Yesterday I listed some questions to help you assess how much you are at risk for suicide. Have you thought about those questions since then?

Whatever your answers, I urge you to get help. The journey you are on is a journey only you can make. Only you make the journey but you don't have to (nor should you) make the journey alone.

God knows the battle for your soul. God knows the war against your life. He wants you to win. He's on your side. Because he is for you, God will put resources in your path that will help you survive this journey and thrive on the other side. This book is one of those resources. It's no accident that you are reading this. God knew you would need this book to make it through this ordeal. He called me to write it and he called you to read it. This is evidence of God's loving care for you.

In addition to written resources, God has placed many other resources for you to tap into during this hard time. I urge you, please reach out and get the help you need.

The following are some suggestions to help you get through this time. Perhaps these suggestions are prompts God is putting in your path to help you right now.

- **Pray** to God. He is listening and much closer to you than you can imagine. He is eager to help you and see you through this. Praying is just talking to God and listening for his response. He longs to hear our cries (see Psalm 62.8).

- **Friends**. We all need a few trusted, loyal, wise friends. Who can you call in the middle of the night who will listen to you, accept you for who you are, and help get you through it? Not everyone will help you but God will give you a few who will.

- **A Pastor**. Pastors are today's unsung heroes. Most pastors are amazing people who give themselves to helping people win victories over the enemy. If you don't have a church, ask around to find a church known for their love for God and their love for people. It takes courage to jump in, but do it. God works through his church. His church is there for you. As a pastor for over 30 years, when someone called me out of the blue and wanted to meet with me, I would immediately and gladly see him/her. Don't hesitate to reach out to a pastor.

- **A Counselor** or **Therapist**. God has put smart people on this planet who are committed to helping people get through hard times. You want this person to be honest and be able to gently confront you when necessary.

- This **website**[91] has hotlines for all kinds of problems.

For years I have told depressed people the same thing: *Don't believe everything you are telling yourself right now. Your thinking is distorted. Instead, listen to what others are saying to you.*

How you are *thinking* now will change. You will have more positive thoughts as time goes by. Hold on!

How you are *feeling* now will change. You will feel better! Hold on!

---

[91] https://brokenbelievers.com/2011/01/23/247-crisis-lines/

Jennifer Hecht succinctly states: *Though we may refuse a version of life, we must also refuse voluntary death.*[92]

You are right to be upset about how your life is right now. Don't choose to change the state of your life, however, by ending it. That is a worse choice with far worse consequences. Instead, hang on, get the help you need, and watch God do his amazing work in your life.

THINK ABOUT IT . . .

> ➤ Get help. Really. Help will help more than you imagine right now.

LIFE COMMITMENT:

I commit to getting the help I need to get through this.

---

[92] Hecht, *Stay*, 183.

Day 56: Sleep is the Great Reset Button

The Word

On my bed I remember you; I think of you through the watches of the night.
Because you are my help, I sing in the shadow of your wings.
My soul clings to you; your right hand upholds me.

— Psalm 63.6–8

Thought for the Day:

I love sleep. My life has the tendency to fall apart
when I'm awake, you know?

~ Ernest Hemingway

WHO NEEDS SLEEP? Not busy, important people. Not people who want to succeed or climb the ladder. The only people who really need sleep is... everyone. Especially when you've been hammered by life.

Earlier I talked about the mighty prophet Elijah (see Day 5). After God had honored Elijah's prayer by consuming the sacrifice (and everything around it) with holy fire, the priests of Baal were wiped out. That was the way of the world back then.

You will recall that though God had clearly won an amazing victory for his glory and the good of Elijah, Elijah shook in his sandals when he heard that Queen Jezebel was after him!

Elijah ran for his life. And then, exhausted, he did what all of us should do when life turns upside down—he collapsed under a tree and slept. The next verses describe the tenderness of God: *All at once*

195

an angel touched him and said, "Get up and eat." [Elijah] looked around, and there by his head was a cake of bread baked over hot coals, and a jar of water. He ate and drank and then lay down again. (1 Kings19:5–6)

How incredible that though Elijah could be considered a coward for being so frightened of this queen, God lovingly cared for him in his exhaustion. Instead of waking up Elijah and berating him, God tenderly put him into a deep, restorative sleep. Imagine that God has actually ordained taking naps!

Amanda Jameson hiked the 2,650-mile-long Pacific Crest Trail. When asked what she learned on that arduous journey, she said, *Sleep is the great reset button.*[93] I like that.

It's thought that during sleep your brain runs a sort of garbage pickup routine. Your brain produces by-products as it works through the day. During sleep these by-products are literally picked up and carried off, performing a cleanup and reset function.[94]

When life tumbles in, your brain is working overtime thereby producing more toxic by-products. You need more sleep to clean out your brain. John Steinbeck said that *it is a common experience that a problem difficult at night is resolved in the morning after the committee of sleep has worked on it.*[95]

When we are Hungry, Angry, Lonely and Tired (HALT) we tend to make poor decisions. The fuse is short and the will is weak when we are tired. Give yourself a break… let your body, mind and soul mend through sleep.

Elijah didn't know all that was going on in his brain when he collapsed into sleep under the tree in the desert, but God did. The result was that through sleep and good food, Elijah was prepared to hear God and take the next step in his life.

Having trouble coping with your pain? Sleep on it.

---

[93] Amanda "Zuul" Jameson, *Advice From a Hiker Who Finished the Pacific Crest Trail*, Backpacker.com, February 14, 2017, accessed February 20, 2017, http://www.back-packer.com/trips/advice-from-a-hiker-who-finished-the-pacific-crest-trail.

[94] "*10 Fascinating Things That Happen While You're Sleeping*," Prevention, March 21, 2016, accessed February 20, 2017, http://www.prevention.com/health/what-happens-during-sleep/slide/9.

[95] "John Steinbeck Quotes," BrainyQuote, accessed September 24, 2017, https://www.brainyquote.com/quotes/quotes/j/johnsteinb103825.html.

Think About It . . .

➤ How much sleep do you get?

➤ If you are having trouble sleeping ask God for help. Check with your doctor and/or therapist to see what they may advise to help you sleep.

➤ Go to this website for tips and tricks for getting and staying asleep: https://www.sleepfoundation.org/articles/healthy-sleep-tips

Life Commitment:

Sleeping doesn't mean I am lazy, it means I'm human. Sleep is designed by God to reset and refresh me. If ever I need good sleep, it's now.

Day 57: Get Moving

The Word

Do you not know that your body is a temple of the Holy Spirit, who is in you, whom you have received from God? You are not your own; you were bought at a price. Therefore honor God with your body.

— 1 Corinthians 6.19–20

Thought for the Day:

Making excuses burns zero calories per hour.

~ Anonymous

Today's encouragement is short and simple. *Start doing something, anything, that gets your heart beating fast and makes you sweat.* You don't have to do it a long time. You don't have to pay anything to do this. No need for special clothes or shoes. The weather doesn't have to be perfect. You don't have to go anywhere special. All you have to do is *do it.* Do **something** that gets your heart beating and your body sweating.

Study after study can give you all the info you could ever want on why exercise is good for you. But the real problem is not *information,* it's *motivation.*

So here's the deal. If you can't do 50 pushups, do 10 today. Do 10 pushups a day for a week. Then next week do 15. Ten pushups today is better than zero. When you do 10 pushups a day this week and then 15 next week, you will see progress and you will be motivated.

If you can't walk 100 yards without your heart coming out of your chest, start with 50. Just do it. *Start today, right now.*

It won't be fun. Putting your heart and lungs into chaos can be exhilarating, but it is not *fun* in the traditional sense of the word. It actually feels more like *work*. Those people who tell you this will be easy and exciting set you up for unrealistic expectations.

I'm not going to tell you it is fun but I can assure you it really feels good. It feels good to drop weight. It feels good to know you can eventually handle that five-mile hike or run with your kids or get on a bike and travel 20 miles on your own power.

It feels good to not have sleep apnea, high blood pressure, acid reflux, chest pains and high blood sugar *simply because you consistently put your heart and lungs into chaos for 30 minutes a day.*

Is this fitness stuff really so complicated? If you eat more calories than you burn, you will get fat. The opposite is true. If you burn more than you eat, you will lose weight. Mean old Mr. Science! But that's the way it works. No matter what anyone tells you, there are no shortcuts or magic pills. Eat less, exercise more, that's it. That's it but that's enough to feel good!

Now is the time to get off the couch and do *something. Something* is better than *nothing* and a bunch of *somethings* add up to *a lot of good things* for you.

If you need a few inspirational quotes, here they are:

- *Better sore than sorry.*

- *Nothing tastes as good as skinny feels.* (My personal favorite)

- *Sweat is just fat crying.*

- *Get comfortable with being uncomfortable.*

- *Pain is weakness leaving the body.*

- *Three months from now you will thank yourself.*

- *No pain. No Gain. Shut up and train.*

- *Work hard. Stay humble.*

- *Sore? Tired? Out of breath? Sweaty? Good . . . It's working.*

- *Good things come to those who sweat.*

- *Sore muscles are the new hangover.*

- *Motivation is what gets you started. Habit keeps you going.*

- *Your fitness is 100% mental. Your body won't go where your mind doesn't push it.*

I guarantee you this: No matter how you feel when you start a workout, you will *not* feel worse after your workout. No matter how you feel when you begin a workout, you will not regret having worked out.

Try me on this one. Get moving. And you will want to check with your doctor before you do anything too strenuous.

THINK ABOUT IT . . .

➤ No . . . don't think about it. Just get up and do SOMETHING to get your heart beating and your body sweating!

➤ Download the motivational quotes above in poster format to put on your fridge.[96]

LIFE COMMITMENT:

I am getting up to do something that will get my heart beating and my body sweating.

---

[96] See here https://storage.googleapis.com/wzukusers/user-25216852/documents/ 5b5dacfc3787aOHWxKa5/Motivation\%20to\%20Get\%20Moving.pdf

DAY 58: LARGER THAN LIFE

THE WORD

He who began a good work in you will carry it on to completion
until the day of Christ Jesus.
— Philippians 1:6

THOUGHT FOR THE DAY:

The rat race speeds up... but it is still a race for rats.
~ Os Guinness

I SLIPPED. I RAGED ON FACEBOOK against the unfairness I experienced. The conversation began when an old friend (literally, 81 years old, and a friend for 30+ years) asked how I was doing. The scab was pulled back and the blood began to flow. My friend is a saint—back in the 1980s when the AIDS epidemic was ravaging the homosexual population, she bucked the evangelical detestation of gays and embraced men who were dying young.

I knew she could take what I had to dish out, so I unloaded my anger and grief right there on Facebook. But a few days later I realized I had let my smaller self gain the upper hand. This was *not* how I wanted to be remembered. I wanted to be remembered as *larger than life* ...

Richard Rohr describers this well:

We describe some people as larger than life. If we could see
their history, we would learn that at some point they were
led to the edge of their own resources and found the actual

201

Source. They suffered a breakdown, which felt like dying. But instead of breaking down, they broke through!

Instead of avoiding, shortchanging, or raging against death, they went through death—a death to their old self, their small life, their imperfections, their illusory dreams, their wounds, their grudges, and their limited sense of their own destiny. When they did this, they came out on the other side knowing that death henceforth could do them no harm.

"What did I ever lose by dying?" they say. This process is supposed to be the baptismal initiation rite into Christianity, where we first "join him in the tomb" and then afterwards "join him in his resurrection"(Romans 5:4-5). We are all supposed to be larger-than-death men, appearing to the world as larger than life. This should be the definition of a Christian man.[97]

God began a good work when he brought you to the planet. That good work, however, is a work in progress and requires your cooperation. When we cooperate with him, we move past the big and little 'deaths' in our lives to his resurrection beyond. If we hang in there with him, he will bring this good work (you!) to completion.

Whatever loss you are experiencing is real and it hurts deeply. Determine, however, to live larger than life, to let your best self get the upper hand and push down your smaller self.

I like how Paul expresses his own pain and victory over it all at the same time:

We are hard pressed on every side, but not crushed; perplexed, but not in despair; persecuted, but not abandoned; struck down, but not destroyed. We always carry around in our body the death of Jesus, so that the life of Jesus may also be revealed in our body. For we who are alive are always being given over to death for Jesus' sake, so that his life may also be revealed in our mortal body. So

---

[97] Rohr, Durepos and McGrath, *On the Threshold of Transformation*, 283. Used with permission.

then, death is at work in us, but life is at work in you. (2
Corinthians 4.8-12)

Paul's pain is real—he clearly expresses it (something not allowed in
our culture). But he also voices victory over that pain. He is in pain,
but his larger self will be victorious through the power of Christ.

The pain of living squeezes our soul. What is leaking out of your
soul today? What comes out will be how others define you . . . Larger
than life or . . . crushed by death?

THINK ABOUT IT . . .

- ➤ The size of your life matters. In your own eyes, are you small
  or large?

- ➤ When you are squeezed, what comes out? Patience, endurance,
  kindness? Or wrath, bitterness, rage?

- ➤ How do you want to be remembered?

LIFE COMMITMENT:

*I have a choice as to how cooperative I am with God's working in me. I
commit to jumping into his jetstream and allowing him to do his work
in me.*

Day 59: It's a War

The Word

*Finally, be strong in the Lord and in his mighty power. Put on the full
armor of God so that you can take your stand against the devil's schemes.
For our struggle is not against flesh and blood, but against the rulers,
against the authorities, against the powers of this dark world and against
the spiritual forces of evil in the heavenly realms.*

— Ephesians 6.10–12

Thought for the Day:

*If you know the enemy and know yourself,
you need not fear the result of a hundred battles.
If you know yourself but not the enemy,
for every victory gained you will also suffer a defeat.
If you know neither the enemy nor yourself,
you will succumb in every battle.*

~ Sun Tzu, The Art of War

THE WORST THING YOU can do when going to war is to underestimate
your enemy. The British underestimated the Americans and the
Americans underestimated the Viet Cong.

Worse than underestimating your enemy is not realizing you
have one. We experienced the terrible results of this fatal error on
September 11, 2001. I experienced it in my church in New England. I
never knew that guy was my enemy or that he was at war with me.

The reality is that we are at war. This war transcends my enemy
who did me in at my last church. This war is even bigger than any

battle fought between humans on earth. This war is cosmic. It's huge and it's ancient, going back to before the beginning of time.

Before we were created, God had a worship leader who wanted to be God. There's only one God and he is (rightfully) jealous of his glory. The worship leader lost his bid to take God's place in the universe. The mutineer and his compatriots were kicked out of heaven. We know this mutinous worship leader as Satan and his fellow mutineers as demons. (See Isaiah 14-12-15, Luke 10.18, Jude 6.)

Ever since that terrible cosmic tragedy, Satan has done all he can to destroy and defame anything of God. The war was won but skirmishes continue. Since Satan can't get to God, he goes for what God loves—his children. The battleground of this war is our mind and heart.

On June 6, 1944, the largest assault in military history took place when the Allies invaded northern France. We know this as D-Day. The success of this initial battle to retake Europe spelled the end of Hitler and his murderous regime. Everyone knew it except Hitler.

Between Normandy and Berlin were 844 miles of German-infested hedgerows, forests, meadows and mountains. To complete the victory meant retaking all that ground stolen by Hitler.

Victory was *assured* on June 6, 1944, D-Day. But victory was not *fully realized* until May 8, 1945, V-E Day, when the Germans surrendered in Berlin. Between D-Day and V-E Day were 336 days and 844 miles of struggle. But each allied soldier fighting those 336 days and 844 miles knew Hitler was doomed.

We are living between a spiritual D-Day and the final V-E Day. Jesus stormed the beaches of Satan's stronghold on Good Friday. Jesus emerged victorious on Resurrection Sunday. The victory was won and secured 2,000 years ago. But the full benefits of that victory will not be realized until Jesus comes again and the Great Renovation of heaven and earth is completed.

Meanwhile, we fight on, knowing the victory is ours and the enemy is defeated.

It helps to know that the battle is bigger than you, your ex-husband, your boss, your flat tire, your _____ (fill in the blank). The real enemy is not a human or situation or circumstance on earth. Your real enemy is Satan, and his target is your head and heart.

It helps to know that a good choice in the midst of your hurt and heartache scores a victory that rings throughout heaven.

It helps to know the battles are temporary. Eventually you will have rest from this struggle. It helps to have hope.

It helps to be angry at the real enemy and to know he is ultimately defeated forever.

THINK ABOUT IT . . .

> ➤ Have I been fighting the right enemy?

> ➤ If all this is true, what does a real victory look like?

LIFE COMMITMENT:

I will know the enemy and I will know myself and my God, so I need not fear the result of a hundred battles.

Day 60: God Wins

The Word

Since everything will be destroyed in this way, what kind of people ought
you to be? You ought to live holy and godly lives as you look forward to the
day of God and speed its coming. That day will bring about the destruction
of the heavens by fire, and the elements will melt in the heat.
But in keeping with his promise we are looking forward to a new heaven
and a new earth, the home of righteousness. So then, dear friends, since
you are looking forward to this, make every effort to be found spotless,
blameless and at peace with him.
— 2 Peter 3.11–14

Thought for the Day:

This is the good news of the gospel. Peace came. Peace lived. Peace died.
Peace rose again. Peace reigns on your behalf. Peace indwells you by the
Spirit. Peace graces you with everything you need. Peace convicts, forgives,
and delivers you. Peace will finish his work in you. Peace will welcome you
into glory, where Peace will live with you in peace and righteousness
forever. Peace isn't a faded dream. No, Peace is real.
Peace is a person, and his name is Jesus.
~ Paul David Tripp

John O'Donohue writes, *It is strange to be here. The mystery never*
leaves you alone. Behind your image, below your words, above your
thoughts, the silence of another world waits.[98]

---

[98] John O'Donohue, *Anam Ċara: A Book of Celtic Wisdom* (New York: Harper
Perennial, 2004), Kindle Location 283.

This mystery is not only in you but far beyond you. There is far more *in* you than you can possibly imagine, and there is far more *beyond* you than you can possibly fathom.

We live out our earthly lives on an extremely thin line (about 10 feet?) where rock and air meet. We exist on a tiny speck of rock in a universe of billions of galaxies. Go outside tonight and look up. You will be humbled. It is indeed, strange to be here.

But we *are* here and we are here because God made us to be here. We are his glorious creation, the ones he has made to love and from whom love is desired. As weird as it is for us to hear it, we are in the middle of a love story.

It makes sense, doesn't it? In the end, don't all good things come down to love, and all the hurt and heartache to misplaced love?

All love stories are about love in the midst of conflict and war. The epic stories we tell and the movies Disney makes are not only creations of our imagination. They are echoes of a deeper reality, a reality we struggle to grasp while stumbling around in our foggy world.

We are in a love story, but a love story gone awry. The battle rages and casualties mount. But here's the thing: as in our epic tales and delightful movies, **in the end, love wins**.

This is crucial for you to understand. In the end, love wins. In the end, God wins. You are on the winning team.

How does this help you manage your grief and suffering? If you know you are on the winning team, you can endure anything until the victory is complete. If you know you are on the winning team, everything *now* becomes training for the ultimate victory *later*. You and I can endure hardship because we know the victory is coming.

The Apostle Paul says it like this:

> For our light and momentary troubles are achieving for
> us an eternal glory that far outweighs them all. So we fix
> our eyes not on what is seen, but on what is unseen. For
> what is seen is temporary, but what is unseen is eternal. (2
> Corinthians 4.17–18)

Knowing you are on the winning team lets you look beyond your current troubles to the victory that is on the way.

THINK ABOUT IT . . .

> ➤ What am I here for?

> ➤ If this is a war, whose side am I on?

> ➤ What would change in my attitude if I really grasped that in the end, all that matters is that God wins?

LIFE COMMITMENT:

It is Friday, but Sunday's coming! I can make it until Sunday.

Day 61: God Restores

The Word

And the God of all grace, who called you to his eternal glory in Christ, after you have suffered a little while, will himself restore you and make you strong, firm and steadfast. To him be the power for ever and ever. Amen.

— 1 Peter 5.10–11

Thought for the Day:

> *Fell sorrow's tooth doth never rankle more*
> *Than when he bites, but lanceth not the sore.*[99]
>
> ~ Shakespeare
> *The Life and Death of Richard the Second*
> ACT I, SCENE III.

The essence of pain is loss. Whether you are the primary cause or not, suffering comes because of devastating costs. Is it possible to regain what has been lost?

Our English word *restore* comes from the French—from *re* which means *back again* and *stauro* which means *to stand, to be firm.*[100]

Traumatic loss events knock us off our feet whether it is a loss of a job, a spouse (to death or divorce), a child, your health, your finances. When we lose something precious to us it feels like a punch

---

[99] *Sorrow hurts most when you treat the pain it creates without curing the cause.*
http://nfs.sparknotes.com/richardii/page_46.html

[100] *"Restore," Online Etymology Dictionary*, accessed July 19, 2017,
http://www.etymonline.com/index.php?allowed_in_frame=0&search=restore.
Our English word *restaurant* comes from the same root as our word, *restore*, and means *food that restores.*

to the gut. We are sometimes left breathless, literally. Sometimes people actually fall to the ground when they receive terrible news of some great loss.

In the old days, to be knocked to the ground in battle was the quickest way to death. For a warrior to live, he had to get back up on his feet. When you are flat on the ground because of your loss, know that God will get you back on your feet—he will pick you up and restore you to a position of strength stronger than you were before.

Don't take my word from it. Consider these promises from God's Word:

> And the God of all grace, who called you to his eternal glory in Christ, after you have suffered a little while, will himself restore [mend] you and make you strong [stable], firm [to make strong of soul and body so you can stand up] and steadfast [to establish]. (1 Peter 5.10–11, AMP)

> Though you have made me see troubles, many and bitter, you will restore my life again; from the depths of the earth you will again bring me up. You will increase my honor and comfort me once again. (Psalm 71:20–21)

> I will repay you for the years the locusts have eaten—the great locust and the young locust, the other locusts and the locust swarm—my great army that I sent among you. You will have plenty to eat, until you are full, and you will praise the name of the Lord your God, who has worked wonders for you; never again will my people be shamed. Then you will know that I am in Israel, that I am the Lord your God, never again will my people be shamed. (Joel 2.25–27)

> "But I will restore you to health and heal your wounds," declares the Lord, "because you are called an outcast, Zion for whom no one cares." (Jeremiah 30.17)

> Instead of their shame my people will receive a double portion, and instead of disgrace they will rejoice in their inheritance; and everlasting joy will be theirs. (Isaiah 61.7)

*Return to your fortress, O prisoners of hope; even now I an-
nounce that I will restore twice as much to you. (Zechariah
9.12)*

*The Lord is my shepherd, I shall not be in want. He makes
me lie down in green pastures, he leads me beside quiet
waters, he restores my soul. (Psalm 23.1–3)*

Does God automatically restore what we have lost? The answer is
no. What are the conditions, then, for restoration?
The following verses show us:

Repent, *then, and turn to God, so that your sins may be wiped
out, that times of refreshing may come from the Lord, and that he may
send the Christ, who has been appointed for you—even Jesus. He must
remain in heaven until the time comes for God to restore everything, as
he promised long ago through his holy prophets. (Acts 3.19–21)*

God wants us to come to him in humility and submit to his
Lordship. Just as a train must submit to the rails to run free and do
what trains do best, so we willingly 'place' ourselves on God's 'rails'
in order to move forward. For a more thorough explanation of how
to come to God, go to Appendix C.

After Job had prayed for his friends, *the Lord made him prosperous again and gave him twice as much as he had before.* (Job 42.10)

Part of our restoration will be moving forward in the process of
forgiveness. Job's friends were unhelpful to him in his time of need.
When Job forgave them, God was free to move forward toward Job's
restoration. Perhaps you need to consider forgiving someone who
has hurt you. Maybe you need to explore if you need to forgive God.
A competent pastor and/or therapist can help guide you through this
difficult journey.

But **seek first his kingdom and his righteousness**, *and all these
things will be given to you as well.* (Matthew 6:33)

As you give yourself to God your priorities will change. The
things of God will become primary in your life. God's Kingdom
will become your first focus. As that happens, the things of earth
will grow less important, and you will know and experience God's
gracious provision for your every earthly need.

God will restore more than you can imagine in ways that will surprise you! It all begins with your willingness to allow God to lead you: *Our response to God determines His response to us.*[101]

Kristin Armstrong has these hopeful words for us: *God will restore your life. In all the ways you think you need it, and in intimate areas where you aren't even aware of your need.*[102]

THINK ABOUT IT . . .

> ➤ What have you lost?

> ➤ What do you expect God to restore to you?

> ➤ What steps do you need to take to make room in your life for God to work? How do you place yourself on God's 'rails' so your train can move freely and fast, fulfilling your purpose?

PRAYER:

Restore to me the joy of your salvation and grant me a willing spirit, to sustain me. (Psalm 51.12)

---

[101] Henry Blackaby and Richard Blackaby, *Experiencing God Day By Day* (Nashville: B&H Publishing, 2006), Kindle Location 3450.

[102] Kristin Armstrong, *Happily Ever After: Walking with Peace and Courage Through a Year of Divorce* (New York: Faith Works, 2008), Kindle Location 3377.

Day 62: Ultimate Hope

The Word

Since, then, you have been raised with Christ, set your hearts on things
above, where Christ is seated at the right hand of God.
Set your minds on things above, not on earthly things.
For you died, and your life is now hidden with Christ in God.
When Christ, who is your life, appears,
then you also will appear with him in glory.
— Colossians 3.1–4

Thought for the Day:

If you don't keep the eyes of your heart focused on the paradise that is to
come, you will try to turn this poor fallen world into the paradise it will
never be.
~ Paul David Tripp

A GOOD FRIEND OF MINE WHO HAD BEEN THROUGH a hard time once
told me, *If you don't have Jesus, this world is as good as it gets. If you*
do have Jesus, this world is as bad as it gets.

If this world is all there is, *all your happiness depends on how*
things are going for you now because now is all you have. Whatever
future you have is limited by death, so you are driven to wring out of
life all that you can while you can. The clock is ticking.

Charles Darwin wrote, *A man who dares to waste one hour of time*
has not discovered the value of life.[103] He is right. But if death ends

---

[103] Charles Darwin, *Life and Letters of Charles Darwin* (Rare Books Club, 2016),
Kindle Location 3485.

it all, time becomes a ruthless taskmaster demanding that you get everything you can out of every minute of this life.

But if you *do* have Jesus, *this life is as bad as it gets* because through Jesus, *this life is not all there is.* In fact, because of Jesus, we have an eternity of problem-free living waiting for us!

A significant portion of pain and suffering is in what we think we have lost in the future. We planned to grow old with our spouse, but divorce or death robs us of that dream. We had plans for a retirement enjoying life and helping others. But Parkinson's intrudes and steals the dream. Loss can be defined as end to our dreams.

At the very least, suffering slows life to a crawl. As you emerge from this dark place, you may resent the time you lost as you experience the pain of shattered dreams. If you believe this life is all there is, your resentment and anger will grow into bitterness because of lost time.

But if you believe in heaven, if you believe the best is yet to be, you will be able to bear the losses with patience and grace. I am not saying this is easy, but it is true that heaven gives you an amazing hope. Heaven frees us from the tyranny of having to get it all now. Heaven gives us room and freedom to live on earth.

Heaven is our ultimate hope. Heaven is forever and it is good. Heaven is home.

THINK ABOUT IT . . .

> ➤ What do you believe about heaven?

> ➤ What would change in your thinking, emotions and actions today if you really believed that this life is not all there is and an amazing heaven awaits you?

PRAYER:

God, deliver me from the tyranny of time. Let heaven settle deep in my soul. Let heaven give me room to breathe, space to live as fully as I can now on earth, knowing that true life awaits me in eternity.

Day 63: Our Life with God (1)

The Word

Therefore we do not lose heart. Though outwardly we are wasting away, yet inwardly we are being renewed day by day. For our light and momentary troubles are achieving for us an eternal glory that far outweighs them all. So we fix our eyes not on what is seen, but on what is unseen. For what is seen is temporary, but what is unseen is eternal.

— 2 Corinthians 4.16–18

Thought for the Day:

God sent me 1,000 hints that he didn't want me to keep doing what I was doing. But I didn't listen, so he set off a nuclear bomb.

~ Jack Abramoff [104]

IT ALL BEGAN WELL ENOUGH. God made two humans for fellowship. He walked with them every day in the Paradise he fashioned just for them. But love isn't love unless it can be rejected, otherwise God would have two robots in his Paradise, not two humans. So he put a temptation in Paradise in the form of a tree. The warning was that if his two humans ate the fruit from that tree, God would see it as a rejection of all that he had provided for them, and he would rightly view that as a rejection of himself.

---

[104]In January 2006, Jack Abramoff was sentenced to six years in federal prison for mail fraud, conspiracy to bribe public officials, and tax evasion. "Jack Abramoff," Wikipedia, accessed February 10, 2017.
https://en.wikipedia.org/wiki/Jack_Abramoff.

Sure enough, the two humans were persuaded that God was less than he said he was and that he was holding out on them. So they turned against God's amazing love and provision. They demonstrated their decision by eating from the one tree God had warned them about. Humanity would now live 'East of Eden,' out from under the provision and protection of God.

Our original sin is that we believed we could go it alone. Our fatal flaw is believing the lie that we don't need God. So the first step in understanding how God works is coming to the realization that we do, indeed, need him.

My daughter is smart and beautiful... and stubborn. When she was about eight she decided to run away. So... she packed her pink Little Mermaid suitcase and headed out the front door *at night!*

How absolutely ridiculous of her! How did she think she would survive alone at night at the tender age of eight? How could she have been so dense?

Well, go look in the mirror! You and I are like my daughter. We are like eight-year-olds running away from a good and kind Father.

The further into the night my daughter went the less sure she was about leaving and the more she questioned her decision. It wasn't far (maybe 100 yards) until she turned around. And when she turned around she found me just behind her, eager to receive her back.

How does God work? He provides for us, but we turn away from him. We fly off into the dark. We stumble along, tripping on that situation here, bumping into that problem there. It's usually not until we are flat on our face that we get it. It's when we're face down on the sidewalk with a bloody nose that we comprehend our profound need for God.

THINK ABOUT IT . . .

- ➤ Did you ever run away from home? If so, what did that feel like? Did it work?

- ➤ Do you know you need God? How do you know?

- ➤ What do you think God thinks when you realize how much you need him?

LIFE COMMITMENT:

I realize that I have been running away from God. I am ready to take steps to go back to him.

Day 64: Our Life with God (2)

The Word

Therefore do not worry about tomorrow, for tomorrow will worry about itself. Each day has enough trouble of its own.
— Jesus as recorded in Matthew 6.34

Thought for the Day:

God can't fix what you pretend isn't broken.
~ Ryan Leek

I WAS NOT IN my daughter's head when she stomped off into the dark one spring evening, determined to run away from her 'mean' parents. But I know what it is like to come to the stark realization that without God I am in deep trouble.

How do you know you are in that moment?

Ask yourself these three questions:

- Am I paralyzed by my PAST? Am I lost in regrets, saying to myself *I should have* rather than *I will*?

- Am I slipping into a Pity Pit in the PRESENT, sliding down a slimy sinkhole where I find only me, myself and I at the bottom?[105]

---

[105]I am indebted to Sarah Young and her book *Jesus Calling* for the concepts of the *Pity Pit* and the *Worry Web*. Sarah Young, *Jesus Calling: Enjoying Peace in His Presence: Devotions for Every Day of the Year* (Nashville: Integrity Publishers, 2016), Kindle Locations 335 and 458.

- Am I tangled up in the Worry Webs of the FUTURE, my mind racing with all the terrible things that could be but aren't yet?

Being paralyzed by the past, sinking into self-pity in the present and/or worrying about your future are sure signs that you aren't connected to God. That's OK for now. Like a thermometer, how you are thinking is only an indication of where you are *now*. Diagnosis is the first step toward an effective treatment.

Know this: God does NOT want you paralyzed by your past, stuck at the bottom of the pity pit or caught in the worry webs of your future. By experiencing his presence and living in trust and gratitude, God will free you from your past, pull you out of the pity pit and untangle you from worry webs.

THINK ABOUT IT . . .

➤ Am I OK with my *past*? Or am I lost in regrets?

➤ Am I taking responsibility for where I am *now* or lost in self-pity?

➤ Am I looking forward to my *future* or dreading what might come?

LIFE COMMITMENT:

I believe God has a better way for me. I commit to finding and following his way for my life.

Day 65: Our Life with God (3)

The Word

Be strong and courageous. Do not be terrified; do not be discouraged,
for the Lord your God will be with you wherever you go.
— Joshua 1.9

Thought for the Day:

Breakdowns often lead to breakthroughs.
~ J.R. Briggs

I'VE READ THE BIBLE through from cover to cover multiple times. The three over-arching themes I see throughout Scripture are **(1) GOD MADE US, (2) GOD IS WITH US** and **(3) GOD PROVIDES FOR US**.

God made us to be with him. The startling thing is that he doesn't need us. He can and does exist completely outside and independently of us. At first this is a troubling thought because our earthly experience regarding the security of our relationships is based on the need of the other for us. For example, we may sometimes say to ourselves, *I won't get fired because my boss needs me.*

God doesn't need us. Yikes! But don't get upset! God's amazing desire for us is not based on *need*, it is based on *desire*. *God wants us!* He wants to be with us! He wants to be with us so much that his own Son died the most horrible death imaginable to break down the wall we had built between us and God:

For God so loved the world that he gave his one and only Son, that whoever believes in him shall not perish but have eternal life. (John 3.16)

If God went to this much trouble to be with us, don't you think he wants you to actually experience his presence in your life?

When my daughter tromped off down the street and then came to her senses, turning around to find me there, do you think that I coldly told her that I was glad she had finally seen things my way and that we should get back into the house?

Heck no! Scared of the darkness in front of her and dreading what our reaction might be behind her, when she turned around, I picked her up and gave her a huge hug! I was thrilled she wanted to be with me, so I made it clear I wanted to be with her.

Suffering and pain can lead to a deep loneliness. Whatever you are going through no one else has gone through it exactly as you are. This realization can make you feel isolated and alone. If you don't feel this loneliness now, unfortunately you most likely will.

Know this: God wants to be with you in a way that *you know he is with you.* He doesn't just want you to know in your head that he is with you. He wants you to know in your heart and soul that he is really with you.

Dallas Willard writes, *The personal presence of Jesus with individuals and groups that trust him was soon understood by Jesus' first students to be the practical reality of the kingdom of God now on earth.*[106]

Living in God's presence is to be the norm for us, not the occasional high we may get at a Christian conference or retreat. I admit it's tough. It's tough to experience God's presence all the time because we live in a fog while on earth. It's a challenge to experience the presence of an invisible God. But it is possible and can actually become the norm.

The Bible is clear: God wants us and he wants us to experience his real and powerful presence.

If you are not experiencing God's presence in your life, ask him to show up. I guarantee you there is no greater invitation from you

---

[106] Willard, *The Divine Conspiracy*, 279.

that God wants than this! Keep your eyes and ears open. Things are about to get interesting for you!

A few days ago the Life Commitment was: *I realize that I have been running away from God. I am ready to take steps to go back to him.* Asking God to make himself known to you is one of these steps you can take toward him. For more information on how to have a relationship with God go to **Appendix C**.

> *Be strong and courageous.*
> *Do not be terrified;*
> *do not be discouraged,*
> *for the Lord your God will be with you*
> *wherever you go.*

Think About It . . .

> ➢ What price did God pay to be with you?

> ➢ Have you ever experienced what you believe to be the presence of God? What happened?

> ➢ What do you think experiencing the presence of God will be like?

Life Commitment:

I am asking God to show up in my life. I commit to having an open and receptive soul to his presence in my life.

DAY 66: OUR LIFE WITH GOD (4)

THE WORD

"Am I only a God nearby," declares the Lord, "and not a God far away?
Can anyone hide in secret places so that I cannot see him?" declares the
Lord. "Do not I fill heaven and earth?" declares the Lord.
— Jeremiah 23.23–24

THOUGHT FOR THE DAY:

We live in a broken world full of broken people.
But isn't it comforting to know God is never broken?
He isn't ever caught off guard, taken by surprise,
or shocked by what happens next.
He can take our worst and add His best.
We just have to make the choice to stay with Him
and keep following Him through it all.
~ Lysa TerKeurst

KIDS ARE AMAZING. THEY never wake up saying to themselves, *Oh no! I wonder if mom and dad got food for me today! I wonder if I will have a house to come home to after school today!* I have *never* heard a kid say that!

Kids have absolute trust in their parents. And where a kid does not have food and shelter, love and affection, shame on the adults for failing those children. And shame on us if we don't do something radical about it.

Most children trust their parents to provide for them. A wise kid will not only trust his/her parents to provide, but express gratitude for that provision.

At the time of this writing I have a 16-year-old son. His life was turned upside-down beginning three years ago. This kid went from a strong, stable situation to a world wrecked by the terrible decisions of some adults that impacted the life of our family in horrendous ways.

A few minutes ago we returned from going out to eat. Despite all that he has been through he said, *Thanks, Dad, for taking me out to eat!* He's that way about everything! He has an amazingly grateful heart.

Our life with God goes something like this: God provides for us. But we foolishly decide we can do this thing on our own. We hit a wall of pain. We cry out to God. God rescues us. Then we get really happy about his rescue!

As we trust him and express our gratitude to him, our souls open wide and we really do know God is with us and for us.

Trusting God and being grateful to him are the two best strategies for staying out of the pity pit and away from the worry webs.

American writer Melody Beattie writes, *Gratitude makes sense of our past, brings peace for today, and creates a vision for tomorrow.*[107] Exactly!

By experiencing his presence with you and living in trust and gratitude, God will free you from your past, pull you out of the pity pit and untangle you from worry webs.

THINK ABOUT IT . . .

➤ What would it look like for you to have the same trust in God that your kids have in you?

➤ You knew this was coming! Make a list of five things you are grateful for:

_____

_____

_____

_____

---

[107] "*Melody Beattie Quotes,*" BrainyQuote, accessed February 13, 2017, https://www.brainyquote.com/quotes/quotes/m/melodybeat134462.html.

LIFE COMMITMENT:

Instead of griping today, I am going to be thankful. Even if it is just for one thing and even if it really hurts to do so.

Day 67: Our Life with God (5)

The Word

You did not choose me, but I chose you and appointed you
to go and bear fruit—fruit that will last.
Then the Father will give you whatever you ask in my name.
— John 15.16

Thought for the Day:

Remembering that I'll be dead soon is the most important tool I've ever
encountered to help me make the big choices in life. Because almost
everything—all external expectations, all pride, all fear of embarrassment
or failure—these things just fall away in the face of death, leaving only
what is truly important.

~ Steve Jobs

As a hospice chaplain I've seen many people die. One man stands out. He was amazingly accomplished. If I told you what he did, you would be stunned, but I can't tell you because of privacy laws.

From the beginning of my only encounter with him, he let me know that he did not have a religious faith but he was not worried about his death.

He was also in agony. He was gasping for air, frantic and wide-eyed with fright. His was not going to be an easy death. You should know that most deaths are not painful or filled with agony. Most people die peacefully.

Back to my guy on his deathbed. As he struggled to breathe, his family kept telling me of his amazing accomplishments, not only in his work life but around the house we were in. *He built this room, he painted that wall, he fixed this light.*

I left the house that day sad. The self-worth of this family was built exclusively on the achievements of their husband/father. And yet in the end, the man was in physical agony and spiritually bankrupt.

As John Ortberg says, *In the end, it all goes back in the box.*[108] Having been with many people at their deaths, I can assure you that there are no do-overs.

God has more for you than a few earthly accomplishments. Once he has rescued you from yourself and planted a heart of gratitude and trust in you, he calls you to your destiny.

It's hard to see this when you are at the bottom after a huge loss. When you're flat on your back with the wind knocked out of you, you can't imagine being back in the game. Winning the game seems totally out of reach.

But God has a plan for you. *In his power* he will lift you up. *In his power* he will heal you. *In his power* he will give you a mission specific to you. And *through his strength* you will accomplish the mission he gives you.

And at the end of the day, when someone like me is sitting beside you, we will celebrate together what God has done in your life for his Kingdom, and we will rejoice together in your final destination.

Think About It . . .

> ➤ If you were on your deathbed right now, what would you tell me about your life?

> ➤ What hope would you have for your future?

> ➤ What legacy would you be leaving?

Life Commitment:

I want to finish well. Where I am today does not define my future. I trust that God will lift me up and set me on the pathway of his choosing.

---

[108] John Ortberg, *When the Game Is Over, It All Goes Back in the Box* (Grand Rapids: Zondervan, 2007), 16.

Day 68: Our Life with God (6)

The Word

*For my own name's sake I delay my wrath; for the sake of my praise I hold
it back from you, so as not to cut you off. See, I have refined you, though
not as silver; I have tested you in the furnace of affliction. For my own
sake, for my own sake, I do this. How can I let myself be defamed? I will
not yield my glory to another.*

— Isaiah 48.9–11

Thought for the Day:

Your desire determines your destiny.

~ John Maxwell

In his book *Sacred Marriage*, Gary Thomas asks a hard question:
*What If God Designed Marriage to Make Us Holy More Than to Make
Us Happy?*[109]

The question Thomas asks of marriage is really a question God
asks each of us no matter where we are in life: *Is God's first job to
make me happy?*

Rick Warren begins his best-selling book *The Purpose Driven Life*
with this simple statement: *It's not about you.*[110] Ouch. We are taught
from the moment we come squealing into the world that it IS about
us! Nearly every decision we make is filtered through the question,
How will this help or hurt me?

---

[109] Gary Thomas, *Sacred Marriage: What If God Designed Marriage to Make Us Holy
More Than to Make Us Happy?* (Grand Rapids: Zondervan, 2015), 1.

[110] Richard Warren, *The Purpose Driven Life* (Cleveland: Findaway World, 2005), 17.

And yet the fact that Rick Warren's book sold well over 40 million copies, landing 90 weeks on the New York Times Bestseller List, should tell us that deep inside we know we were made for more than just personal happiness.

In Isaiah, God makes clear that our happiness is secondary to his holiness and glory: *I will not yield my glory to another.* If our happiness were God's first job, then he would have to make his glory secondary to our happiness. No, everything is first about God's glory.

Nearly 400 years ago a group of English and Scottish Theologians came to the same conclusion. The Westminster Catechism's first question is: *What is the chief end of man?*

The answer? *Man's chief end is to glorify God, and to enjoy him forever.*[111]

The Hebrew word translated *glory* means '*weight*.' Each of us has only so much 'weight' to throw around. We have only so much 'weight' to give to people and things. Where do you throw your weight, toward God's glory or toward your own happiness?

The losses of life can mount up quickly and painfully. In a short period, I lost my hard-earned reputation, my status in society, a huge chunk of my career, lots of money—the list goes on and on. I went from a beautiful home tucked in the New Hampshire forest to a one-bedroom apartment with a cat. I went from Superhero to Superzero.

If I measured my life in terms of circumstances, I would be very unhappy. But I know that my happiness is secondary to God's glory. God's amazing glory is far bigger than my puny little speck of happiness. What this means is that if I can stay tuned in to God's glory, I am attached to something bigger and better than my little life, and nothing can touch that!

Through these terrible ordeals I have tried to stay focused on glorifying God despite my afflictions. And here's the deal: staying tuned into God's glory has kept me sane. But that's what tomorrow is all about.

---

[111] Philip Schaff, *Creeds of Christendom*, Vol. 1, (New York: Harper & Brothers, 1919), 1659.

THINK ABOUT IT . . .

- ➤ Where do you throw your 'weight'?
- ➤ Are you plugged into God's glory or your own happiness?

LIFE COMMITMENT:

Life is first about God's glory, not my happiness.

Day 69: Our Life With God (7)

The Word

All this is for your benefit, so that the grace that is reaching more and more people may cause thanksgiving to overflow to the glory of God.
— 2 Corinthians 4:14–15

Thought for the Day:

To please God... to be a real ingredient in the divine happiness... to be loved by God, not merely pitied, but delighted in as an artist delights in his work or a father in a son—it seems impossible, a weight or burden of glory which our thoughts can hardly sustain. But so it is.
~ C.S. Lewis

THE MAN BEFORE ME was shaking like a leaf. He shouldn't have been. He had just retired young with tons of money. To the world he was a raging success. He appeared to have it all. But like so many men, he had reached the top of the mountain only to find that he had climbed the wrong mountain.

As he stood before me trembling with anxiety I told him what I had told many other men in his position: *The second half of his life would be far better than the first half.*

The first half of a man's life is all about me. I work hard to build my life around what the culture tells me will make me happy and significant.

But if we work hard enough and achieve whatever it is that our culture tells us will make us happy and significant, at some point it all comes tumbling down. The tower that we so carefully constructed crashes around us.

Women's journeys are a bit different—women more clearly understand suffering— they give birth to and nurture their children often out of the spotlight. But however success is defined by both men and women, it can be taken away in a heartbeat.

Apart from God, success and adversity are two sides of the same coin. For my newly retired but unhappy friend, success was a hollow shell of what he expected it to be. At some pint on the life journey for all of us, adversity rips at us until we are empty inside.

As we saw yesterday, however, it's not first about our happiness, it's about God's glory. God is passionate for his glory. Whatever God does is first for his glory, as he says in Isaiah, *I will not yield my glory to another.* (Isaiah 48.11)

But here's the awesome thing about God's Kingdom: When we make God's glory first in our lives, *we find true and lasting happiness and satisfaction.*

The catechism asks: *What is the chief end of man?* The glorious answer is *Man's chief end is to glorify God, and to enjoy him forever.*

Those old guys got it right! In putting God's glory first we get to enjoy him forever! And when we enjoy him, we enjoy all the things that bring him delight such as his astounding creation, loving others, even working through hard times.

This is the promise Paul makes: *All this is **for your benefit**, so that the grace that is reaching more and more people may cause thanksgiving to **overflow to the glory of God**.* (2 Corinthians 4.14-15, emphasis mine)

God calls us to glorify him with our lives. In putting his glory first, we find our true purpose. When we live out his purpose for us, we find amazing fulfillment, satisfaction and happiness.

A Hellfire missile has come screaming into your life and you may think all is destroyed. Far from it. God is using all you have lost to highlight what is of first importance: Him and his glory.

When you get this—when you really understand and submit to this truth—you will find relief, joy and an eagerness to discover God's next step for you.

THINK ABOUT IT . . .

> ➤ Fill in the blank: If _____ would happen, I would be happy.

> ➤ Is the answer in the question above about you or about God and his glory?

> ➤ What would living for God's glory look like in your life right now?

LIFE COMMITMENT:

I have lived my life for me, myself and I. It is time to live for God the Father, Jesus the Son, and the Holy Spirit.

Day 70: Slow Down Fast

The Word

Very early in the morning, while it was still dark, Jesus got up,
left the house and went off to a solitary place, where he prayed.
— Mark 1.35

Thought for the Day:

Let us leave a little room for reflection in our lives, room too for silence.
Let us look within ourselves and
see whether there is some delightful hidden place inside
where we can be free of noise and argument.
Let us hear the Word of God in stillness and
perhaps we will then come to understand it.

~ Augustine of Hippo

Your soul is like a tire. No, I didn't say your soul is tired, though your soul may *feel* very tired. Let me suggest a different way to view your soul. Your soul is not *tired*, it is *flat*.

Ever since I can remember I have lived on my bike. Back in the day, we rode our bikes without helmets and common sense. There was nothing like flying my banana seat bike off a homemade plywood ramp and onto that ever so unforgiving asphalt! Now I ride 25 miles dodging cars, rocks and the heat.

If you are a cyclist *you know that your tires leak.* In fact, every time I get ready for a ride I pump a little air in my tires. Low tires translate into a slow and sluggish bike. Slow and sluggish is not me. I want to ride high and clean, fast and efficient.

Your soul is like a bike tire. It leaks. All kinds of things steal the air out of your soul—people poking at you, financial worries, expectations of others that go unmet.

Every time I ride my bike I must put a little air in the tires. Every day you and I must put a little air back into our souls. If you don't, you will be flat. Tired, flat souls need air. Whether your soul is flat all the way to the ground or just a little low, what do you use to put the air back in?

In 'Christian speak,' the means by which we put air back into our souls are called *Spiritual Disciplines*.[112] There are many spiritual disciplines but for you right here, right now, I want to recommend the following (we will explore a few in detail in the next few days):

- **Solitude**—Spending time alone to be with God.

- **Prayer**—Honest conversation with your True Father.

- **Fellowship**—Being with other Christians who nourish your soul through understanding, challenge and encouragement.[113]

- **Guidance**—Positioning yourself to follow God's best path for his glory, your good and the good of those around you.[114]

- **Study**—Reading and really thinking about what God is saying to you through his Word, the Bible.

- **Worship**—Giving back to God the worth he is due.

- **Confession**—Talking openly and honestly about your life with a trusted circle of friends.

- **Submission**—Humbling yourself before God, trusting that in God's economy, the way up is down.

---

[112]The best definition of the Spiritual Disciplines I have found is: *Spiritual Disciplines are instruments of God's grace which, through the Spirit, transform us daily into people who reflect Jesus' love, obedience, humility, and connection to God.* This comes from a pamphlet from Rose Publishing: Spiritual Disciplines, (Peabody, MA: Rose Publishing, July 7, 2014).

[113]Bill Donahue, *Leading Life-Changing Small Groups: Groups that Grow*, (Zondervan, 2012), Kindle Locations 782-783.

[114]Richard J. Foster, *Celebration of Discipline* (Harper Collins, 2009), 175.

- **Service/Giving**—Learning to live with an open hand.

I have ridden my bike hundreds of miles without a flat. But in one ride I had two! Life is like that. Whether cruising fast and efficient or stuck by the side of the road, you need air. Let God pump your soul back up.

The first habit of the heart, the first lesson in our training is to practice the discipline of **SOLITUDE**.

Solitude is really simple: *Slow slow slow slow down.*

Actually, just stop. Stop your body. Quit moving your body. Quit fidgeting.

Stop your mind. Let the constant internal conversation in your head slow to a crawl. Stop the frantic thoughts. Quit thinking about what you have to do. Just stop it! You can do it! Push that stuff out of your brain.

Stop your eyes. Stop your eyes from roving to and fro. Relax your gaze upon God. Focus on him.

Stop your breathing. Well, don't *stop* breathing, but try to slow it down! Let all the air out of your chest. Now relax your chest. Now take a really deep breath. Let the air fill your lungs. Slowly let it go. In my personal walk with God, this moment of deeply relaxing my chest is the moment I know I have entered into real solitude and time with God.

The bottom-line is this: *You will not have a meaningful and fulfilling relationship with God unless you slow down and just sit still.* Don't complain that you can't hear God if, in reality, you are unwilling to stop moving enough to actually hear him.

Psalm 46.10 says, *Be still, and know that I am God; I will be exalted among the nations, I will be exalted in the earth.*

The Hebrew word translated "be still" is *raphah.* This Hebrew word means to sink down, to let drop, to relax, to withdraw, to abandon, to forsake, to let go, to be quiet. Get the idea?

Being in solitude feels awkward at first just as walking through a forest for the first time feels strange and unfamiliar. But as you practice the discipline of solitude, you will become more comfortable with the silence. As you continue to sit in silence, the background static of your life will slowly recede and you will begin to 'hear' the deeper things of your own life.

As you keep practicing solitude, enough noise will drop out of your life to actually hear God's whisper. This is an amazing moment and you will know when it happens.

In that moment many things will change in your life. The most important change will be a deep inner awareness, untouchable by time and space and flesh, that you will be OK, that nothing can take God away from you, that all you really have is God and he is enough. More than enough. Nothing can touch that. It's worth the wait, believe me.

How to have time alone with God:

First, **choose a time**... morning, lunch, evening. I like morning. Really early morning. I promise that you won't die if you get up an hour earlier. No one died from getting up an hour early. You can do it. But if this doesn't work, try something different. Life is an experiment. If something doesn't work, ditch it and try something else.

Next, **find a quiet place** free from distractions. Definitely do NOT sit close to your computer. Your computer or phone will beckon you. They will whisper to you, telling you how busy you are, how many things you have to get done today, how good you will feel if you just get started *right now* on getting things done. Don't give in. All that stuff can wait. Remember that when you die your inbox will be full. You cannot empty it today or ever.

Now, **settle your mind**. Ask God to quiet your thoughts. But don't worry if your brain is still cluttered. It's OK. Just showing up is a great start and God smiles despite all the crazy cluttered brain stuff going on between your ears.

Ask God to give you peace. Rest in his care. Breathe.

Listen to worship songs. Music has amazing power to settle your soul and put your mind back on track with God. If you are able to, **play** or **sing along** with the worship songs.

Now take time to **pray** (more on that in the coming days).

Finally, **be open to variety**. God speaks in many ways. Don't be a slave to your routine. Just be WITH God... he loves to be with you!

Solitude means being alone but solitude is not lonely. God is there. But like a forest, you have to sit in it long enough to start to get a sense of the unseen but visible, the silent but raucous world the busy people miss.

Henri Nouwen writes, *Solitude is not a private therapeutic place. Rather it is a place of conversion, the place where the old self dies, the place where the new self is born, the place where the emergence of the new man and new woman occurs.*[115]

THINK ABOUT IT . . .

➤ When was the last time you were really still (besides sleeping)?

LIFE COMMITMENT:

I want to know God. I mean, I want to KNOW God. I don't just want to know about him. I want to know him. I know this will take some time. I am willing to give solitude a whirl.

---

[115] Quoted in Robert J. Wicks, *Spiritual Resilience: 30 Days to Refresh Your Soul* (Cincinnati: Franciscan Media 2015), 118.

Day 71: Hearing God

The Word

"Then you will call upon me and come and pray to me, and I will listen to you. You will seek me and find me when you seek me with all your heart. I will be found by you," declares the Lord, "and will bring you back from captivity."
— Jeremiah 29.12–14

Thought for the Day:

People are meant to live in an ongoing conversation with God, speaking and being spoken to by him.
~ Dallas Willard

Do you believe God wants to speak to you? Many of us have been taught that we can and should talk to God (prayer) *but we should never expect him to talk back to us.* For years this is what I was taught, if not explicitly, then implicitly. If someone ever said, "God told me..." they were to be regarded with suspicion.

But I was also taught that Christianity is a *relationship*, not a *religion.* As far as I could tell, relationships involved communication—two-way communication!

Jesus told his disciples, *My sheep listen to my voice; I know them, and they follow me. I give them eternal life, and they shall never perish; no one can snatch them out of my hand.* (John 10:27–28)

I didn't understand this shepherding thing until we lived in Africa for almost a year. I grew up in Texas where land is fenced. Sheep, cows and horses were kept in with a fence. There are very few fences in Africa, however.

One day while driving down the road in Tanzania I saw a little boy, about six years old, herding 30 cows, sheep and donkeys down the side the road. The only tools this little boy had to manage all these animals were his voice and a small stick!

It was clear that the cows, sheep and donkeys knew the boy's voice and they listened to him. The boy was in constant communication with his animals, walking to and fro, chatting it up with them, gently pushing animals back in line with his stick. The shepherd wanted to speak to his sheep, and the sheep needed and expected to hear from him.

Here's the thing: *sheep don't come out of the womb knowing the shepherd's voice.* They must learn the voice of their shepherd, and since survival depends on knowing the shepherd's voice, they are motivated.

Jesus clearly said that our relationship to him is just like the sheep's relationship to their shepherd. Jesus wants to talk to us. He longs to have a relationship with us. He wants to guide us, protect us, comfort and heal us, just like the good shepherds back in his day. But we have to learn to hear his voice. To learn the voice of the shepherd takes several steps:

- **A desire to sit with the shepherd.** If you don't want to hear God speak to you, you won't. But if you don't have any desire to hear God, *ask him to give you a strong desire to want to know him and his voice.* God forms and shapes our desires. Expect to have an increasing desire to be with him.

- **Unhurried time sitting with the shepherd away from the thousands of voices and sounds that is the cacophony of modern life.** I love the New England forest. The woods behind our house in New Hampshire became sacred ground as I walked through and sat in the midst of the trees throughout the seasons. One thing I learned: *the longer you sit in the woods and just listen, the more sounds you will hear.* More than just hearing sounds, however, you will get to *know* that forest. Through the years my ears slowly tuned into the deep forest sounds around me—the black-capped chickadee to my left, the chipmunks behind me, the woodpecker 100 yards to the south. In the same way, to learn the voice of the shepherd takes time being still and listening.

- **Learning from his Word, the Bible.** The Bible is God's voice passed down through the centuries. It's his love letter and owner's manual wrapped up in one. The Bible is the primary way God communicates to us, but it is not the only way. To get a sense of God's voice, however, start with the Bible. Nothing you hear from God will contradict what the Bible says, but the Bible doesn't say everything he wants you to know, especially about the specifics of your own life. To hear God's specific word to you, immerse yourself in his words to all humanity.

- **Learning from others.** Others have journeyed this path before us. We can and must learn from those who have discerned the Shepherd's voice in the constant static of life.

- **Testing what you hear with others.** One of the jobs of the community of faith (the church) is to give us a place to test what we believe God is telling us. Imagine a flock of sheep. The shepherd calls out a command. At least that's what you *think* you heard. Unsure, you turn to the sheep next to you: *Was that our shepherd hollerin' at us?* The reply comes back: Y-e-e-e-e-e-e-p!

Think About It . . .

- ➤ Do you believe God still speaks to people today?

- ➤ Do you believe God *can* speak to you today?

- ➤ Do you believe God *wants* to speak to you today?

- ➤ Do you want to hear what God has to say to you?

Life Commitment:

This is an either/or kind of thing: I believe God still speaks today and that he actually wants to speak to me, or I don't. I choose to believe that God still speaks to his people, and that he wants to speak to me.

Day 72: God Hears You

The Word

Trust in him at all times, O people; pour out your hearts to him,
for God is our refuge.
— Psalm 62.8

Thought for the Day:

Gentlemen, I have lived a long time and am convinced that God governs in
the affairs of men. If a sparrow cannot fall to the ground without His
notice, is it probable that an empire can rise without His aid? I move that
prayer imploring the assistance of Heaven be held every morning before we
proceed to business.
~ Benjamin Franklin, Constitutional Convention, July 28, 1787

When Aaron, my second son, was about five years old, I was to care for him for an entire Saturday. We spent that day doing stuff around the house and yard.

Like any five-year-old, Aaron asked a lot of questions and lots of needs. He would begin every single one of these questions or demands with a hearty, "***DAD!***"

Dad*, why do we have to mow the yard today?*

Dad*, when do we eat lunch?*

Dad*, look at that bird!*

Toward the end of the day I was just finishing mowing the front yard. Aaron was in the backyard. Sure enough, I heard his little five-year-old voice holler, '***DAD!***'

243

After a day of what seemed like a thousand '*DAD!*'s, I'd had it! Hot, tired, covered in grass and dust, I had heard my name enough for one day!

But God is gracious. Before I could say something I would regret, it hit me: *My Father in Heaven relishes it when I cry out to him!* Unlike me, he NEVER tires of me hollering out to him! He actually LIKES it when I call out his name!

When I think about the countless times I had cried out to him, I was so grateful that he *always hears me when I pray,* and, what is more, *his greatest desire is for me to call out to him.*

Our sin is believing the lie that we can live as if God does not exist. Our greatest downfall is believing the lie that we are independent, the lie that we are not dependent on God for anything.

What an incredible lie! Every breath you and I take is a gracious gift from the Father. We have nothing that didn't come from God's gracious hand. Best of all, this same God who so generously provides us with all things, wants—more than anything—to have a deep, abiding, personal love relationship with us.

The heart of any relationship is a foundation of trust expressed in frequent, passionate and honest communication. All this to say, *God loves it when we cry out to him in our deepest need.*

Not only that, he relishes it when we praise him for an awesome sunset, a cup of hot coffee, a warm house on a cold day. Unlike me, he actually enjoys being 'bothered' by us hollering out to him. God never tires of us calling his name.

This is the promise David gives to us in Psalm 62.8: *Trust in him at all times, O people; pour out your hearts to him, for God is our refuge.*

Yesterday we asked a simple question: Do you believe God still speaks today and that he wants to speak to you?

Today we ask the reverse question: Do you believe God hears us, and that he will hear you when you talk to him?

The answer to both questions is a resounding YES that rings throughout the universe and through all time: **Our God hears us**!

He hears us because he wants to hear us. He hears us because of all the things he created, he uniquely designed us to talk to him. *His ears are bent toward us, his heart leans into ours to listen to us.*

Think About It . . .

> ➤ Do you believe the God of this universe hears you?

Prayer:

God, I believe you hear me. Thank you that you never tire of me hollering out to you, even if what I holler sometimes isn't very civilized or even friendly toward you.

Day 73: It's Not What You Think It Is

The Word

*And when you pray, do not be like the hypocrites, for they love to pray
standing in the synagogues and on the street corners to be seen by men. I
tell you the truth, they have received their reward in full. But when you
pray, go into your room, close the door and pray to your Father, who is
unseen. Then your Father, who sees what is done in secret, will reward you.
And when you pray, do not keep on babbling like pagans, for they think
they will be heard because of their many words. Do not be like them, for
your Father knows what you need before you ask him.*
— Jesus, as recorded in Matthew 6.5–8

Thought for the Day:

*On some given day when grace overtook me and I returned to prayer,
I half-expected Jesus to ask, "Who dat?"*
~ Brennan Manning

THREE OLD RANCHERS WERE sitting in a Dairy Queen in a small West
Texas town early on a Monday morning (as ranchers in small Texas
towns are known to do). The topic of conversation was the preacher's
sermon from the day before, which was on prayer.

These old guys started to talk about the best posture for prayer.

The first rancher said, *I believe the best way to pray is with your
head bowed and eyes closed.*

*I think we should be kneeling beside our beds, like my mama taught
me,* said the second.

The third rancher chimed in: *The best way to pray is upside-down
in a well!*

That third guy was on to something! The best prayers are when we *want* to pray, and for us humans, we most *want* to pray when we are upside-down in a well, that is, when life has kicked us in the teeth and we are down on the turf. Whatever tragedy or trauma you are facing, it is a face-down-in-the-turf moment. *Pray, pray, pray.*

I've heard it said that too many people use God like a spare tire—pulling him out only when needed—instead of letting him be the driver. That may be true, but God wants us to cry out to him (**see Day 72**). When trouble slams into our life a good and right thing to do is pray. When you need a spare tire, a spare tire is a fantastic thing to have!

Our ultimate goal, of course, is to be in such a relationship with God that we carry on a conversation with him all through the day, putting him in the driver's seat. Later we will talk about how to do that.

But for today, know that a lot of confusing things have been said about prayer. As with most things, however, prayer is much easier than we have been led to believe.

Prayer is simply talking to God and letting him talk to you.

There are **no special words or phrases** to use. Use whatever language God blessed you with to talk with him. He is as happy to hear your Bronx accent as he is to hear the finest Georgia drawl. Really. He doesn't care. He just wants you to show up.

There is **no special place** to pray. God is not more in a church than outside it. God is everywhere so you can pray to him anywhere. Place is simply not an issue.

You **don't have to go through any special person** to pray. You don't have to have a priest or a pastor to help you pray. Just talk to God. That's it. You can tell him anything. It's that simple.

Anne Lamott writes, *I don't know much about God and prayer, but I have come to believe, over the past twenty-five years, that there's something to be said about keeping prayer simple.*[116]

Her three simple prayers are *Help, Thanks, Wow.*

Nice!

---

[116] Anne Lamott, *Help, Thanks, Wow: The Three Essential Prayers* (London: Hodder & Stoughton, 2015), 1.

Jesus' disciples asked him to teach them to pray. Jesus gave them what Protestants call *The Lord's Prayer* and Catholics call *The 'Our Father.'* The most stunning thing about this prayer is how short it is. Back in that day the religious leaders addressed God like a subject would address their king—ridiculously long adjectives and titles, running on for what must have seemed like forever.

Jesus trashed that idea. He called God his *Abba*, his *Dad*. Dads want informal, intimate conversations with their kids. At least good dads do.

So that's how to pray. Just do it. Stop right now and just talk to God.

THINK ABOUT IT . . .

- ➤ What is prayer to you?

- ➤ Where and from whom did you learn to pray?

- ➤ What misconceptions about prayer were passed down to you?

- ➤ Did you pray a second ago when I said to stop and pray? If not, stop and pray. It's super simple.

LIFE COMMITMENT:

God, show me the truth about prayer. And... thanks for hearing the prayer I just prayed! Thanks for simple. I can do simple.

Day 74: God Answers Our Prayers

The Word

> *The righteous cry out, and the Lord hears them;*
> *The Lord is close to the brokenhearted and saves*
> *those who are crushed in spirit.*
> — Psalm 34.17–18

Thought for the Day:

> *I don't pretend to know how God makes it all work,*
> *but somehow there are tangible benefits*
> *when we pray in accordance with God's will.*
> ~ Tony Dungy

It's one thing to know that we can talk to God. It's another to know he hears us. *It is yet another to know if this conversation actually makes a difference.* Does God answer our prayers? Do our prayers matter?

One of the greatest mysteries of the universe is this: God hears our prayers and responds to each and every one with an answer.[117]

---

[117] Oswald Chambers writes: *God answers prayer in the best way—not just sometimes, but every time.* Oswald Chambers, *My utmost for His Highest: Selections for the Year* (Uhrichsville, OH: Barbour and Co, 1992), 353.

Henry Blackaby writes: *It is overwhelming to consider that holy, Almighty God would speak directly to us! What a privilege that He would care enough to challenge our destructive thoughts or practices. No matter whether His words are praising us or chastising us, we ought to consider it joy to receive life-changing words from our Master! Every time we prepare to worship the Lord, we ought to do so with*

How can our Almighty Amazing Enormous God even care about us? We are unbelievably tiny and insignificant in an unfathomably vast universe! And yet, he does. If God knows the number of the hairs on our head (Matthew 10.30) he hears our prayers. The cry of your heart is more important than the number of hairs on your head. And if he hears your prayers, he promises to answer each one.

We claim by *faith* that Almighty God hears and answers our prayers. Anyone who walks with God for very long can also claim this by *experience*. Your loss broke your heart. God is close to the brokenhearted. He is close to you. He hears your prayers.

This morning I woke up worried and concerned about a situation. The problem is serious and if you knew it, you would know why I was distressed.

I sat down at 0500 for my time with God. I listened to a song (*Blessed Be Your Name* by Matt Redman), then I read this from Sarah Young's devotional, *Jesus Calling*:

> *When things don't go as you would like, accept the situation immediately. If you indulge in feelings of regret, they can easily spill over the line into resentment. Remember that I am sovereign over your circumstances, and humble yourself under My mighty hand. Rejoice in what I am doing in your life, even though it is beyond your understanding.*[118]

Bingo. God knew every aspect of my situation. He wasn't surprised by a single circumstance in my life. The negative things I am dealing with are not caused by God, but he knows about them and is already in my future working out solutions that will bring glory to him and good to me. When I sat down to spend time with him this morning, he knew exactly what I needed to take my heart off my worries and put

---

anticipation that Almighty God may have something to say to us. *Whenever we open our Bibles, we should expect that God has something to tell us in our time with Him. We ought to be far more concerned with what God will say to us during our prayer times than with what we intend to tell Him. When you receive a word from your Lord, whether it be of praise or of correction, consider it joy that Almighty God would speak to you.* Blackaby and Blackaby, *Experiencing God Day by Day*, Kindle Location 2605.

[118]Young, *Jesus Calling*, Kindle Location 768.

my affections squarely on him. Knowing of his intimate knowledge and care of these details of my life brought peace to my soul.

If we could pull back the curtain on all that God is doing in your life, you would be as amazed as if you could somehow suddenly understand all the amazingly complex biological processes that keep your body alive. God is with you and in you. He is involved in every detail of your life.

Remember, this is NOT a WYSIWYG world. God is doing stunning things in your life and in your future. Because he is at work, we can trust his answers to our prayers.

So... how does God answer prayer? God gives us one of four answers: NO, SLOW, GROW, or GO.

Sometimes God answers with a **NO**.

Looking back on my life, I am so glad God gave me a NO to some of my requests! Like a parent who knows a steady diet of donuts is not good for a five-year-old, so God knows what is best for us. His 'no's' come to us for our good.

Sometimes God answers with a **SLOW**. We are on the right track but the timing is not right. He calls us to wait on him.

Wayne Stiles insightfully notes about waiting on God:

> We want God to change situations. God wants us to change in them. We want relief. God wants repentance. We want happiness. God wants holiness. We want pleasure. God wants piety. It's like a game of Ping-Pong. Or tug-of-war.
>
> In the end, if we really knew the big picture, we too would want what God wants for us—and in the exact way and timing he wants it to occur. It's just that our pain often blinds us to that perspective. We see only the red light. God sees the purpose—his good and loving purpose—for the delay. And although we cannot understand why the light is there, we do know what the red light means. Wait. I'm convinced the primary way we apply God's providence to our lives is by waiting. We apply sovereignty by waiting on God.[119]

---

[119]Stiles, *Waiting on God*, Kindle Location 93.

Waiting is not an American virtue. But waiting on God to do the work he needs to do is crucial. When God gives you *wait* for an answer, sit back and wait. Trust him with peace in your heart.

Sometimes God answers with a **GROW**. What we ask for is in his plan for us but we have to grow into it first. He has some soul-work that needs doing in our lives.

Oswald Chambers emphasizes:

> *You did not do anything to achieve your salvation, but you must do something to exhibit it. You must "work out your own salvation" which God has worked in you already (Philippians 2:12). Are your speech, your thinking, and your emotions evidence that you are working it "out"? If you are still the same miserable, grouchy person, set on having your own way, then it is a lie to say that God has saved and sanctified you.*[120]

If you don't hear response to your prayer, submit to God's work of growth in your life.

Sometimes God answers with a **GO**. The purpose is right, the timing is right, and you're ready to go for it! This may be the answer we were hoping for. But ironically we may also feel a sense of hesitation because God's GO *always* means adjustments to our lives. If the answer is GO, trust God, make the adjustments in faith, and get moving!

Always remember this, however: God gave us the gift of free will. That means that God chooses not to coerce us or the people in our lives. If the answer to your prayer depends on someone else, that person must choose to follow God as well. If they don't obey God, however, be assured that God can take their NO and turn it into something good for his glory and your good.

Think About It . . .

> ➤ What are you praying for right now?

> ➤ What have you sensed God's answer to be?

---

[120] Chambers, *My Utmost for His Highest*, 135.

➤ What are your next steps?

LIFE COMMITMENT:

If God knows how many hairs I have on my head he knows every detail of my life. I can't explain it but I believe it. I am trusting him for however he chooses to answer my prayers. I know this: However he answers my prayers will be for his glory and for my good. This I believe.

Day 75: The Discipline of Gratitude

The Word

> *Give thanks to the Lord, for he is good. His love endures forever.*
> — Psalm 136.1

Thought for the Day:

> *No longer dependent on our good works and performance, with the destination of our souls secured for all eternity, you'd expect that the energy of sheer gratitude, if nothing else, would propel us to never-ending acts of worship and service.*
> ~ Nancy Leigh DeMoss

No single attitude adjustment has more power to transform our lives than that of gratitude. And no single adjustment of attitude presents so stark a choice in real time.

Paul David Tripp writes, *Today you will spend solitary moments of conversation with yourself, either listing your complaints or counting your blessings.*[121]

When it comes to our thought life, it really is *either/or. Either* I will choose to meditate on my complaints *or* I will choose to meditate on my blessings.

The discipline of gratitude is a discipline and disciplines are hard. This discipline requires commitment, resolve, determination and strength to choose thankfulness over complaint.

---

[121] Tripp, *New Morning Mercies*, 478.

At the heart of ingratitude is believing that your life is out of God's control and/or that he cannot take the bad stuff and transform it into the good he promised in that famous verse, Romans 8.28. At the heart of ingratitude are faulty beliefs: God has lost control, he never had control, and/or he doesn't care.

To be grateful, then, is to replace this faulty belief system with the reality that nothing surprises God and that all that is happening in your life can be redeemed by God. The Apostle Paul reminds us that *we live by faith, not by sight.* (2 Corinthians 5:7)

To exercise this discipline is to believe that not *all* of life is terrible. Bad things have happened and the consequences of those bad things really are devastating. Though it may seem like we have lost everything through our tragedy, we haven't. We still have much in our lives for which you and I can be grateful.

Melodie Beattie summarizes the transformative power of gratitude: *Gratitude unlocks the fullness of life. It turns what we have into enough, and more. It turns denial into acceptance, chaos to order, confusion to clarity. It can turn a meal into a feast, a house into a home, a stranger into a friend.*[122]

To exercise this discipline is to choose to let go of some things.

- To be grateful requires letting go of *anger*, because you cannot be angry and grateful at the same time.

- To be grateful will mean letting go of *self-pity*, because gratitude is not on your pity party's guest list.

- To be grateful means letting go of *revenge*. The gladness in a grateful heart pushes out the bitterness that drives revenge.

- To be grateful is to *expand and project your perspective from this moment into eternity*, believing that in the long run, things will, indeed, work out for you

This is a tough discipline for me. Anger, revenge, self-pity—I struggle with these. For my sake, I'm going to hammer this point home with this long but poignant quote from Richard Rohr:

---

[122] Melody Beattie, *"Melody Beattie Quotes."* BrainyQuote, accessed June 11, 2017. https://www.brainyquote.com/quotes/authors/m/melody_beattie.html.

Things go right more often than they go wrong. Our legs carry us where we are going, our eyes let us see the road ahead, and our ears let us hear the world around us. Our bodies, and our lives, work pretty much as they should, which is why we become so unsettled when we confront any failure or injustice. This is not so true for people born into intense poverty or social injustice, of course. And we had best never forget that.

Nevertheless, we must stop a moment and look clearly and honestly at our life thus far. For most of us, life has been pretty good. We shouldn't be naive about evil, but perhaps the most appropriate attitude on a day-to-day basis should be simple and overwhelming gratitude for what has been given.[123]

THINK ABOUT IT . . .

➤ Eugene Peterson writes, *All true prayer pursued far enough, becomes praise.*[124] What do you think he means by this?

➤ You knew this was coming: Take a sheet of paper and make a list of things for which you can be grateful. Ask God to open your heart and show you the good things he has brought into your life. If you are struggling, check out this website[125]. Caution: When you read a list like this you will come across items that you *don't* have! This may send you spiraling down into negative thinking. Skip over those items quickly, and move on to the things you *do* have. If a list like this does more harm than good, skip the list!

➤ Note: If you are stuck in a pattern of negative, cynical thinking, you may be depressed. If you know you should be grateful but your mind can't go there despite your best efforts, see a pastor, a counselor/therapist and your medical doctor. Living

---

[123] Rohr, Durepos and McGrath, *On the Threshold of Transformation*, 285.

[124] Peterson, *God's Message for Each Day*, 239.

[125] https://www.lifehack.org/articles/communication/60-things-thankful-for-life.html

with depression is incredibly debilitating, and counseling, along with medication (if needed) can literally save your life. There is no shame in getting the help you need.

PRAYER:

God, open my heart and mind to your goodness in my life. Push away anger, thoughts of revenge and indulgences in self-pity to make way for glad thoughts of the good in my life.

This concludes our short foray into the Spiritual Disciplines. But don't let the brevity with which we have treated this subject undermine their importance. It is critical that you and I train ourselves with the disciplines. For more insight, I highly recommend: Richard Foster's *Celebration of Discipline* (Harper Collins) and Dallas Willard's *The Spirit of the Disciplines: Understanding How God Changes Lives* (HarperOne).

Day 76: God Can Repair the Damage Done to You (1)

The Word

Therefore, as God's chosen people, holy and dearly loved, clothe yourselves with compassion, kindness, humility, gentleness and patience. Bear with each other and forgive whatever grievances you may have against one another. Forgive as the Lord forgave you. And over all these virtues put on love, which binds them all together in perfect unity.

— Colossians 3.12–14

Thought for the Day:

> *Thou hast been ...*
> *A man that Fortune's buffets and rewards*
> *Has taken with equal thanks ...*
> *Give me that man*
> *That is not passion's slave, and I will wear him*
> *In my heart's core, aye, in my heart of hearts*
> *As I do thee....*
> ~ Hamlet to his friend Horatio
> Shakespeare, *Hamlet*, Act 3, Scene 2

WHY IN THE HECK do we do the things we do? Why did I throw a screwdriver when I was angry during The Great Door Disaster? (See Day 27) Any rational person, including myself, could easily make a determination that throwing a screwdriver inside a house with other people in the room is dangerous and reckless!

When teaching an intro class on pastoral ministry to Master-level students I clear stated: *You will never ever benefit from losing your temper. NEVER have I lost my temper as a pastor and later thought it was a good idea.*

Six weeks later on a Sunday night after church I was nose-to-nose with one of my church members! Seriously? I lost my temper *that quickly* after telling 50 students not to?! How can emotions so easily override reason?

The answer is that all of us have been wounded. There is absolutely no way anyone will get through childhood without being beat up verbally, physically, emotionally and sometimes sexually.

Painful memories deeply embed themselves into our mind. This is for our survival—we are designed to quickly and efficiently process potentially painful stimuli to avoid dangerous situations. When our senses detect circumstances similar to those from which we were initially wounded, the part of our brain that deals with emotions (the amygdala) takes over from the part of our brain that processes stimuli using reason and sound judgement (the prefrontal cortex). If we touch a hot stove our brain is good at remembering not to do that again. We quickly (without deliberate thought) react emotionally and behaviorally in the interest of self-preservation.

The problem is that all these memories of wounds become tapes we play every time we're in a similar situation.

The summer between second and third grade I went to our school gym to goof around. A bunch of kids were shooting baskets and tossing around those maroon utility balls. One of those utility balls came my way so I kicked it as hard as I could. The ball sailed under the basketball goal, bounced off the wall, and smacked this big fifth grader in the face as he was coming in for a layup! Ouch.

This kid marched over to me and, looking down at me, said something to the effect that he would kill me if I ever did that again. Almost 50 years later this memory is alive and well.

But painful experiences are more than just remembered for a long time. Painful memories inform and instinctively direct our behavior. After I was told I would die at the hands of this fifth grader, *I became afraid of kids older than me and avoided them for years afterward.* That's the power of a single event that took place in less than five minutes.

The events surrounding your trauma have seared new painful memories into your consciousness. What is more, many of the behaviors that led to your painful situation were probably instinctive reactions driven by the tapes in your head. In other words, the painful things done to you decades ago can make you do things you would not think possible, like throw a screwdriver across a room.

The great news is that God can *repair* the damage done *to you.* In fact, this is the perfect time to allow God to bring those memories to the surface and heal them.

Determine to get those old tapes out of your head! If you don't, you will continue to *react instinctively* to life rather than *respond thoughtfully.*

The second half of your life can be far better than the first half. For that to happen, however, old tapes need to be ejected and tossed in the garbage. More on that the next few days...

THINK ABOUT IT . . .

➤ Think back on a time when you reacted in a way that was more instinctive than rational. What were you thinking? What were you feeling?

➤ What are the most painful memories in your life? How do you think those memories may be influencing your emotions and behaviors today?

➤ Dredging up old memories can be a daunting task. If you were severely wounded, seek to do this journey with a competent counselor or therapist.

LIFE COMMITMENT:

I have tapes in my head that short-circuit my thinking. Time to get rid of those old 8-tracks!

Day 77: God Can Repair the Damage Done to You (2)

The Word

Brothers, I do not consider myself yet to have taken hold of it. But one thing I do: Forgetting what is behind and straining toward what is ahead, I press on toward the goal to win the prize for which God has called me heavenward in Christ Jesus.

— Philippians 3.13-14

Thought for the Day:

Nature has placed mankind under the governance
of two sovereign masters, pain and pleasure.
It is for them alone to point out what we ought to do,
as well as to determine what we shall do.
~ Jeremy Bentham

Nobel Prize winning psychologist Daniel Kahneman[126] helps us understand how bad memories get out-sized in our minds. God can use our understanding of this dynamic to help put our past in perspective.

Kahneman believes we have two selves, the *Experiencing Self* and the *Remembering Self.* The Experiencing Self are the experiences you have in everyday living. For the most part our experiences are not horrifically bad. In fact, for most of us most of the time, we are

---

[126] Daniel Kahneman, *Thinking, Fast and Slow* (New York: Farrar, Straus and Giroux, 2015), 912-14.

reasonably physically comfortable and in a state of relative emotional equilibrium.

But even as we experience a mostly comfortable and tolerably happy life, a single bad experience can become the author of our memories. In other words, memories overwrite experiences as we 'write' our life history. The *Remembering Self* has power over the *Experiencing Self.*

When I really think back on my childhood I was mostly happy. Seldom was I physically or emotionally uncomfortable. But it's not the normal experiences of day-to-day living that inform most of my memories. I remember the time my dad swung me by ears and threw me into the dining room table. I remember being yelled at and criticized. But I wasn't *always* criticized. And I was tossed around *only one time.* In reality, my dad often affirmed and encouraged me and took good care of me.

What's more, Kahneman has shown that a *good experience that ends badly* will be remembered *only as a bad and painful experience.* Let's say you go on vacation with your spouse. For 99.99% of this vacation things are wonderful. But on the way home from the airport you get into an argument. Years later you will tend to remember the argument, not the great vacation, and you will think of the entire vacation as an unpleasant experience.

What does this mean for you right now? As God repairs your past, consider these points:

- **Allow God to 'right-size' your memories.** Realize that your painful memories describe only a tiny fraction of your overall life experience. What should be a brief memory has overwhelmed how you think about your past. Ask God to shrink these overly huge negative memories to their proper size. Don't let the negative override the positive in your life.

- **Determine to go forward with God.** The Apostle Paul says, *One thing I do: Forgetting what is behind and straining toward what is ahead.* (Philippians 3.13) Paul had a lot to forget. Before he came to Christ Paul focused his considerable energy into destroying Christ's church. But in God's power, Paul put that behind him and reached for the goal in front of him.

God has a future for you. You won't reach God's future for you if the tapes of outsized memories from your past constantly replace thoughts of his presence and power in your life. Paul goes on to say, *I press on toward the goal to win the prize for which God has called me heavenward in Christ Jesus.* How positive is that?!

- **Be patient**. Paul says, *Brothers, I do not consider myself yet to have taken hold of it.* Amen to honesty! Paul acknowledges that the battle in our minds is constant but it *is* winnable!

THINK ABOUT IT . . .

➤ What do you think about most of the time?

➤ When you recall the past, what thoughts usually come to mind? Are they negative, unhappy remembrances or mostly positive?

➤ What negative tapes hold you back from the pursuit of God's future for you?

LIFE COMMITMENT:

I do not consider myself yet to have taken hold of it. But one thing I do: Forgetting what is behind and straining toward what is ahead, I press on toward the goal to win the prize for which God has called me heavenward in Christ Jesus. (Philippians 3.13-14)

Day 78: God Can Repair the Damage Done to You (3)

The Word

> *Do not conform any longer to the pattern of this world,*
> *but be transformed by the renewing of your mind.*
> — Romans 12.2

Thought for the Day:

> *The human capacity for burden is like bamboo—*
> *far more flexible than you'd ever believe at first glance.*
> ~ Jodi Picoult

GOD CAN *REPAIR* THE DAMAGE done *to you.*

In September 2009, my (then) wife and I traveled to Gulu in the northern part of Uganda. Just weeks before we arrived, Joseph Kony, the evil leader of the terribly misnamed *Lord's Resistance Army*, had just been pushed out of Uganda into the Central African Republic. We visited a church and an orphanage in this war-ravaged part of the world.

Kony's brutality is infamous. To build his army, Kony's soldiers raided schools and homes stealing children in the night. As the terror spread, thousands of children in northern Uganda would walk from the countryside into the towns, including Gulu, spending the night wherever they could, usually on the streets.

At least 30,000 children were abducted and forced to become child soldiers. Kids as young as six were taught to shoot and kill. Often they were forced to slaughter family members or friends. The brutality is beyond the capacity of language to describe and the human soul to fully absorb. My wife and I left Gulu on the charter flight back to Kampala amazed that anyone could survive such cruelty.

That night at a conference at Kampala Pentecostal Church we heard several former child soldiers tell their stories. These young men and women had been trapped in Kony's icy grip just a year before. While I had been sleeping in a nice bed and enjoying good food and friends, these young women and men were sleeping on the ground, terrified at what the morning would bring and living with the horror of what they had been forced to do to others.

Remember what we talked about yesterday—how a single bad experience will be remembered over all the good experiences in life. These children's experiences were *not* good. Their experiences were overwhelmingly horrific *most of the time.* Surely the memories of those horrible experiences would dominate their every waking moment. *But these kids proved that God is bigger than our experiences and he can right-size our memories—*even the most horrific memories.

God's power to repair their past was clear as these young men and women told their stories. Their tales all started the same way— they were happy children sleeping in their home or dorm when LRA soldiers raided their village or school and snatched them. They were ripped from family and friends. They were made to do atrocious things. Then they planned and executed a daring escape.

Here's what stuck out in my mind as I listened. The amount of time each speaker dedicated to the horror of his/her experience was only about 10%. The rest of their story (90%) was about God's victory in their lives.

These kids had experienced more trauma in their short lives than most people will in a lifetime. But these young men and women did not let that trauma define them. Instead, they did exactly what Paul encouraged: *Forget what is behind and strain toward what is ahead... press on toward the goal to win the prize for which God has called us heavenward in Christ Jesus.* (Philippians 3.13-14)

With huge smiles and contagious joy, these former child soldiers told of how God rescued them from their plight. They overflowed with gratitude as they shared how God was healing them of the trauma they experienced. They were overwhelmingly hopeful about their future. Filled with optimism of their future with God, each young man and woman knew that telling their story was a rich opportunity to give glory to God and to make him famous. They were *pressing on toward the goal to win the prize for which God has called [them] heavenward in Christ Jesus.*

Repairing your past is not a simple, one-time event accomplished by any single thing you can do. It's a process that takes time. But these young women and men proved that God *can* take our pain, right-size it, and move us into an amazingly bright and hopeful future.

Your traumatic experience of loss is an experience where you have been *snatched up* into a new and painful reality. It hurts. If you have just been recently snatched into this reality, hold on. Don't give up. God can rescue you and repair your heart and soul from this experience.

Maybe you are further down the road of the grief journey. The immediate crisis has passed and you are settling into a new but uncomfortable reality. And yet you keep playing the painful tapes. You are counting your losses and you alternate between intense anger and sadness. If this is you, don't despair. God can repair the damage done to you. If you cooperate with God, one day you will be able to tell others of God's rescue, repair and restoration of your life.

To repair your past God needs your cooperation. Gary Thomas writes, *God is the agent of change, but we have a responsibility to surrender ourselves to God's change.*[127]

If the negative, painful tapes of what has happened to you—either recently or in your distant past—are ruling your mind, surrender to God. Ask him to change the tape. Tell him you are ready to cooperate with his transformative work in your mind.

THINK ABOUT IT . . .

> ➤ When you read the story of the child soldiers of Uganda, what came to mind?

---

[127] Gary Thomas, *Simply Sacred: Daily Readings* (Grand Rapids: Zondervan, 2011), Kindle Location 1239.

➤ What childhood memories dominate your thinking? Can you trust God to re-size those memories and repair them?

PRAYER:

God, only you can repair me. I surrender myself to you and your power to resize my memories and give me hope for my future.

Day 79: God Can Repair the Damage Done to You (4)

The Word

Finally, brothers, whatever is true, whatever is noble, whatever is right, whatever is pure, whatever is lovely, whatever is admirable—if anything is excellent or praiseworthy—think about such things.

— Philippians 4.8–9

Thought for the Day:

Never let the inmates run the asylum.

~ Chrissy Scivicque

ALL OF US TALK to ourselves. The moment we wake up in the morning this conversation from one 'self' to the other 'self' begins. Part of you is talking to your deeper self.

This internal conversation is the stuff of life and determines the course of your life. What are you saying to yourself?

Humans have the unique capacity to step away from ourselves and become our own observers. The more we do this the more human we are. The less we do this the more animal-like we are.

So... stop and listen to the conversation you are having with yourself. The content of this conversation will tell you what you believe. Some of the things you believe empower you, moving you forward in life. Some of your beliefs hold you back.

To determine the beliefs that are holding you back, ***pay attention to your thoughts that make you feel fear***. Beliefs that cause you to feel fear are mostly likely the beliefs holding you back.

I like adventures—hiking, cycling, kayaking. My favorite is cycling. I have two bikes I ride, one for outside and a second mounted on an indoor trainer. Winters are made for the indoor trainer. Summers are for glorious outside rides. Every year as winter turns to summer *it takes me a while to get on my outside bike!* Why?

Honestly, I am slow to ride outside because my indoor trainer is familiar and safe. In contrast, outside rides pose very real dangers. Last summer I almost got tangled up with a pickup truck and the huge boat he was hauling behind him. A slight miscalculation would have sent me under the wheels of the boat trailer and that couldn't have possibly turned out good.

On another occasion, I ingloriously slid through an intersection on a rainy day. Embarrassing and painful! Another time my wheels caught the edge of the road and I fell over the curb. I wasn't going fast but I jacked my hand when I hit the grass. It took a year for it to not hurt when I shook hands with someone.

So even when the spring brings a much-welcomed warm day, I have a twinge of fear as I think about making the ride outside. *This fear is irrational.* Riding outside is far better than watching Netflix while pounding away on my indoor trainer! And though I have taken a few spills on my bike outside, the reality is that I have ridden tens of thousands of miles accident free.

My irrational and out-sized fear is driven by a belief that is limiting me.

All of us have these limiting beliefs. Loss and trauma will inevitably bring these beliefs to the surface and may even become so dominant as to paralyze you.

Ask God to show you these limiting beliefs that dominate your self-talk. The roots of these limiting beliefs are most likely the result of something traumatic done to you in the past, even decades ago.

What are you telling yourself? Think about this: The truth of the matter is that if we spoke to others the way we speak to ourselves, they'd probably accuse us of emotional abuse.[128]

---

[128] *"How to Delete That Negative Voice in Your Brain,"* accessed March 06, 2017, https://www.dumblittleman.com/how-to-delete-that-negative-voice-in/. I also recommend Chris Thurman, *The Lies We Believe* (Nashville: T. Nelson, 2003).

Wow, that is probably true for most of us! Would you say to others what you are saying to yourself? If you did, how do you think they would feel after you hammered them the same way you are hammering yourself? How do you think they would eventually begin to behave if you kept pounding away at them?

Now that you have insight into what you are saying, why you are saying what you are saying, and how your internal conversation is probably impacting your attitude, emotions, happiness and behaviors, *throw those thoughts away!* Get rid of them.

In their place, put something POSITIVE and TRUE.

For my bike and me, fears of crashing are replaced with the thought of sinking my hot sweaty body into the cool Blanco River at mile 15 on my bike ride! Doubts about if I can make it are met with the truth that I *have* made this 25-mile ride often, and when I finish *I never regret having made the ride!*

What would you tell someone who is going through a hard time? Now, tell those things to yourself!

THINK ABOUT IT . . .

➤ Step back and analyze the conversations you have with yourself.

➤ Write down the fear-based lies you say to yourself:

_____

_____

_____

_____

_____

_____

➤ Would you say to others any of these things you are saying to yourself?

➤ Now write down three truths about yourself that you can use to replace the negative self-talk that has been running through your head. If you are having trouble coming up with something, refer to http://www.yourlifeyourvoice.org/Pages/tip-101-positive-things-to-say-to-myself.aspx.

_____

_____

_____

_____

_____

_____

LIFE COMMITMENT:

I am more than the lies I keep telling myself. I refute those lies and replace them with the truth about who I am and what I am capable of.

Day 80: The Four P's of Identity

The Word

Those who are led by the Spirit of God are sons of God.
For you did not receive a spirit that makes you a slave again to fear,
but you received the Spirit of sonship. And by him we cry, "Abba, Father."
— Romans 8.14–15

Thought for the Day:

We are never-ending. We are warriors and creators.
We are divine and sacred and worthy.
You are worthy without caveat or exception.

~ Teresa Pasquale

From the moment of our birth we are seeking our identity. The first task is to separate ourselves from our parents. But to define ourselves by what we are *not* leaves a huge hole. We fill that hole with things from the horizontal.

Richard Rohr writes:

> *Without a transcendent connection, each of us is stuck in his own little psyche, struggling to create meaning and produce an identity all by himself. When we inevitably fail at this—because we can't do it alone—we suffer shame and self-defeat. Or we try to pretend that our small universe of country, ethnicity, team, or denomination is actually the center of the world. This can bear dire results. We need a wider universe in which to realize our own significance and a bigger story in which to find meaning. Not only does*

*a man need to hear that he is beloved, that he is a son, he
needs to believe that he is a beloved son "of God."* [129]

Rohr identifies a person's horizontal pursuit of identity by the 'Four
P's': *Possessions, Perks, Prestige, and Power.*[130]

When we suffer a great loss, at least some of the trappings of
the Four P's are stripped away. In the end, for every person on the
planet, the great awakening is that *finding happiness, satisfaction and
contentment in the horizontal is empty and fruitless.* The horizontal is
composed of the *gifts.* True happiness, satisfaction and contentment
are found (vertically) in the *Giver.*

And what does the Giver think about us? He radically, wildly,
passionately loves us and pursues us!

The Bible says that Jesus began his ministry with his Baptism.
Matthew says that *As soon as Jesus was baptized, he went up out of
the water. At that moment heaven was opened, and he saw the Spirit
of God descending like a dove and lighting on him. And a voice from
heaven said, "This is my Son, whom I love; with him I am well pleased."*
(Matthew 3.16–17)

The amazing thing about this is that God declared Jesus his Son
and stated his love, pleasure and acceptance of him *before Jesus did
anything.*

The same is true of us. *Because* you are a child of God, you are of
immeasurable worth and happiness to God. And you are a child of
God because he has declared you his son or daughter and paid the
price through Jesus to make you his child.

Brennan Manning writes,

> *It takes a profound conversion to accept that God is re-
> lentlessly tender and compassionate toward us just as we
> are—not in spite of our sins and faults (that would not be
> total acceptance), but with them. Though God does not
> condone or sanction evil, He does not withhold His love
> because there is evil in us.*[131]

---

[129] Rohr, Durepos and McGrath, *On the Threshold of Transformation*, 254.

[130] Ibid., 95.

[131] Brennan Manning, John Blase, and Jonathan Foreman, *Abbas Child: The Cry of
the Heart for Intimate Belonging* (Colorado Springs: NavPress, 2015), 19.

Your identity is in God, the Giver, not in acquisition of the gifts. Your identity is as a child of God, not a product of this world. Your identity is rooted in the eternal, not the temporal. No one can take your identity in God away from you. He holds you safe and secure.

THINK ABOUT IT . . .

➤ Go back to **Days 36-41** to remind yourself what it means to be accepted by God.

➤ Think about what you have lost. What role did that person or those things play in defining you? How can firmly rooting your identity vertically in God replace the pain of losing these horizontal things.

➤ In 100 years, what will the Four P's have given you (Possessions, Perks, Prestige, and Power)?

➤ In 100 years, what will having rooted your identity in God have given you?

LIFE COMMITMENT:

Though building my identity around Possessions, Perks, Prestige, and Power is tempting, I choose to find my identity in God and in him alone.

Day 81: Thin Skin, Hard Heart Or...

The Word

When [Jesus] saw the crowds, he had compassion on them,
because they were harassed and helpless, like sheep without a shepherd.
— Matthew 9.36

Thought for the Day:

[God] will use the brokenness of the world that is your present address to
complete the loving work of personal transformation that he has begun.
~ Paul David Tripp

IT'S CRAZY HOW OUR CULTURE GLORIFIES PEOPLE who have a *thin skin* and *hard heart*. Movies and TV celebrate 'tough guys' who take quick and violent action against anyone who slightly provokes them. Their 'toughness' is measured in how violently they respond to the slightest offense rather than their ability to absorb offenses without being rattled.

Thin-skinned people are easily provoked. A simple phrase or look can offend them. Everything is about them so anything or anyone who makes them uncomfortable in any way *gets under their skin*. They wear their feelings on their sleeve, which means that everyone knows what they are feeling, which is usually anger at some offense.

Thin-skinned people have a hard heart. Since they believe they are the center of the universe they lack the ability to put themselves in the other's shoes. They can't envision what it is like to be the other person because their imagination is limited to their own narrow lives.

Thin-skinned, hard-hearted people are usually angry, resentful, and bitter. And they let the world know it because they don't care how their words fall on others. Though they are easily offended, they believe others should not be. Thin-skinned, hard-hearted people believe they should be allowed to criticize everyone else. But when criticized, thin-skinned, hard-hearted people react with disbelief, anger and hostility. They can dish it out but they can't take it.

Thin-skinned, hard-hearted people believe they are powerful and that their angry outbursts show them to be so. In reality, however, thin-skinned, hard-hearted people have given their power away to others.

Thin-skinned, hard-hearted people are the opposite of self-differentiated people. Thin-skinned people's thoughts, emotions and actions are completely controlled by what other people think, feel, say and do. Thin-skinned, hard-hearted people believe that they are controlling others when, in fact, they are controlled *by* others.

Jesus was not like this. Jesus had a thick skin, that is, he was able to hear what others said and then respond (or not respond) according to what God the Father wanted, not according to his own wants or desires.

For example, during his trial before Pilate, Jesus fearlessly spoke truth to power. At the same time, he allowed Pilate to send him to the cross for crimes he didn't commit because Jesus knew that his death would bring life to us. (See John 18.28-40)

Jesus' thick skin allowed him to take what others were hurling against him. At the same time, his soft heart drove him to act with complete compassion toward those who were hurting, including those who were hurting him.

We are to be like Jesus, not Charlie Sheen. We are to be like Jesus, not the Godfather.

Losses—whatever their source—are a radical assault on our soul. Grief slams through our skin and slashes our heart. If left unchecked, the wounds of loss can make our skin thinner and our hearts harder.

This is your moment to allow God to transform your thin skin and hard heart. God can thicken up your skin and soften your heart. Everything in you right now is reinforcing the old thin-skinned, hard-hearted person you were. Push back on that. Surrender to God's work of transformation. Let him toughen up your skin and soften your heart.

Think About It . . .

> ➤ How thin is your skin? How hard is your heart? You can measure both by simply thinking about what you *think*, how you *feel* and what you *do* when you are criticized.

> ➤ What would change in your life if you were more like Jesus—thick-skinned and soft-hearted?

Prayer:

God, show me where my skin is thin and my heart is hard. I want you to thicken my skin and soften my heart.

Day 82: Between Surviving & Thriving

The Word

It is good and proper for a man to eat and drink,
and to find satisfaction in his toilsome labor
under the sun during the few days of life God has given him.
— Ecclesiastes 5.18

Thought for the Day:

To be broken is no reason to see all things as broken.
~ Mark Nepo

I DESCRIBED EARLIER WHAT I EXPERIENCED when I walked in from a 38-hour journey from Tanzania that October day only to have my wife inform that she was leaving me. I was crushed beyond words. My thoughts spiraled out of control as my soul struggled to figure out what *had happened,* what *was happening* and *what could possibly happen* to my future.

I distinctly remember saying to myself that my goal was to ride this wave, to grab on to the Rock and hold on through the storm. I knew that whatever my long-term future looked like I would never make it there if I didn't survive this short-term hurricane.

When people are devastated by crushing news the first order of business is survival. But God made us for more than mere survival. He designed us to thrive as we live out the purpose for which we are created.

I fervently believe you will survive and I believe you will even thrive beyond your loss.

You may be in survival mode. You are riding out the storm. You are clinging to the Rock. Survival for you may look doubtful. If surviving seems iffy, thriving will definitely seem a distant, diminishing hope.

But here is some hope for you right now: There is a place between merely surviving and totally thriving. It is in this place that God will give you some moments of enjoyment.

As you move through the survival stage you can expect God to give you moments of pleasure and happiness. They will probably be brief but these moments are real.

These glimpses of joy and hope may come from the things that gave you joy before like being with friends or hiking or woodworking or reading or fishing. As you regain strength, try to do some of the things that brought joy to you in the past.

On the other hand, God may bring some new things into your life. Who knew bird watching could be so energizing! The symphony? Seriously? Country music? Rap? OK, maybe we're pushing the limits! Or maybe not.

You just never know what God will do in your future! Just know this: He loves you and has a plan for you that will include your deepest desires coupled with the world's greatest needs. It is in that happy place that you will know you are thriving. Until then, look for some spots along the trail where the views are stunning, the breeze refreshing, the water crystal clear.

Think About It . . .

> - Where are you on this journey? Are you in survival mode? Are you fully thriving? Or are you somewhere along the path between these two places?

> - As you think of your life right now, where are some places of enjoyment and happiness?

> - Has God brought into your life some new desires? Has he put you into unexpected places of hope and healing?

LIFE COMMITMENT:

Even if life looks totally black right now, I can expect God to bring into my life some new places of happiness and enjoyment, even if briefly.

Day 83: Play Your Position

The Word

In his heart a man plans his course, but the Lord determines his steps.
— Proverbs 16.9

Thought for the Day:

No one ever healed from a blow to the head
by hitting themselves there again.
~ Leslie Becker-Phelps

My favorite position in football is linebacker. The linebacker plays the rush and covers the pass. He's on the move, mentally covering the entire field, but singularly focused on where the football might be and being there when it is. Linebackers have to be smart, fast and tough.

Even though linebackers cover more of the football field than any other defensive player, *linebackers still have to play their position.* In fact, everyone does. Success in football requires that each player *knows* his position, *stays* in his position and *plays* his position to the best of his ability.

The quarterback calls a pass play in the huddle. Each guy immediately knows his position. Most important to the success of the play will be the determination of the receiver to know his route and then run it with precision. When the ball is snapped the quarterback drops back and—if the receiver is open—throws the ball to the pre-planned and much-practiced tiny spot on the 57,600 square-foot football field where the receiver will eventually be. Everyone on the team knows the route and believes in it. Each runs here and pushes there, trusting that if everyone plays his position, the plan will work.

As I write this, the USA Women's Soccer Team just beat England in the semi-finals of the World Cup. To advance this far these women had to have great skill but also great restraint to only play their position. If everyone on the soccer field ran to the ball wherever it was, it would be chaos!

But as Helmuth von Moltke famously said, *No battle plan survives contact with the enemy.*[132] That's why the coaches watch hours of the tapes of the other team's defense. The idea is to anticipate how the enemy will react, and adjust accordingly.

But what if the coaching staff had a video of the game they were *going to play*? Every move could be planned with precision! I know this is a bit *Back to the Future-ish*, but in a way, that's what God does for us. He has a position for us to play. But he knows how everything plays out. Though it seems we have been knocked *out of position*, God helps us recover and get back *in position*.

Trauma is like a quarterback blindsided by a wild-eyed Mike Singletary or hammered by Lawrence Taylor. The hard blows of life knock you out of position. But God is bigger than this giant blow in your life.

God gave us free will. He doesn't cause these body-blows—we cause them from our poor choices and/or they happen to us because of the terrible choices of others. The amazing thing is that God's grace is stronger than evil and his plan supersedes the chaos of life on earth.

Can you trust the plan? Can you play your position? Surrendering to God's plan is one of the best ways to handle your anger, sadness, sorrow, hurt and pain.

Despite all the chaos around you, know that God is not surprised by what has happened in your life. Trust him to take this pain and transform it into something better than you imagined. When you release control of your present and future to him, you will experience

---

[132]Helmuth von Moltke, *No Battle Plan Survives Contact with the Enemy*, accessed September 24, 2017, http://www.lexician.com/lexblog/2010/11/no-battle-plan-survives-contact-with-the-enemy/.

relief that is far better than any of the other things you might have tried.

God is in the game and so are you. It's not over till it's over. Trust him to get you to victory.

Think About It . . .

- ➤ What positions did you play before the your life was upended? How have those positions changed?

- ➤ Trust God to take you from where you are to where he wants you to be. Trust him that his plan is good and right. Commit your ways to his care, then follow his direction.

Life Commitment:

Though I am flat on the turf, I trust that God will get me back up and give me a new route.

Day 84: Occupation or Vocation?

The Word

Fight the good fight of the faith. *Take hold* of the eternal life to which
you were called when you made your good confession in the presence of
many witnesses. In the sight of God, who gives life to everything, and of
Christ Jesus, who while testifying before Pontius Pilate made the good
confession, *I charge you to keep* this command without spot or blame
until the appearing of our Lord Jesus Christ, which God will bring about in
his own time—God, the blessed and only Ruler, the King of kings and Lord
of lords, who alone is immortal and who lives in unapproachable light,
whom no one has seen or can see.
To him be honor and might forever. Amen.

— 1 Timothy 6.12-16, emphasis mine

Thought for the Day:

> Grace not only forgives you, but enables you to
> live for something hugely bigger than yourself.
> Why go back to your little kingdom of one?
>
> ~ Paul David Tripp

God has something much bigger for you than just punching a clock
until you can hit a little white ball around a nicely manicured lawn.
He calls us to a life of risk and adventure, not for our own sakes but
for the sake of the world.

One benefit of loss is that we may lose some things that were
blocking us from fulfilling God's true calling in our lives. God may
be tearing you down so he can rebuild you into the person he called
you to be—a strong, confident woman or man, given over to God and

to the world he created, using your energy for others instead of only yourself.

Do you merely have an *occupation*? Or has God called you into his *vocation*? The root meaning of the word *vocation* means *voice*. You hear it in other words like *vocal*. To fulfill God's mission in your life means *hearing his voice in your life and following him into the task to which he calls you.*

How do you live in the power and energy of your *vocation* rather than merely live in the drudgery of an *occupation*?

First, Till the Soil.

If the farmer wants a crop in the fall he tears up the soil in the spring. God can't plant a vision, a dream, a mission into a hard, bitter, crusty heart. Take the plow to your heart. We do that by practicing the Spiritual Disciplines, the *habits of the heart* that make room for God to speak to us. If you plow the soil of your heart God will honor your movement toward him by speaking to you. Be patient. The farmer doesn't plow and plant on Monday and get the harvest on Friday.

Second, Listen for God's Call.

The call of God upon our lives is *God's call.* He initiates and invites. We don't come up with a good idea and then ask him to bless it. We don't ask God to join us in *our* mission. No, this is about God, not us. Let God speak. Expect him to speak. He has a huge mission in this world. Why would he not call you to your place in that mission?

Henry Blackaby writes:

> *The most dramatic changes in your life will come from God's initiative, not yours. The people God used mightily in Scripture were all ordinary people to whom He gave divine assignments that they never could have initiated. The Lord often took them by surprise, for they were not seeking significant mandates from God. Even so, He saw their hearts, and He knew they were trustworthy.*
>
> *The Lord may be initiating some new things in your life. When He tells you what His plans are, trust Him and walk closely with Him. Don't let the busyness of your present activity keep you from experiencing all that God has in store*

for you. You will see Him accomplish things through your life that you never dreamed were possible (Eph. 3:20).[133]

Third, Trust.

Trust that the call is from God. God wants you to do his will. He is for you! He wants you to succeed for his glory, for your good, and for the good of the world.

Trust that he will accomplish his will through you. I heard the testimony of a man named Jimmy Heald. By all accounts, Jimmy should be dead. Growing up with drug abusing parents, his dad was murdered when Jimmy was a boy, his mom hooking. But God reached Jimmy, rescued him, and set him on a path to becoming a staff member of a large, growing new church, all in the course of a few years! Jimmy could testify from his own amazing experience: *If God is calling me to it he will see me through it.*[134]

Fourth, Obey.

C.S. Lewis throws down the challenge before us: *[God] is calling us. It remains with us to follow or not, to die in this winter, or to go on into that spring and that summer.*[135]

Losses bring us into a winter season, but if we wait patiently, winter turns to spring. This is *always* true in the earth, but *only* true in our lives if we plow the soil, let God plant the seed, and then obey him through the summer all the way to the harvest. If God calls, obey. Don't hesitate.

Think About It . . .

> ➤ Have you heard God speak to you?

> ➤ Have you heard God call you to a ministry inside the church or beyond its walls?

> ➤ Consider this statement by Rick Warren: *God never wastes anything. He would not give you abilities, interests, talents, gifts,*

---

[133] Blackaby and Blackaby, *Experiencing God Day By Day*, Kindle Location 3510.

[134] Sermon by Jimmy Heald, Real Life Church, Austin, Texas, 2017

[135] C. S. Lewis and Walter Hooper, *The Business of Heaven: Daily Readings from the Writings of C.S. Lewis* (London: Fount, 1999), Kindle Location 1828.

personality, and life experiences unless he intended to use them for his glory.[136] What abilities, interests, talents, gifts, and life experiences do you have that God is calling you to use for others?

LIFE COMMITMENT:

Life is too short to spend it on myself. I give myself to God, asking him to plant the seed of his vision for my life in my heart. I will hear and respond to him in obedience.

---

[136] Rick Warren in Erik Rees, *S.H.A.P.E.: Finding and Fulfilling Your Unique Purpose for Life* (Grand Rapids: Zondervan, 2006), 6.

Day 85: Getting Passion Back

The Word

The heart of a man is like deep water.
— Proverbs 20.5

Thought for the Day:

Do more than belong: participate.
Do more than care: help.
Do more than believe: practice.
Do more than be fair: be kind.
Do more than forgive: forget.
Do more than dream: work.
~ William Arthur Ward

I RODE MY BIKE OVER 5,000 MILES LAST YEAR. On one ride I was only two miles away from home when I noticed my front tire making an odd noise. Then it got really hard to peddle. My tire was flat to the ground. Most flats are slow leaks. Not this one. My tire was at zero psi and there was no moving forward without a fix. A big Texas thorn made short work of my tire and tube.

Sometimes life produces slow leaks in our soul. A few times throughout our lives, a great tragedy is a thorn that takes the air out of your life. Whatever passion you had before is gone. But why do we view the flat tire of loss as a permanent state of deflation? When my bike stopped on the highway I didn't believe for a second that I would spend the rest of my life sitting on the side of the road with a flat tire. I didn't even believe that this flat could hold me up for more than 15 minutes.

But there is a difference between a tire and your soul. When a tire is flat, we know how to fix it. When the soul deflates, we may not know how to patch the hole, blow it back up and get back on the road. But lack of knowledge is no excuse to sink into despair. It is possible to regain your passion. Or, more likely, to actually get a real passion for your life perhaps for the first time.

The truth is most of us are stumbling through life with no sense of mission or purpose. If you are one of those folks, *now is your chance to discover who you are and what you are made to do.* In other words, this is your opportunity to slow down and look into the deep waters of your soul to find your passion.

John Maxwell asks penetrating questions: *Do you know your life's mission? What stirs your heart? What do you dream about?*[137]

Now is the time to find out who you are and what you are made for. Determine to seriously pursue finding and fulfilling your passion. *Know that your flat tire can be fixed!*

Here are some suggestions from Maxwell on discovering your passion:

1. *Get next to people who possess great desire [passion].*

2. *Develop discontent with the status quo.*

3. *Search for a goal that excites you.*

4. *Put your most vital possessions into that goal.*

5. *Visualize yourself enjoying the rewards of that goal.*[138]

A win looks like being clear about where you are now and clear about your passion for your future.

THINK ABOUT IT . . .

➤ Do you know your life's mission?

➤ What stirs your heart?

➤ What do you dream about?

---

[137] John C. Maxwell, *The Maxwell Daily Reader*, 385.

[138] John C. Maxwell, *Failing Forward: Turning Mistakes into Stepping-Stones for Success* (Nashville: Thomas Nelson Publishers, 2000), 171.

LIFE COMMITMENT:

I commit to asking God to give me clarity about who he wants me to be and what he wants me to do with the rest of my life.

Day 86: The Next Right Thing

The Word

In all my prayers for all of you, I always pray with joy because of your partnership in the gospel from the first day until now, being confident of this, that he who began a good work in you will carry it on to completion until the day of Christ Jesus.
— Philippians 1:4-6

Thought for the Day:

Perhaps it's not such a bad thing to come to the end of your rope if at the end of your rope you find a strong and willing Savior.
~ Paul David Tripp

You will find yourself at your wits' end but at the beginning of God's wisdom. When you come to your wits' end and feel inclined to panic—don't! Stand true to God and He will bring out His truth in a way that will make your life an expression of worship.
~ Oswald Chambers

With time, great good can come from great sorrow.
~ Desmond Tutu

Every spiritual problem has an individual genesis and therefore requires an individual exodus.
~ Gary Thomas

Ahhh, what a time in which to live! Everything seems to be getting stronger and lighter with so many choices it leaves the head spinning! One such product caught my attention recently: Duct Tape.

Duct tape was the brainchild of Vesta Stoudt, mother of two Navy sailors in World War II. Working in a factory making ordnance, she had the idea for duct tape as a way to seal ammo boxes so that the boxes would stay closed but could also be easily opened during battle.

She wrote the President who forwarded her idea to the War Production Board. They sent it to Johnson & Johnson who developed duct tape.[139] Today duct tape comes in so many colors and patterns it boggles the mind. Not only is it strong, it's pretty. Go figure.

Competition to produce ever-better duct tape is fierce. I recently saw one such product: T-Rex Duct Tape. I haven't bought any yet but I probably will before the zombie apocalypse. It pays to be prepared.

What caught my eye about the T-Rex Duct Tape ad was its tag line: *T-Rex Ferociously Strong Tape… All Weather, Works Longer, Holds Stronger.*

I want to be like T-Rex Duct Tape: *Ferociously Strong, All Weather, Works Longer, Holds Stronger.*

In the end, this is who God calls us to be: *Ferociously Strong, All Weather, Working Longer, Holding Stronger.*

The circumstances of my life caused me to change residences five times in 38 months, and this for a guy who really likes to hang out in the same place forever! In my last move I ran across a box that had been sealed long ago with duct tape. The gray plastic top layer was either faded to white or completely gone. The fabric showed underneath. But it was still holding.

The grind of life can weather us. Traumatic events can rip us apart. But in the end, we want to be *Ferociously Strong, All Weather, Working Longer, Holding Stronger.*

By now this truth has sunk into you: Whatever happens *circumstantially* in your life is secondary to what is going on *spiritually.* And above all, by now you understand that what God wants—more than anything—is for **you to come to him so he can invade your soul and grow you into the woman or man he calls you to be.**

Circumstances are what they are. I certainly didn't want to lose two churches and a wife in 18 months. In fact, I worked like heck to

---

[139] *Duct tape*, Wikipedia. July 28, 2017, accessed August 11, 2017.
    https://en.wikipedia.org/wiki/Duct_tape.

keep that from happening, but it happened anyway. I didn't choose to have my life turned upside-down and to lose hundreds of thousands of dollars in the process. But it happened.

What I did choose to do was to go to God. In him I found something, or rather Someone, who could never be taken away from me. I found my Heavenly Father, my *true* Father, glad to receive me, eager to comfort me, and firmly calling me into a future with him.

I know God did not cause my life to fall apart—people did. But I also know God is the pro at taking the horrible things in our lives and, with our cooperation, turning them into amazing displays of his grace, love and strength.

Tony Dungy captures this reality:

> *Have you thought about all the events that led up to this moment in your life—why you're here, how you've been shaped, what caused you to read this book or seek God's plans for your life? Have you wondered how much of it is accidental or random and how much is designed? I believe God knew exactly where you would be right now and exactly what you would be like. He knew about your passions and gifts and the platform you have. In fact, I believe He was very purposeful in designing your life. He made you to be uniquely significant and to have an eternal impact on the world around you.*[140]

When life comes crashing in we can either choose hope or despair, action or depression, life or suicide. Choose hope, engage in constructive, purposeful action, and embrace the life God has given you now and the life he will give you as you are healed and restored.

Life will continue to be a challenge. As long as we have breath on this planet we will struggle. But how much better to know this world is not all there is? How much better is God's invitation into a future with him? How much better to know that God can turn your pain into promises for others? How much better to know that your life counts and can be spent doing things of eternal significance?

---

[140]Dungy and Whitaker, *The One Year Uncommon Life*, Kindle Location 202.

It all begins when we say *Yes* to God. As Henry Blackaby points out, *Our response to God determines His response to us.*[141] Have you said *yes* to God? He has already said *yes* to you! With God at your side your future is far brighter and more significant and meaningful than you can imagine!

In the old days they said . . . *Nulla tenaci invia est via . . .* (*For the tenacious, no road is impassable*).

In today's language we might say: *Ferociously Strong, All Weather, Working Longer, Holding Stronger.*

THINK ABOUT IT . . .

> ➤ Where are you with God?

> ➤ What are your next steps?

LIFE COMMITMENT:

I am a wounded warrior being rehabilitated into a magnificent person who will give back to the very world that beat me to the ground. In God's strength and love, I am ferociously strong, working longer, holding stronger.

---

[141] Blackaby and Blackaby, *Experiencing God Day By Day*, Kindle Location 3450.

Day 87: Moving into the New Normal

The Word

When you were dead in your sins and in the uncircumcision of your flesh,
God made you alive with Christ. He forgave us all our sins, having
canceled the charge of our legal indebtedness, which stood against us and
condemned us; he has taken it away, nailing it to the cross. And having
disarmed the powers and authorities, he made a public spectacle of them,
triumphing over them by the cross.
— Colossians 2.13-15

Thought for the Day:

Attitude is everything—or at least a great, big piece of everything!
Check your attitude as you do small tasks and then take on greater things.
~ Tony Dungy

Twice in two years I experienced moments that I knew everything changed for me, and not for the better.

The first was December 16, 2013. By the time I left what should have been a routine meeting of my church's elders, I understood that I could not trust them or my staff anymore. At that point everything I had believed in and worked so hard for radically changed. The foundation of my vocational life was shattered. The future of what I had worked to achieve was completely up for grabs.

The second came nearly two years later. On October 23, 2015, I arrived home after a two-week teaching trip to Africa only to have my wife meet me in the carport of the church parsonage and tell me she had left me. As I walked into the house I knew that my life was further radically changed. I knew that I was losing things I had struggled to achieve. I knew the losses would pile up and would be felt for years to come. I knew that the things by which I identified myself were being stripped away before my eyes.

The journey since those moments has been like something I have never experienced. I cannot find words to wrap around the heartache and pain.

But this I know: *God has walked with me every step of this treacherous path.* Whatever was normal before is gone and can't be recovered. But with God at my side, he is moving me into a new 'normal,' whatever 'normal' is.

You can't let what has happened to you or what you have done to others stop you in your tracks now. Too much is at stake and God has so much planned for you.

Life is more like pedaling a bike uphill than it is a cruise downhill. If you are going uphill and you stop pedaling, you tump over! So... keep pedaling!

In the end, I want to be able to say with the Apostle Paul: *I have fought the good fight, I have finished the race, I have kept the faith.* (2 Timothy 4:7)

Think About It . . .

> ➤ What is 'normal' to you?

> ➤ How has your life been turned upside-down?

> ➤ What could a new 'normal' look like to you?

> ➤ What steps do you need to take today to move into the future God has for you?

Life Commitment:

God is for me. He has a future for me that includes a deeper, richer, more profound life. I want to live for him and eternity rather than for myself and this brief life on earth. I want to fight the good fight, finish the race, keep the faith.

Day 88: All in for Jesus

The Word

But whatever was to my profit I now consider loss for the sake of Christ.
What is more, I consider everything a loss compared to the surpassing
greatness of knowing Christ Jesus my Lord, for whose sake I have lost all
things. I consider them rubbish, that I may gain Christ and be found in
him, not having a righteousness of my own that comes from the law, but
that which is through faith in Christ—the righteousness that comes from
God and is by faith. I want to know Christ and the power of his resurrection
and the fellowship of sharing in his sufferings, becoming like him in his
death, and so, somehow, to attain to the resurrection from the dead.
— Philippians 3.7–11

Thought for the Day:

Obedience is not a stodgy plodding in the ruts of religion,
it is a hopeful race toward God's promises.
~ Eugene Peterson

At some point in life we must make a major decision. After we make
this huge decision, the rest of life is filled with many decisions either
supporting or undermining this decision. The decision of which I
speak is what to do with Jesus.

Are you all-in for Jesus? Have you given control of your life over
to him? Is he your leader now? Have you bent your knee before
him in submission, then experienced him raising you up to a new,
challenging, fulfilling life?

Or, is one foot in the 'religious' world and your other foot still in the secular world? Are you still trying to play both sides? Are you sitting on the fence?

Another way to ask this question is: Imagine you are on your deathbed. In that moment, who or what will you be trusting in to get you to the other side? Luck? Your 'good' life or good deeds? A philosophy that claims that when you die you just go away? Or will you be trusting Jesus?

God calls you to himself through his Son Jesus who gave himself on the cross so that you could, in humble, exhilarating gratitude, give yourself back to him.

Chris Tiegreen asks this penetrating question:

> *Imagine God giving you these two options: (1) to live a mediocre existence without too many highs or lows; or (2) to lay it all on the line and experience ultimate joy and rewards along with genuine sacrifices. Which would you choose? Most of us would say we want the second option— to live life to its fullest, in spite of the costs. But that's exactly the choice God gives us, and most of us tend to opt for average on a daily basis.*[142]

Jesus doesn't call you to average. He calls you to himself to allow him to propel you into his Kingdom in whatever way he chooses. One thing I have learned: following Jesus completely is not easy by any means, but it is *best*.

When Jesus walked the earth he was constantly calling people to decision:

> *Then Jesus said to his disciples, "If anyone would come after me, he must deny himself and take up his cross and follow me. For whoever wants to save his life will lose it, but whoever loses his life for me will find it. What good will it be for a man if he gains the whole world, yet forfeits his soul? Or what can a man give in exchange for his soul?"* (Matthew 16.24–26)

[142] Chris Tiegreen, *The One Year Hearing His Voice Devotional*, (Carol Stream: Tyndale Momentum, 2014) 685.

What is so precious on earth that you want to hold onto it at the price of your soul? What has the world given you that is so worth keeping? Why not surrender to Jesus and follow him wherever he leads?

Oswald Chambers said that...

> *It is only through abandonment of yourself and your circumstances that you will recognize Him. You will only recognize His voice more clearly through recklessness—being willing to risk your all.*
>
> *As soon as we abandon ourselves to God and do the task He has placed closest to us, He begins to fill our lives with surprises.*
>
> *God ventured His all in Jesus Christ to save us, and now He wants us to venture our all with total abandoned confidence in Him.*[143]

God risked all for us. He calls us to surrender our lives completely to him. This is risk. This is adventure. This is the thing for which you were made.

THINK ABOUT IT . . .

> ➤ When did you surrender to Jesus? If you can't remember the experience, you may not have done this yet.

> ➤ What is holding you back? What are you afraid you will lose?

> ➤ If you are struggling with this decision, seek out a pastor or a good friend who has taken the plunge.

LIFE COMMITMENT:

I surrender. I give up my little life to become part of God's bigger, eternal reality. I realize I am giving up on my own petty desires and dreams, but in the end, I want to be able to say with the Apostle Paul, "I consider [it all] rubbish, that I may gain Christ and be found in him...."

---

[143] Chambers, *My Utmost for His Highest*, 169, 120, 129.

Day 89: Steady Strum

The Word

*By the grace God has given me, I laid a foundation as an expert builder,
and someone else is building on it. But each one should be careful how he
builds. For no one can lay any foundation other than the one already laid,
which is Jesus Christ.*
— 1 Corinthians 3.10–11

Thought for the Day:

Nothing resembles pride so much as discouragement.
~ Henri Frédéric Amiel

I've been playing the guitar for only a few years and it's been
good for my soul.

As a new student to the guitar I have realized that it takes both
the left and right hands doing the right things at the right time to
make good sound. But my hands do different things.

The notes established by the fingers of the left hand pushing down
on the strings on the fretboard are the foundation of good sound.
To make solid and clear sound, the fingers must be on the fretboard
pushing down hard in the right place at the right time. No matter
how great my strumming, if my fingers on the left hand are weak
and/or misplaced, the sound will be muddled and out of tune.

At the same time, the right-hand strums or picks. Unlike the
fingers of the left hand—which must be firm, secure, stable and tight—
the right hand is free to strum or pick as the song dictates.

What is true of my guitar is true of my life. On the one hand, my life must be pushing in on the right foundation. Like the fingers of my left hand on the fretboard, I must have a firm grasp of my values, my convictions—the things in my life I am willing to die for and will not give up at any cost. I must be clear and firm about the principles, values and core truths that define the 'sound' of my life.

Some folks have found it helpful to ask God to give them a personal Mission Statement. God clearly gave me mine: *My life mission is to fervently love God and people, expressing this love frequently and persevering in it forever.*

I haven't always strummed well to this mission statement, but at least I have something to ground me.[144]

With my foundation firmly in place, I am free to strum or pick as life demands. Sometimes I can strum my life with a slow, steady peaceful rhythm. At other times I have to strum hard and fast to make the music that fits the moment. At other times, finessed picking sounds best. As a beginning guitarist, I'm still working on strumming. Finessed picking is sometime in my future!

As we come to the close of this devotional, think about your core truths. What are your values? Are you pushing down hard on these values? Are these truths deeply ingrained in your soul and second nature to you?

How about your strumming? Do you know when to strum slow and when to strum fast?

Think About It . . .

> Do you have a Mission Statement? If not, check out *The Purpose-Driven Life* by Rick Warren to figure out yours.

Life Commitment:

I may not be Jimi Hendrix on a real guitar, but with God's help and the right values, I can strum well to life.

---

[144]For help with developing your own Mission Statement, see Rick Warren, *The Purpose-Driven Life*, 312-319.

Day 90: Finishing Well

The Word

For I am already being poured out like a drink offering,
and the time has come for my departure.
I have fought the good fight, I have finished the race, I have kept the faith.
Now there is in store for me the crown of righteousness,
which the Lord, the righteous Judge, will award to me on that day—
and not only to me, but also to all who have longed for his appearing.
— 2 Timothy 4.6–8

Thought for the Day:

According to legend, the Great Plains warriors would say to their sons first
thing in the morning, "It is a good day to do great things."
~ Richard Rohr

Here's what I have observed from watching people die:

- Few people have thought about life, how they will end theirs, and if they have much to celebrate or regret. Most folks—it would seem—really have lived lives of quiet desperation.[145]

- Not a single person has ever said to me, *I had the best lawn in the neighborhood* or *I wish I had spent more time at the office* or *How 'bout them Cowboys?*

---

[145] Henry David Thoreau wrote: *The mass of men lead lives of quiet desperation. What is called resignation is confirmed desperation. From the desperate city you go into the desperate country.... A stereotyped but unconscious despair is concealed even under what are called the games and amusements of mankind.* Henry David Thoreau, *Works of Henry David Thoreau* (Boston: MobileReference.com, 2008), Kindle Location 5599.

- Most people the world would consider highly successful (high achievers such as physicians, lawyers, successful businessmen) go out kicking and screaming. They are angry that they have to die. But death is beyond their control and they hate that.

- Godly folks are few and far between. These few are gentle, humble, and full of joy when they die. They are grateful for the lives they were given and they are full of hope for the new life they know is coming.

These observations bring up important questions:

- Why do so few people think deeply about their lives?

- Why do so many folks spend their lives in such trivial pursuits such as football fanaticism, being beautiful or having the perfect lawn?

- Why do highly successful people sometimes end life so angry?

- Why are so few people finishing well?

We've always heard that life is a journey. When we were young we believed the journey would last forever. There comes a time, however, when we know it won't. For many men that time comes in the middle of life and it comes like a train barreling down the tracks. For women this time may come when their children move out of the house.

Perhaps you are in this moment as you face your tragedy, the thing that has robbed you of so much. *This is a moment we all face* whether brought on by death of a loved one, divorce, a job loss, financial ruin, a health crisis or any number of catastrophic events.

It's at this point that you and I decide how we will finish the journey. Imagine your life 30 years from now. When you are an old woman or man, how do you want people to think of you? What do you want to be remembered for? What kind of person do you want to be?

Most folks don't think this through and consequently, most people don't finish well. Your personal disaster has given you the opportunity not to be one of those people.

At this point in the journey we have a choice to make: (1) keep trying to be successful according to the four 'P's of the world; (2)

surrender to anger and cynicism, ending up bitter, or (3) humble yourself before the King of kings and join him in the adventure he has for you.

If you choose to surrender to God, you will end well. Determine that at the end of the day, you will be able to say with the Apostle Paul: *I have fought the good fight, I have finished the race, I have kept the faith.*

I recently had a hospice patient who was nearly 100 years old. As she reflected back on her life, a look of chagrin crossed her face, and she said, *"You know, I don't think I have done very much with my life."*

At 100, it's too late for a do-over. But it's not too late for you. Finish well!

THINK ABOUT IT . . .

> ➤ Are you still defining yourself by what you have, what you do (or did), and who or what you control?

> ➤ Have you given in to bitterness, determined to make it to the end with gritted teeth? Or...

> ➤ Have you surrendered to God and heard his call upon the rest of your life?

LIFE COMMITMENT:

I don't want to end up a bitter old man/woman. I want God to use me as he sees fit, and, at the end of the day, finish well.

Was this book helpful? If so, please write a review!

Here's how to write a review of this book:

- Go to the Amazon page were my book is sold under this title: *Disaster to Deliverance: 90 Days of Hope & Healing*

- Under the title, click "Customer Reviews."

- On the next page click the 'Write a Customer Review".

- Click the number of stars you give my book... then

- Write your review... then post it!

Thank you!

APPENDIX A: SUICIDE RISK ASSESSMENT

WORDS OF LIFE

*So do not fear, for I am with you; do not be dismayed, for I am your God. I
will strengthen you and help you;
I will uphold you with my righteous right hand.*
— Isaiah 41.10

*The Lord is close to the brokenhearted and saves those who are crushed in
spirit. A righteous man may have many troubles,
but the Lord delivers him from them all.*
— Psalm 34.18–19

A GOOD AND TRUE THOUGHT:

God's agenda is never elimination but transformation.
~ Richard Rohr

National Suicide Prevention Lifeline: 800-273-8255

A stunning study by the CDC in 2018 revealed that the suicide rate
has increased dramatically in the past 20 years in the US, with a
significant uptick in the period 2006 to 2016.[146] Ironically, the rate
of suicide declined globally. Countries with either high affluence or
dramatically dire circumstances experienced increased suicide rates.

---

[146] *Suicide rising across the US: More than a mental health concern*, Center for Disease
Control *Vital Signs*, last updated June 2018, accessed July 8, 2019,
https://www.cdc.gov/vitalsigns/suicide/index.html

Taking one's life is the tenth leading cause of death in the US. The tragedy of suicide is an important but often overlooked issue in our culture. Let's change that.

If you have thoughts of taking your life you are not alone nor are you abnormal. I believe that the vast majority of people think of taking their own life at some point in their lives. As stated earlier, my observation is that people either think about taking their life or they don't. Those who never think about ending their lives wonder how anyone could think such a thing. But those of us who have considered suicide as a viable option to the pain we are in really do struggle with it.

I know I did. For about four days a few months after my divorce was final, suicide became one of several options. What was strange about this was how casually I laid this option on the table. As I considered what to do, suicide seemed a viable choice. Death by my hand was laid out there along with other options on how to escape the pain.

A newly divorced man named Philip writes:

> As a divorced man, I can honestly say I contemplated suicide for the first time in my life during the first year or two of my separation. It's incredibly difficult to have your entire family life—children, home and wife—pulled away from you. Prior to the divorce, I was very happy, making a good salary and living in a nice neighborhood. Soon after the divorce, I was saddled with very high child support payments, debt from legal fees and barely enough left over to pay the rent of my small one bedroom apartment.[147]

Tremendous pain is caused through the tragedies of life because these tragedies result in real losses. Added to this is the fact that our society largely ignores pain and suffering. This creates more isolation for people suffering loss, which only increases the pain. Suicide can seem like one way to escape our pain.

---

[147] *Why does divorce make men more suicidal than women?* Jack Cafferty, last updated March 11, 2010, accessed July 13, 2017, http://caffertyfile.blogs.cnn.com/2010/03/11/why-does-divorce-make-men-more-suicidal-than-women/.

Edwin Shneidman writes:

> *Suicide haunts our literature and our culture. It is the taboo subtext to our successes and our happiness. The reporting of a suicide of any public figure disturbs each of us. Amid our dreams of happiness and achievement lurk our nightmares of self-destruction. Who is not mindful of the potential self-defeating elements within our own personality? Each new day contains the threat of failure and assaults by others, but it is the threat of self-destruction that we are most afraid to touch, except in our secret moments or the hidden recesses of our minds.*[148]

H. Norman Wright believes there are four main reasons for suicide:

> ➤ **Depression [Rage]**—*The person is sitting on a high level of unacceptable rage that has developed because of a series of events in life over which he or she has no control. Eventually this repressed rage is turned against himself or herself in suicide.*

> ➤ **Relief of Pain**—*Those with high levels of pain usually have three [unhealthy] choices: a psychotic distortion that reduces the pain, drugs or alcohol, or suicide. They often say, "I don't want to die, but I don't know any other way out—I just can't stand it."*

> ➤ **Revenge**—*Some [people] feel overwhelmed by hurt or rejection from another person. Their desire to hurt back is stronger than the desire to live.*

> ➤ **Hopelessness**—*Twenty-five percent of those who commit suicide do so after giving it quiet consideration and weighing the pros and cons of living and dying.*[149]

Though there are many reasons we may want to take our lives, it is always a bad choice.

The story of Kevin Hines is instructive. On September 25, 2000, Kevin jumped off the Golden Gate Bridge. He hit the water 220 feet

---

[148] Edwin Shneidman, *The Suicidal Mind* (Oxford: Oxford University Press, 1995), Kindle Location 60.

[149] H. Norman Wright, *The New Guide to Crisis and Trauma*, Kindle Locations 3120-3126.

below and lived to tell about it. He is only one of 33 people to have survived the fall among an estimated 2,000 people who have jumped.

As I read his story his words leapt out at me:

> *In the midst of my free fall, I said to myself these words,*
> *words I thought no one would ever hear me repeat: "What*
> *have I done? I don't want to die. God, please save me!" As*
> *I fell, I somehow possessed the mind-set that all I wanted*
> *to do was live—by any means necessary.*[150]

I wonder how many of the more than 45,000 people who take their lives every year in the United States have had the same thought the instant after they jumped or pulled the trigger or hit the tree or swallowed the pills or cut their wrists?

Teacher, author, and historian Jennifer Michael Hecht lost two friends to suicide. In her own grief she decided to research and write about it. She wrote her thoughts in a blog called "The Best American Poetry." In the blog she made an appeal to those contemplating suicide:

> *I want to say this, . . . Don't kill yourself. Life has always*
> *been almost too hard to bear, for a lot of the people, a lot of*
> *the time. It's awful. But it isn't too hard to bear, it's only*
> *almost too hard to bear . . .*
>
> *I'm issuing a rule. You are not allowed to kill yourself.*
> *When a person kills himself, he does wrenching damage*
> *to the community. One of the best predictors of suicide is*
> *knowing a suicide. That means that suicide is also delayed*
> *homicide. You have to stay.*
>
> *I'm throwing you a rope, you don't have to explain it to*
> *the monster in you, just tell the monster it can do whatever*
> *it wants, but not that. Later we'll get rid of the monster,*
> *for now just hang on to the rope.*

---

[150] *He jumped off the Golden Gate Bridge . . . and lived!* New York Post, last updated June 20, 2013, accessed July 13, 2017,
http://nypost.com/2013/06/30/he-jumped-off-the-golden-gate-bridge-and-lived/.
See also his book, Kevin Hines, *Cracked, Not Broken: Surviving and Thriving After a Suicide Attempt.*

*Don't kill yourself. Suffer here with us instead. We need
you with us, we have not forgotten you, you are our hero.
Stay.*[151]

When I was struggling those four days, here is what I kept in my
head in order to choose to stay:

> **I will get through this.** Life has always been almost too hard
> to bear for a lot of the people, a lot of the time. It's awful. But
> it isn't too hard to bear, it's only almost too hard to bear. What
> I feel today will not be what I feel tomorrow.

> *I would severely hurt the people I love the most*—my (now
> wife) Kelly, my kids and many others. I knew the pain I was in.
> Why would I want to increase the pain of those I love? Even if
> you have convinced yourself that the people in your life don't
> love you or care (surely a huge distortion of your thinking)
> they do care and you will hurt them immeasurably. I didn't
> want to add pain to the world.

> *If I take my life, this is what I will be remembered for.* No
> matter all my accomplishments, the first thing people will think
> of when my name is mentioned will be that I took my life. I
> didn't want that.

> *By taking my own life, I may contribute to someone else's
> suicide.* Survivors of those who take their lives are more likely
> to take their own life. I didn't want to potentially contribute to
> the death by suicide of anyone among my family or friends.

> *I will deprive the world of what God has planned to do
> through me.* God showed me that I had many years to serve
> him and that many people would be helped if I chose to stay. I
> have much to offer this world. I really do and so do you.

> *Why would I destroy this most amazing of all creations,
> my body?* I would never take a hammer to a Ferrari! Why

---

[151] Hecht, *Stay: A History of Suicide and the Philosophies Against It*, 7-8 (emphasis
mine).

would I destroy my body which is exponentially more wonderful than a Ferrari?

> I would be making a decision which belongs to God alone.

> I would defame God's reputation in the world.

> It would show a lack of trust in God's plan for my life.

> It would show a lack of trust in God's ability to provide for me.

> It would show a lack of trust in God's ability to restore to me what has been lost or stolen.

> It is only almost too much to bear. This will pass. ***God has me and it will be OK.***

When I thought of these realities, suicide remained an option, but one among many options. If I had not considered these realities, suicide as an option could have become my *only* option, at least in my mind. If suicide becomes the *only option*, alarm bells should be going off in your head.

Assessment

Are you thinking of taking our life? Take your thoughts seriously.

If you are thinking of suicide as one of several options, pay attention to your thinking. Seek out professional help now to assess how serious your situation is. If you are not sure, go to the website below to take this simple risk assessment.[152]

If you have come to the conclusion that suicide is your *only* option, **YOUR THINKING HAS BECOME DISTORTED AND YOU NEED IMMEDIATE HELP**.

Call the suicide prevention hotline (**800-273-8255**) *immediately.* Don't hesitate. Put this book down and call **NOW**.

If you are thinking any of the following **thoughts** or taking any of the following **actions**, you are at a higher risk for attempting to take your life by your own hand. Ask yourself these questions:

---

[152]https://www.choosehelp.com/topics/depression/suicide-risk-assessment-the-sbq-r-a-4-question-test

➤ *How much of my 'brain space' is taken up by thinking of suicide?* If your thoughts are dominated by reasons why you should take your life, you are at higher risk for following through. *Now is the time to seek help.*

➤ *Are my thoughts turning into plans?* Have you thought of a *time* and a *place*? Have you thought of *how* you would do it? Have you rehearsed how you would do it? Have you obtained the *means* to do it such as purchasing a gun or obtaining pills? If you are thinking any or all of these thoughts, <u>**STOP**</u> and <u>**SEEK HELP**</u> immediately.

➤ *Am I considering what people would say?* If you are thinking of how people will react to your suicide, <u>**STOP**</u> and get help immediately.

➤ *Am I preparing others for my leaving?* Have you told anyone you will miss them? Have you written out your will? Have you given away personal belongings? If you are doing these things, <u>**STOP and seek help immediately**</u>.

➤ Have you decided if you want your attempted suicide to be your final act on earth, or do you plan for it to be only self-injurious—that is, not lethal? In other words, are you using a means that will lead to sure success or a means that may leave you here but injured? **Either way, your thinking is distorted and you need to STOP and get help now.**

If you answered *yes* to any of these questions, I urge you, I plead with you, get help immediately. Call this number: **800-273-8255**.

What the Psalmist wrote 3,000 years ago is as true today as it was then: *The Lord is close to the brokenhearted and saves those who are crushed in spirit. A righteous man may have many troubles, but the Lord delivers him from them all.* (Psalm 34.18–19)

In 1997 my 50-year-old sister, Jackie, took her life. Jackie was an amazing woman, a fantastic big sister and fervent Christian. Through some terrible choices of others, her life became very painful. But the other day as I was thinking of her, I thought of all the people she could have helped these past 23 years that she didn't because she is not here. God could have used her to add so much more life to the world. Instead, she effectively robbed the world of her and God's help he wanted to give to her and through her.

Don't do what my sister did. Please stay. I did, and I'm glad I did.

I and many others want you to stay. I would imagine that if the people in your life got inside your head right now and knew your thoughts, they would be traumatized and horrified. They would want you to get help now.

I got up at 4:30 every morning for months so that I could write this book *so that you would choose to stay*. One reason I chose to stay is to help others in the same situation choose to stay. You are wanted and needed. Please stay.

From a spiritual perspective (which is the eternal and thus most important perspective), you and I are in a war and Satan is your enemy. Satan hates God, but since Satan can't destroy God, his driving passion is to deface God by defacing and/or destroying you. Suicide is the ultimate destruction of God's amazing creation.

King David wrote: *When I consider your heavens, the work of your fingers, the moon and the stars, which you have set in place, what is mankind that you are mindful of them, human beings that you care for them? You made them a little lower than the angels, and crowned them with glory and honor.* (Psalm 8:3–5)

Wow! You and I are God's amazing creation! No wonder Satan wants to take you out! **Don't let him!**

In my office I have a plastic anatomical human skull that can be taken apart. Inside is a model of the brain. Sometimes when people come into my office who are troubled and depressed, I take out my plastic skull and pull out the plastic model of the brain.

I say to them:

> *I know you are suffering and that you are in pain because of your loss. But did you know that you still have this amazing thing between your ears—your brain! Your brain is the second most incredible thing in all the universe. Did you get that? That three-pound mass of cells in your head is the second most astounding thing in the entire universe! The first is, of course, God himself. Whatever you have*

lost, you still have this amazing thing! And, you have God!
What can be better than that?

To take your life by suicide is to destroy this second most amazing thing in all the universe! Don't do it. Don't give Satan the victory. Don't let the thief come in and destroy. Instead, cry out to God. He WILL rescue you!

I urge you to get help. The journey you are on is a journey only you can make. Only you make the journey but *you don't have to make the journey alone.*

God knows the battle for your soul. God knows the war against your life. He wants you to win. He's on your side. Because he is for you, God will put resources in your path to help you survive this journey and thrive on the other side. This book is one of those resources. It's no accident that you are reading this. God knew you would need this book to make it through this ordeal. He called me to write it and he called you to read it. This is clear evidence of God's loving care for you.

God has given many resources for you during this hard time. I urge you, please reach out and get the help you need. The following are some suggestions. Perhaps these suggestions will be prompts God is putting in your path to help you right now.

> **Pray** to God. He is listening and much closer to you than you can imagine. He is eager to help you and see you through this.

> **See a Counselor** or **Therapist**. God has put smart people on this planet who commit themselves to helping people get through hard times. Ask around for a counselor or therapist who is known for his/her skills in helping people through hard times. You want someone who is tender and compassionate. You also want this person to be honest and be able to gently confront you when necessary.

> **Call a Friend**. We all need a few trusted, loyal, wise friends. Who can you call in the middle of the night who will listen to you, accept you for who you are, and help get you through? Not everyone will help you but God will give you a few who

will. If you have no one at this time, pray for God to send someone. He will. You will be amazed when he does.

> **Call a Pastor.** Pastors are today's unsung heroes. Most pastors are amazing people who help people win victories over the enemy. If you don't have a church, ask around to find a church known for their love for God and their love for people. It takes courage to jump in, but do it. God works through his church. His church is there for you. Pastors get calls all the time from desperate people. They are used to these calls and welcome them.

For years I have told depressed people the same thing: *Don't believe everything you are telling yourself right now. Your thinking is distorted. Instead, listen to what others are saying to you.*

If you need more encouragement to push against thoughts of suicide...

> **Don't put a period where a comma belongs.** Tens of thousands of people in our country put the ultimate period in their lives—they kill themselves. But crushing life problems are only commas. Don't make a comma into a period.

> **Suicide is a huge mistake.** Suicide is a permanent (and terrible) solution to a temporary problem. Failure is a temporary problem. You will move past this time into a better future.

> **Be assured that how you are thinking now will change.** You will have more positive thoughts as time goes by. Hold on!

> How you are **feeling** now will change. You will feel better! Hold on!

> **There are many kinds of treatment for struggling folks like you and me**—medications, talk therapy, etc. There are many options for help and that should give you hope. Don't think there is only thing that can help you, and if that thing doesn't help you, then there is no hope. Again, this is a lie from Satan. God has many ways to help his hurting children. Try something. If it doesn't work, let God use the smart professionals move you on to another solution.

Jennifer Hecht succinctly states: *Though we may refuse a version of life, we must also refuse voluntary death.*[153]

You are right to be upset about how your life is right now. Don't choose to change the state of your life, however, by ending it. That is a worse choice with far worse consequences. Instead, hang on, get the help you need, and watch God do his amazing work in your life.

Here again is the Suicide Prevention Hotline. Call this number: **800-273-8255**.

---

[153] Hecht, *Stay*, 183.

Appendix B: Our Discomfort
with Discomfort

Two things have become glaringly obvious to me these past four years of heartbreak and loss: (1) people, especially men, are not supposed to feel pain and (2) people who are in pain are not to expect much empathy, sympathy, comfort or consolation during their hard times.

Whenever I would express any sort of pain or complaint about my situation I would be shut down by either being ignored or given the pat answers of *You must learn to forgive* or *Things will get better.* Dealing with the pain of loss is not taught by our culture in any significant, meaningful, deep or lasting way.[154]

People in our culture are uncomfortable being with hurting people. People don't want to hear about your troubles. But just because friends and family are uncomfortable with raw pain doesn't mean we who suffer don't feel the pain.

People all around us are mired in troubles and heartache. People all around us suffer losses on a scale most people don't know unless they, too, have been there. These losses can push us to consider suicide as a viable option especially when appropriate avenues and methods of expressing grief and anger are shut down by our culture.

---

[154]Tim Keller notes that *Sociologists and anthropologists have analyzed and compared the various ways that cultures train its members for grief, pain, and loss. And when this comparison is done, it is often noted that our own contemporary secular, Western culture is one of the weakest and worst in history at doing so.... Our own contemporary Western society gives its members no explanation for suffering and very little guidance as to how to deal with it.* Timothy Keller, *Walking with God through Pain and Suffering*, 18.

I lost my family, my career, my reputation, my income. These losses hurt so much because they were real. Millions of people experience this pain, but it goes unspoken and unaddressed because our culture says that we cannot feel that way. But I did. I felt anger, loneliness, exhaustion, shame, embarrassment, sadness and deep grief. Despite the world saying that I should feel nothing, I felt deep and powerful emotions. You can't will away emotions. You can't decide not to feel.

When you're in pain, being told to 'man-up' is not going to get it done. Being told to pull yourself up by your bootstraps is not helpful. Being ignored only adds to the suffering and drives us into further isolation where we may find comfort in a bottle or shopping or porn or some other addiction. What this means for us is that when we hurt, we may not be able to find folks to listen to us and simply be with us.[155]

But we *must* express our suffering. Or, put another way, suffering *will be expressed.* As someone said *Talk it out or you will take it out.* No human can endure profoundly damaging events and go unscathed. Wounds to the soul find expression. Untransformed pain will flare outward or inward or both, torching ourselves and others in the process.

The Bible doesn't share our culture's discomfort with pain and suffering. In fact, Jesus always recognized pain and moved toward

---

[155]The story of Job in the Bible is a perfect illustration of this. Job suffered incredible losses, and his friends were not much help. Job complains about them in the verses that follow:

When desperate people give up on God Almighty, their friends, at least, should stick with them. But my brothers are fickle as a gulch in the desert—one day they're gushing with water from melting ice and snow cascading out of the mountains, but by midsummer they're dry gullies baked dry in the sun. Travelers who spot them and go out of their way for a drink end up in a waterless gulch and die of thirst. Merchant caravans from Tema see them and expect water, tourists from Sheba hope for a cool drink. They arrive so confident—but what a disappointment! They get there, and their faces fall! **And you, my so-called friends, are no better—there's nothing to you! One look at a hard scene and you shrink in fear.** *It's not as though I asked you for anything—I didn't ask you for one red cent—Nor did I beg you to go out on a limb for me.* **So why all this dodging and shuffling?** (Job 6:14–23, MSG, emphasis mine)

it, not away from it. This was true whether the bearer of the pain was male or female, perpetrator or victim.[156] This is a huge comfort because it means that God is moving toward you, not away from you.

Nowhere does the Bible indicate that to be a real man means you never express anger, sadness, heartache or heartbreak or that you never seek comfort and consolation. Quite the opposite. It is more than OK to say out loud what is happening in your head and heart. If the mighty prophet Elijah could tell God, *Take my life; I am no better than my ancestors* (see 1 Kings19.4), you and I have permission to verbally express our pain.

King David was as manly a man as there ever ways. But he wrote: *How long must I wrestle with my thoughts and every day have sorrow in my heart? How long will my enemy triumph over me?* (Psalm 13:2) If I posted that on Facebook as if it were coming from me, I would be slammed!

I cannot emphasize enough how our culture shuts down, explains away and radically ignores real suffering. When you are suffering deeply, to be shut down and/or ignored amplifies and exacerbates suffering.

I believe that if friends and family would allow grieving people to really grieve, hurting people to really hurt, angry people to really be angry, sad people to really be sad, much of the transmitted pain would be transformed in our society, making us stronger, not weaker.

And therein lies the most significant myth about pain: that pain is weakness. Weakness is perceived as vulnerability, and vulnerability is defined as failure and failure is exactly the opposite of everything American. To express pain—to reveal your suffering—is to express everything un-American. Americans are not weak, we are strong. Americans aren't vulnerable, we are impenetrable. Americans don't suffer, we conquer. To acknowledge our suffering is to fail, and failure is un-American.[157]

---

[156] See Matthew 8.1-4; Luke 13.10-17; Matthew 18.1-5; Mark 5.35-42.

[157] Megan Divine notes that *Our culture sees grief as a kind of malady: a terrifying, messy emotion that needs to be cleaned up and put behind us as soon as possible. As a result, we have outdated beliefs around how long grief should last and what it should look like. We see it as something to overcome, something to fix, rather than something to tend or support. Even our clinicians are trained to see grief as a*

But Americans also take tons of anti-depressants, drink ourselves under the table, view untold hours of pornography. We do everything possible to deny, avoid or medicate our pain. It's not working.

I'm convinced that uncountable numbers of people take their own lives or end up bitter and weak because no one wants to hear their pain and shepherd them through it. This ought not be.

How is our Pain Transformed so it is not Transmitted?

Look at the graphic on the next page. In the upper left corner notice that our culture's 'discomfort with discomfort' leads people to disrespect you if you express your pain. You are regarded as 'playing the victim' if you state any negative emotion regarding your situation.

On the far right of the graphic, we find that people expect you to only take responsibility for how you handle it. And there's truth to this notion that how we handle our pain is our responsibility. You may be the victim in this thing, but how you and I respond is our responsibility. But our culture makes the false assumption that a person who expresses his/her hurt is not handling the situation responsibly and is, therefore, defaulting to the 'victim mentality.' The two appear to be mutually exclusive **but they are not**. This is a critical distinction.

If we express our pain, a second false assumption is made: that we are not moving forward, we are not 'accepting' our situation, we are not working on it. People assume we are 'stuck' and that we like it that way. They assume that we feel good when we feel bad. If we would just shut our complaining mouths and shut down our raging emotions, we could get on with our lives (and quit bothering everybody with our heartache).

Is it possible to express your hurt, anger, grief and mount a defense of yourself (if you are not the primary perpetrator) without being labeled a victim, or, worse yet, actually falling into the victim role?

Society is right in pushing us away from a victim mentality. If we complain to everyone and engage in destructive behaviors, we

---

disorder rather than a natural response to deep loss... those outdated ideas add unnecessary suffering on top of natural, normal pain. Megan Devine and Mark Nepo, *It's OK That You're Not OK: Meeting Grief and Loss in a Culture That Doesn't Understand* (Boulder: Sounds True, 2017), Kindle Locations 134-140.

The Difference Between Fault & Responsibility

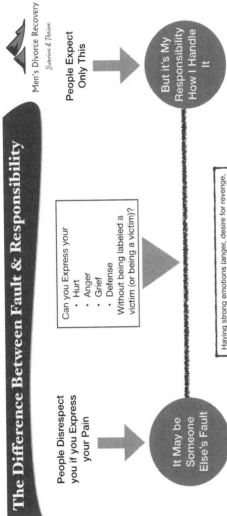

Men's Divorce Recovery
Survive & Thrive

People Disrespect you if you Express your Pain

People Expect Only This

It May be Someone Else's Fault

But it's My Responsibility How I Handle It

If we complain to everyone and engage in destructive behaviors, we are playing the victim.

Pain that is not Transformed is Transmitted.
– Richard Rohr

Can you Express your
- Hurt
- Anger
- Grief
- Defense

Without being labeled a victim (or being a victim)?

Having strong emotions (anger, desire for revenge, grief) at what someone has done to us can be expressed even while moving forward.

Expressing emotions does not mean we are playing the victim, as long as our actions show we are moving forward.

Expressing our Emotions & Moving Forward are not Mutually Exclusive.

How long must I wrestle with my thoughts and every day have sorrow in my heart? How long will my enemy triumph over me?
~ Psalm 13:2

If we are taking steps to
- Stay engaged with life, especially with people
- Work on self-improvement
- Going to work
- Not harming self or others...

... we can be said to be moving forward.

are playing the victim. If we define ourselves by our wounds and let everyone know it, we are playing the victim. If we wallow in our despair, paralyzed by our pain, we are playing the victim. But I'm convinced that if we have just one or two people who really seek to understand our hurt and pain, the need to verbally vomit on everybody diminishes and eventually goes away.[158]

If we find one or two people who really understand our heartache but care enough not to leave us there, we can move forward into healing and recovery. Those few who get it understand that having strong emotions (anger, desire for revenge, grief) at what we have lost can be expressed even while we are moving forward. Expressing emotions does not mean we are playing the victim, as long as our actions show we are moving forward. Expressing our emotions and moving forward are not mutually exclusive.

The Bible commands us to *Carry each other's burdens, and in this way you will fulfill the law of Christ.* (Galatians 6.2).[159] The church

---

[158] McKay et al, state: *There is only one requirement for listening with empathy: simply know that everyone is trying to survive. You don't have to like everyone or agree with everyone, but recognize that you do share the same struggles.* Matthew McKay, Martha Davis and Patrick Fanning, *Messages: The Communication Skills Book* (Oakland: 2009), Kindle Locations 364-366.

[159] John McArthur writes, *It is our duty as believers to help bear one another's burdens. When someone staggers, we help steady the load. If he is straining, we help bear the burden. And if he stumbles, we lift him up. Helping fellow believers carry the weight of their worldly troubles is one of the chief practical duties that ought to consume every Christian.... When Paul suggests that burden-bearing "fulfill[s] the law of Christ," he makes it clear that he has the whole moral law in view. Every act of compassion and self-sacrifice on behalf of our brethren is a practical means of displaying the love of Christ and thereby fulfilling the moral demands of His law.*

But the apostle clearly has in mind spiritual, emotional, and temperamental encumbrances — not physical freight only. The burdens we need to help carry for one another include guilt, worry, sorrow, anxiety, and all other similar loads.

Do you want to fulfill the moral requirements of the Law? Love your neighbor. How do you love him? By bearing his burdens.

It's interesting that Paul would emphasize this theme in an epistle written to confront people who were falling into legalism. It's as if he were saying, "You want to observe a law? Let it be the law of Christ. If you have to impose burdens on yourselves, let it be through acts of love toward your neighbor." If you will do that faithfully, your own burden won't seem so heavy. Best of all, you will find it easier

must bear one another's burdens. The church must not make burdens more unbearable by denying the burden or telling the one suffering that the burden is not as heavy as he/she thinks it is.

Finding someone who can absorb some of our pain helps free us to move forward responding responsibly to our situation. What does moving forward look like?

If we are taking steps to

- Stay engaged with life, especially with people...

- Work on self-improvement by acknowledging the parts of our lives that need to change...

- Resist addictions such as alcohol/drugs, pornography, materialism...

- Go to work, take care of the kids, fulfill other daily obligations...

- Not harm ourselves or others... we can be said to be moving forward.

Unfortunately finding people in our lives who can walk this journey with us in a balanced and helpful way is difficult. Most people are not capable or trained to do it. That's why a therapist or counselor should be engaged as soon as possible.

It is possible and necessary to express our pain without falling into victimhood. We are successful in doing this if we are taking active steps to get better, be healed, and move forward along the path God has for us.

---

to keep your focus heavenward, regardless of the trials you suffer in this life. John McArthur, *Bearing One Another's Burdens*, last updated January 1, 2010, https://www.ligonier.org/learn/articles/bearing-one-anothers-burdens/accessed%20May%206https://www.ligonier.org/learn/articles/bearing-one-anothers-burdens/accessed May 6, 2018.

Appendix C: You Need Jesus

When loss comes screaming in at us we often attempt to bargain: *God, I will change my ways, I will go to church, I will give money, if you only make this problem go away.* Severe pain causes us to think extreme thoughts.

Many folks have sat in my office as a pastor sharing their heart-break, seeking ways to ease their pain. I tell these folks the same thing: *I don't know if your problem can be solved, but I do know that God loves you and that your relationship to him is what we need to work on first. And I know that if you are tight with God, no matter what happens regarding your life, the second half of your life can be far better than the first half, if you live it for the Lord.*

Why We Feel Far from God

When I was a kid my friends and I would get into rock fights, that is, we would throw rocks at each other. We also had a tendency to try to shoot each other with BB guns. That's what boys do. Boys like to shoot things, burn things, and blow things up. And I define 'boys' here loosely!

One day my friend and I got into rock fight at my house. My friend threw a rock at me and missed. That was the good news. The bad news was that the rock hit my dad's car and put a significant dent just below the back window on the passenger side.

Oh, this was very very bad. My dad was definitely *not* the kind of dad who you just walked up to and said, *Father, I have failed you. My friend just threw a rock at me and instead of hitting me it hit your car. Please forgive us.* To say such a thing to my dad was to sign your death warrant.

But here's the thing. Even though my dad had no clue what we had done, my guilt and fear of him drove me to avoid him. My fear of what he would do to me if we were discovered made me avoid him.

That's the way we are with God. God made us and then gave us rules to live by. Those rules are for our own good but they are also a test of our love for God. If we love God we obey his rules, just like a husband who loves his wife doesn't cheat on her but instead, remains faithful to her, not out of begrudging obligation but from a heart of joyful love.

Ever since Adam and Eve turned against God, however, we've been rebels. We are like my daughter, who at the age of eight decided she could do better without us. So she packed her little suitcase and walked right out the front door *at night*. I think all of us would agree that had we not rescued her, a night alone for a 7-year-old would not have ended well.

What we see around us is the result of humanity trying to live without God. The daily cable news channels bear 24/7 witness to the folly of this strategy. We may not be consciously aware of it, but deep inside we know we have done what God has told us not to do, and we have failed to do what God requires of us. The Biblical word for rebellion and rule-breaking is *sin*. The Bible is clear: *For all have sinned and fall short of the glory of God.* (Romans 3.23)

So, just like I tried to avoid my dad out of fear of what he would do to me, we avoid God out of fear of what he will do to us. Unlike my dad, however, God is all-knowing *and* he is all-powerful. As much as I feared my dad, my dad didn't know everything (though he acted at times as if he did!) and he wasn't all-powerful (though he felt very powerful in my life).

Sin separates us from God. Our rebellion against God has put a very real gap between God and us. We avoid God because we fear his punishment. When we sin we are rebelling against a perfect and holy God. Our sin separates us from God. Our sin is our running away from God in a hopeless bid for autonomy rather than living in dependence upon him and submission to him. Because of our sin we are far from him.

Our sin causes unspeakable damage to ourselves, to the people around us and to our world. The cost of sin is immeasurable. When my friend threw the rock that put the dent in my dad's car, damage was done and repairing the car would be costly. Someone would have to pay to have the car fixed. Our sin puts us in debt to God because of the damage it causes to his creation. Because we have turned away from God, we are far from him and the cost to repair the damage is far beyond us.

The great news is this: God loves us too much to leave us in our lost, separated and miserable state. Since we couldn't go to him he came to us. He sent his son Jesus, fully God and fully human, to be the bridge between him and us.

When Jesus hung on the cross he was taking upon himself all the hell you and I rightfully deserve for the damage we have caused by our rebelling against God. When Jesus hung on the cross he not only suffered terribly physically (as portrayed in the movie *The Passion*) but he suffered far more spiritually when he paid the price to repair the damage we have caused. That's why out of the billions of people who have died, only Jesus' death can affect your life on earth and your life after you die.

The Apostle Peter wrote about Jesus: *[Jesus] himself bore our sins in his body on the tree, so that we might die to sins and live for righteousness.* (1 Peter 2.24)

And Jesus said about himself: *For even the Son of Man did not come to be served, but to serve, and to give his life as a ransom for many.* (Mark 10.44-45)

Jesus paid this unspeakably high price so our debt to God would be paid and we would be forgiven of every sin we have committed and all the sins we will commit.

When Jesus hung on the cross he took upon himself your sin, and when he died, your sin was killed on that cross. In exchange for our sin, Jesus gives us his righteousness. He exchanged our black for his white, our infection for his healing, our damage for his restoration.

What we see on banners in end zones of countless football games is the most important truth the world could ever know: *For God so loved the world that he gave his one and only Son, that whoever believes in him shall not perish but have eternal life. For God did not send his Son into the world to condemn the world, but to save the world through him.* (John 3.16–17)

Or as the Apostle Paul wrote: *[God] made [Jesus] who knew no sin to be sin for us, that we might become the righteousness of God in Him.* (2 Corinthians 5.21)

Tim Keller is right when he says, *Jesus lived the life we should have lived and died the death we should have died.*

When Jesus died on the cross *all your sins were put upon him and he paid for every one of your sins on that terrible and amazing day.* It's a done deal. It's not something that *might* happen. *It happened.* It's not something that could be, *it is.* You don't have to hope Jesus paid for your sins. He did. You don't have to plead with him to forgive you. He has.

Your sins are paid for, your debt erased. You are forgiven. God won this battle for his glory and your good!

What is our part in receiving God's forgiveness through Jesus's sacrifice on the cross?

Ray Pritchard says there are three elements to receiving God's gift of salvation: *True saving faith involves the **intellect**, the **emotions**, and the **will** . . . Faith starts with **knowledge**, moves to **conviction**, and ends with **commitment**.*[160]

To receive forgiveness now and heaven forever, you need to <u>**know some facts**</u>, be <u>**convinced they are true**</u>, and then <u>**make a decision**</u>.

What you need to <u>**KNOW**</u>:
Here are the basics:

- We don't get to heaven based on our goodness. Instead, we get there only by God's grace because **no one is good enough. Our rebellion against God, expressed as sin, separates us from God.**

- Since we can't go to God, he came to us. God sent his Son, Jesus, to take the punishment we deserve for our sin. **On the cross Jesus took upon himself your sin**, and when he died, your sin was killed on that cross. In exchange for our sin, Jesus gives us his righteousness.

---

[160]Ray Pritchard, *An Anchor for the Soul: Help for the Present, Hope for the Future* (Chicago: Moody Publishers, 2011), 123. Emphasis mine.

- After Jesus died on the cross **he rose again**, proving he is who he said he is, and proving his power over our greatest enemy which is death.

To solve any problem you have to understand it and then map out the solution. You and I have a problem: we are separated from God because of our sin. God provided the solution by sending his own Son to die in our place. These are the basics of what you need to know about your problem and its solution.

Do you know these facts and are you convinced they are true? If you need more convincing, ask! Ask a pastor or a friend who is close to God. Find answers to your questions. Many smart people for hundreds of years have thought about the answers to questions regarding Jesus and God's plan of salvation for us.[161]

Once you are convinced these facts are true, you must **make a decision**.

John 3.16 says, *For God so loved the world that he gave his one and only Son, that whoever **believes** in him shall not perish but have eternal life.*

The best way I can describe what believing looks like in today's world is getting on an airplane.

Suppose someone gave you a free ticket to Hawaii. You didn't earn this ticket. It's a free gift. But to get to Hawaii, you have to exercise tremendous faith in an airplane, which, I might remind you, is an aluminum tube hurtling through the air at 600 mph seven miles above the earth!

The reality is that you probably wouldn't hesitate to get on that plane because at some point in your life you had learned about airplanes and modern flying. You had decided that your knowledge about airplanes is trustworthy and true. You came to believe that airplanes are remarkably safe and that if you choose to fly, there is a very high probability you will safely arrive at your destination.

But no matter how much you know about flying or how much you believe in the safety of modern air travel, *You won't get to your*

---

[161] For answers to your questions about the Bible, Christianity, etc. see https://www.christianityexplored.org/Groups/276317/CE\ORG/Tough_ Questions/Tough_Questions.aspx

destination unless you actually get on the airplane.

The same is true of getting to heaven. Faith starts with **knowledge**, moves to **conviction**, and ends with **commitment**.[162]

To receive forgiveness now and heaven forever, you need to **know some things**, be **convinced they are true**, and then **make a decision**.

We have talked about some facts as revealed in the Bible about our problem (sin) and God's solution (Jesus). Do you believe those facts? Do you trust they are true?

If so, now is the time to make a decision. To be right with God you must get on the plane. To get to heaven, you have to walk down the jetway, step into the airplane and take your seat. Your trip is bought and paid for by Jesus Christ. But to get to your final destination, you have to trust the ride.

What does this look like when it comes to placing our trust in Jesus? My experience is that at some point a person's heart that has been leaning away from God *leans toward God.* When your heart leans toward God (and you will know when it does), you are saved. That moment is usually expressed with words spoken in your heart and/or verbally (see below).

Another way to think of what trusting Jesus looks like is to project your life forward to your deathbed. Think about who or what you will trust in that moment to get to you to the other side. The only right answer is Jesus.

Pritchard writes, *How much faith does it take to go to heaven? It depends. The answer is not much but all you've got. If you are willing to trust Jesus Christ with as much faith as you happen to have, you can be saved.*[163] I like that!

The good news is that though we are not good enough to get to heaven, Jesus is. Through his death on the cross he has taken our sins upon himself and given us his righteousness instead.

Is your heart leaning away from God or toward God? Are you trusting your own good works to get you to heaven?

---

[162]Pritchard, *An Anchor for the Soul*, 123. Emphasis mine.
[163]Ibid., 129.

Or perhaps you feel you have sinned so much God can never forgive you. You aren't good enough to get into heaven, but you have not done anything so horrendous to keep you out of heaven. Jesus paid the price for your sins (all your sins!) so you can be free and clear, forgiven and heaven-bound. (If you are struggling with God's acceptance of you, go back and re-read Days 58-63).

If you are ready to make this commitment to God, if you are ready to get on God's airplane, trusting him with your life, simply say that to him. Using your own words, express your need for his forgiveness because of your sin and your desire to accept this gift of salvation through Jesus and what he did for you.

Your prayer may be something like this:

Dear God, I know that I am a sinner and there is nothing that I can do to save myself. I confess my complete helplessness to forgive my own sin or to work my way to heaven. At this moment I trust Christ alone as the One who bore my sin when He died on the cross. I believe that He did all that will ever be necessary for me to stand in your holy presence. I thank you that Christ was raised from the dead as a guarantee of my own resurrection. As best as I can, I now transfer my trust to Him. I am grateful that He has promised to receive me despite my many sins and failures. Father, I take you at your word. I thank you that I can face death now that you are my Savior. Thank you for the assurance that you will walk with me through the deep valley. Thank you for hearing this prayer. In Jesus' Name. Amen.[164]

When you come to Jesus your life changes!

Despite where you are today, God promises that when we come to him, *he will grow you into the man or woman he always wanted you to be.* What looks to us like an ending becomes a new beginning. What looks like a funeral is a celebration of new birth. In fact, the Bible describes those who have come to him for salvation as being

---

[164]Prayer by John Barnett: https://www.crosswalk.com/faith/prayer/prayers/the-sinners-prayer-4-examples.html, accessed May 12, 2018.

born again. Your spiritual birthday is today and your new life begins today! Now you will want to grow up in your faith.

Growing in your faith means that you will become more and more like Jesus. You will come to *love the things God loves and grieve the things he grieves.* You will react to the situations in your life as Jesus did—with *wisdom and peace, confidence and gentleness.*

You will come to see people as God sees them. You will live with an open hand and warm spirit. You will know what to fight and when to fight, what weapons to use and what constitutes a victory.

God will transform you from the inside out. He will change your desires. You will want to experience God's presence in your life through prayer, reading and consuming his Word (the Bible), being with other Christians, and serving God through your church. Following God will not be a burden but a natural outgrowth of your life as you experience more of God's love.

The best is yet to be for you. The second half of your life can be better than the first half. You have a hope and future. You will give yourself to something much bigger and far more lasting than anything you have sold out for up to now.

For specific teachings on growing in Christ, check out CRU.[165]

To grow in Christ begin with the following steps:

1. Tell someone you have decided to follow Jesus.

2. Pray! Just talk to God. It is really simple. Don't make this complicated.

3. Read your Bible. Start with the Gospel of John in the New Testament. Start with Psalms in the Old Testament (sometimes called the Hebrew Bible).

4. Find a local church. Jump in! This is tough but you will be rewarded.

5. Be baptized. When you are ready, follow Christ's command to be baptized. This happens in the local church.

6. Give. Live with an open hand and heart. Nothing will grow you like giving.

---

[165] https://www.cru.org/us/en/train-and-grow/10-basic-steps.html

These are just beginning steps. God is so happy to have you in his kingdom!

Brennan Manning wrote, *My deepest awareness of myself is that I am deeply loved by Jesus Christ and I have done nothing to earn it or deserve it.*[166] Amen!

To see an excellent video presentation of this good news, see https://vimeo.com/14035242

---

[166] Brennan Manning, *The Ragamuffin Gospel: Good News for the Bedraggled, Beat-Up and Burnt Out* (Colorado Springs: Multhomah Press, 2005) 25.

Works Cited

Anderson, Neil T., and Joanne Anderson. 1993. *Daily in Christ: A Devotional.* Eugene, Oregon: Harvest House.

Armstrong, Kristin. 2008. *Happily Ever After: Walking with Peace and Courage Through a Year of Divorce.* New York: Faith Words.

Blackaby, Henry, and Richard Blackaby. 2006. *Experiencing God Day by Day.* Nashville: B&H Publishing.

Brown, Brené. 2017. *Rising Strong: How the Ability to Reset Transforms the Way We Live, Love, Parent, and Lead.* New York: Random House.

Chambers, Oswald. 1992. *My Utmost for His Highest: Selections for The Year.* Uhrichsville, OH: Barbour & Co.

Cordeiro, Wayne. 2009. *Leading on Empty: Refilling Your Tank and Renewing Your Passion.* Minneapolis: Bethany House.

Darwin, Charles. 2016. *Life and Letters of Charles Darwin.* Rare Books Club.

Descartes, René. 2015. *The Passions of The Soul: And Other Late Philosophical Writings.* Oxford: Oxford University Press.

Devine, Megan, and Mark Nepo. 2017. *It's OK That You're Not OK: Meeting Grief and Loss in a Culture That Doesn't Understand.* Boulder: Sounds True.

Donahue, Bill. 2012. *Leading Life-Changing Small Groups: Groups that Grow.* Zondervan.

Driscoll, Mark. 2013. *Who Do You Think You Are? Finding Your True Identity in Christ.* Nashville: Thomas Nelson.

Dungy, Tony, and Nathan Whitaker. 2011. *The One Year Uncommon Life Daily Challenge.* Carol Stream, IL: Tyndale House Publishers.

Fisher, Bruce, and Robert Alberti. 2016. *Rebuilding: When Your Relationship Ends*. 4th ed. Oakland: New Harbinger Publications.

Foster, Richard J. 2009. *Celebration of Discipline*. New York: Harper Collins.

Grylls, Bear. 2014. *A Survival Guide for Life: How to Achieve Your Goals, Thrive in Adversity, and Grow in Character*. New York: William Morrow.

Hecht, Jennifer Michael. 2015. *Stay: A History of Suicide and the Philosophies Against It*. New Haven: Yale University Press.

Hines, Kevin. 2013. *Cracked, Not Broken: Surviving and Thriving After a Suicide Attempt*. Lanham, MD: Rowman & Littlefield Publishers.

Keller, Tim. 2013. *Walking with God through Pain and Suffering*. New York: Penguin.

Manning, Brennan. 2005. *The Ragamuffin Gospel: Good News for the Bedraggled, Beat-Up, and Burnt Out*. Colorado Springs: Multnomah Press.

Manning, Brennan, John Blase, and Jonathan Foreman. 2015. *Abba's Child: The Cry of the Heart for Intimate Belonging*. Colorado Springs: NavPress.

Martin, Keturah C. 2014. *Jesus Never Wastes Pain but Can Bring Eternal Gain*. Bloomington, IN: Xlibris Corp.

Maxwell, John C. 2000. *Failing Forward: Turning Mistakes into Stepping-Stones for Success*. Nashville: Thomas Nelson Publishers.

———. 2007. *The Maxwell Daily Reader: 365 Days of Insight to Develop the Leader Within You and Influence Those Around You*. Nashville: Thomas Nelson.

McKay, Martha Davis, Matthew, and Patrick Fannin. 2009. *Messages: The Communication Skills Book*. Oakland: New Harbinger Publications.

Nakken, Craig. 1988. *The Addictive Personality: Roots, Rituals, and Recovery*. Center City, MN: Hazelden.

O'Donohue, John. 2004. *Anam Ċara: A Book of Celtic Wisdom*. New York: Harper Perennial.

Pascal, Blaise. 1966. *Pensées*. Harmondsworth: Penguin Books.

Peterson, Eugene. 2006. *God's Message for Each Day: Wisdom from the Word of God*. Nashville: Thomas Nelson.

Peterson, Eugene H., Dale Larsen, and Sandy Larsen. 1996. *A Long Obedience in The Same Direction: 6 Studies for Individuals or Groups. With Guidelines for Leaders & Study Notes*. Downers Grove: InterVarsity Press.

Pritchard, Ray. 2011. *An Anchor for the Soul: Help for the Present, Hope for the Future*. Chicago: Moody Publishers.

Rees, Erik. 2006. *S.H.A.P.E.: Finding and Fulfilling Your Unique Purpose for Life*. Grand Rapids: Zondervan.

Reich, Alex J. Zautra, John W., and John Stuart Hall, eds. 2012. *Handbook of Adult Resilience*. New York: Guilford Publications.

Rohr, Richard, Joseph Durepos, and Tom McGrath. 2010. *On the Threshold of Transformation: Daily Meditations for Men*. Chicago: Loyola Press.

Shneidman, Edwin. 1995. *The Suicidal Mind*. Oxford: Oxford University Press.

Stiles, Wayne. 2015. *Waiting on God: What to Do When God Does Nothing*. Grand Rapids: Baker Books.

Thomas, Gary. 2009. *Holy Available: What If Holiness Is About More Than What We Don't Do?* Grand Rapids: Zondervan.

———. 2011. *Simply Sacred: Daily Readings*. Grand Rapids: Zondervan.

———. 2014. *The One Year Hearing His Voice Devotional*. Carol Stream: Tyndale Momentum.

Thoreau, Henry David. 2010. *Works of Henry David Thoreau*. Hustonville, KY: Golgotha Press.

Tiegreen, Chris. 2010. *The One Year Worship the King Devotional*. Carol Strem: Tyndale Momentum.

Tozer, A. W. 1961. *The Knowledge of The Holy: The Attributes of God, Their Meaning in The Christian Life*. New York: Harper & Row.

Tripp, Paul David. 2014. *New Morning Mercies: A Daily Gospel Devotional*. Wheaton, IL: Crossway.

Walton, John H. 2009. *The Lost World of Genesis One: Ancient Cosmology and the Origins Debate*. Downers Grove: IVP Academic.

———. 2015. *The Lost World of Adam And Eve: Genesis 2-3 and the Human Origins Debate*. Downers Grove: IVP Academic.

Warren, Rick. 2005. *The Purpose Driven Life*. Cleveland: Findaway World.

Wicks, Robert J. 2015. *Spiritual Resilience: 30 Days to Refresh Your Soul*. Cincinnati: Franciscan Media.

Willard, Dallas. 1998. *The Divine Conspiracy: Rediscovering Our Hidden Life in God*. San Francisco: HarperSanFrancisco.

————. 1999. *Hearing God: Developing A Conversational Relationship with God*. Downers Grove: IVP Academic.

————. 2002. *Renovation of the Heart: Putting on the Character of Christ*. Colorado Springs: NavPress.

Witwer, Sean. 2016. *Divorce Recovery 101: A Step by Step Guide to Reinvent Yourself in 30 Days*. Amazon Digital Services.

Worthington, Everett L. 2003. *Forgiving and Reconciling: Bridges to Wholeness and Hope*. Downers Grove: IVP Academic.

Wright, H. Norman. 2003a. *Experiencing Divorce*. Downers Grove: InterVarsity Press.

————. 2003b. *The New Guide to Crisis and Trauma Counseling*. Ventura: Regal Books.

Young, Sarah. 2016. *Jesus Calling: Enjoying Peace in His Presence: Devotions for Every Day of the Year*. Nashville: Integrity Publishers.

ABOUT THE AUTHOR

Dale Brown, Ph.D., has pastored six churches in Texas and New England, lived, traveled and taught overseas and led Men's Retreats and Conferences. He has served as a chaplain with hospice, several hospitals and volunteer Fire Departments. He has taught and ministered in various prisons and has worked with sex offenders and victims. He holds a B.S. degree from the University of Texas and the M.Div. and Ph.D. degrees from Southwestern Baptist Theological Seminary. Dale has a passion to see men make a lasting impact on the world and finish well. Dale is husband to Kelly and dad to Lindsey, Davis and Aaron. Dale enjoys hiking, hunting, backpacking, guitar, swing and two-step.

Sooner or later, a beat dog bites.

Beat Dog Press

Made in the USA
Columbia, SC
09 August 2021

42836046R00196